Harvard Historical Studies,   152

Published under the auspices
of the Department of History
from the income of the
Paul Revere Frothingham Bequest
Robert Louis Stroock Fund
Henry Warren Torrey Fund

Globalizing Sport

National Rivalry and International Community in the 1930s

Barbara J. Keys

HARVARD UNIVERSITY PRESS

Cambridge, Massachusetts

London, England

First Harvard University Press paperback edition, 2013

Library of Congress Cataloging-in-Publication Data

Keys, Barbara J.
  Globalizing sport : national rivalry and international community in the
1930s / Barbara J. Keys.
    p.   cm.—(Harvard historical studies ; 152)
  Includes bibliographical references and index.
  ISBN 978-0-674-02326-0 (cloth)
  ISBN 978-0-674-72570-6 (pbk.)
    1. Nationalism and sports.   2. Sports and globalization.   3. Sports—
History—20th century.   I. Title.   II. Harvard historical studies ; v. 152

GV706.34.K48 2006
306.4'83—dc22

                                                              2006043381

To Jeff

Contents

Illustrations

Acknowledgments

Despite long, lonely stretches in archives and in front of the computer, writing a scholarly book is not the solitary endeavor that the single name on the author line implies. To paraphrase Hillary Clinton, it takes a village to write a book. This one owes much of its inspiration to Akira Iriye. He was a patient and supportive graduate adviser, and although sport is far from his own field of interest, it would have been impossible to conceive of this study without the influence of his groundbreaking work on intercultural relations. Loren Graham first suggested that I add sport to my long list of potential topics and then steered my project in the right direction at a crucial time.

I am also grateful to Ernest May, for advice and comments on chapter drafts, and to Terry Martin, who stepped in as a late addition to my dissertation committee and offered valuable insights that prodded me to think more deeply about the ramifications of my argument. Bob Edelman has been a valued source of guidance and expert advice over the years, providing recommendations on sources and careful readings of numerous iterations of chapters and conference papers. This book would not have been possible without the work of Bob and many other pioneering historians and sociologists who made sport not just a respectable but also a fruitful subject of study.

Among the many friends and colleagues who assisted me in various ways, I am especially grateful to those who were on the front lines at the beginning. Erika Dreifus, Adrienne Edgar, and Paul Hagenloh offered advice, moral support, and critical readings of early chapter drafts or papers. Jeff Vanke and David Brandenberger helped me negotiate the German and Russian archives (respectively) and recommended sources. Nina Zuzykina and Evgenyi Pogrebniak were extremely helpful in Moscow. Frank Schauff provided valuable citations to documents in the Comintern archives that I would not otherwise have found. Others who read and commented on draft chapters include Jessica Gienow-Hecht, David Large, Erez Manela, David Margolick, Maria Mitchell, Charles Postel, Mona Siegel, and Lee Simpson. Peter Beck gave the entire manuscript a detailed critique; Frank Ninkovich also read the whole thing and pressed me to think more deeply about the relationship between culture, politics, and ideology. Anonymous reviewers for Harvard University Press provided useful comments. Workshops at the Davis Center and the Center for European Studies at Harvard and at Cal State Sacramento provided critiques of chapters. Curtis Murphy and Stephanie Varrelman provided first-rate research assistance.

The research and writing of this book received support from the Social Science Research Council; the Kennan Institute for Advanced Russian Studies at the Woodrow Wilson International Center for Scholars; the International Olympic Committee; California State University at Sacramento; the University of Melbourne; and the International Research and Exchanges Board, with funds provided by the National Endowment for the Humanities, the U.S. Department of State, and the U.S. Information Agency. At Harvard University, the History Department, the Davis Center for Russian Studies, the Warren Center for American Studies, the Minda de Gunzburg Center for European Studies, and the Weatherhead Center for International Affairs all provided assistance. None of these organizations is responsible for the views expressed herein.

Many librarians and archivists helped along the way. I am especially grateful to Wayne Wilson and his staff at the marvelous Paul Ziffren Sports Resource Center in Los Angeles, who went above and beyond the call of duty to help me and whose remarkable digital archive offers a treasure trove of valuable sources; to Patricia Eckert and her staff at the International Olympic Committee's Documentation Centre in Lausanne, Switzerland; and to Liudmila Finogenova and Valentina Melnikova at the Rossiiskaia Gosudarstvennaia Akademiia Fizicheskoi Kultury.

I am grateful to Sage Publications for allowing me to reprint, in revised form, parts of my article "Soviet Sport and Transnational Mass Culture in the 1930s," originally published in *Journal of Contemporary History* 38, no. 3 (2003), 413–434; to Blackwell Publishing for permission to reprint revised parts of "Spreading Peace, Democracy, and Coca-Cola: Sport and American Cultural Expansion in the 1930s," originally published in *Diplomatic History* 28, no. 2 (2004), 165–196; and to Imprint Publications, which published "The Internationalization of Sport,

1919–1939," an earlier examination of some of the ideas in this book, in *The Cultural Turn: Essays in the History of U.S. Foreign Relations,* edited by Frank A. Ninkovich and Liping Bu (Chicago, 2001), 201–219.

Convention holds that I thank last those to whom I am most indebted. My husband, Jeff Shimeta, and more recently my son, McKinley Keys (who finished his first book before I finished mine), have supported my work in many ways, not least by reminding me of all the reasons to finish and move on.

Globalizing Sport

Abbreviations

AAU   Amateur Athletic Union of the United States

AOC   American Olympic Committee

DRA   Deutscher Reichsausschuß für Leibesübungen

FIFA   Fédération Internationale de Football Association

IAAF   International Amateur Athletic Federation

IOC   International Olympic Committee

VOKS   All-Union Society for Cultural Relations Abroad

Introduction

> The first laws ever to be voluntarily embraced by men from a wide variety
> of cultures and backgrounds are the laws of sport.
>
> —Ali Mazrui

When the Olympic flag climbed to the top of the central mast in Berlin's impressive new stadium on August 1, 1936, it signaled not just the opening of the Eleventh Olympic Games but also, in one observer's eyes, the creation of "a new sovereign state." According to the publicity director of the American Olympic Committee, during the sixteen days of the Olympic Games the five continents of the globe had united to establish an "independent government," the boundaries of which extended "to the limits of the arena, the Stadium, the Olympic Village, and all the accessory fields and buildings" where contests were held. Within these boundaries was "an international state, ruled over by the International Olympic Committee," whose supreme law was the Olympic statutes. It was not, the publicist claimed, merely a "make-believe or cardboard domain"; it was "actual and real, in effect superseding the regular civil, police and military power."[1]

The U.S. publicist overstated the independent powers of the Olympics, but the press release nevertheless pointed to a fundamental truth. In the years leading to the Berlin Games, a form of "international sovereignty"—limited but real—had come to govern the playing fields where nations now pitted their representatives. The stadiums and arenas of international sports competitions became deterritorialized, penetrated and shaped less by the cultural contexts of their immediate physical locations than by distant, transnational influences. They had local inflections, as the Third Reich's grandiose Olympic Stadium vividly demonstrated, but their structure and functions were constrained by a universal idiom, one whose grammar would have been understood by

1

any of the growing numbers of fans who clamored for seats in countries large and small across the globe. Uniforms, victory ceremonies, scores, times, distances, the rules of the game: these were symbols and terms that increasingly constituted a universal form of communication. Newspaper and radio (and later television) coverage of events lifted the arenas of competition even further from their geographic locations, as fans could participate in the spectacle whether the action was taking place in Copenhagen or Rio de Janeiro.[2]

Stadiums were the focal point of a system of relationships that constituted the international sovereignty of sport, a system that took shape in the decades before World War II. In those years international sport came to constitute an "imagined world" in much the same way that a nation can be seen as an "imagined community."[3] Like the imagined community of a nation, the imagined world of sport was governed by distinctive laws and practices, linked by its own repertoire of invented symbols and traditions, referring to a common past and common heroes. Sport has been an important means of introducing "empty time" into everyday life, from the halves of a soccer match, clocked according to the same time everywhere, to the quadrennial cycle of the World Cup and Olympic Games, which have synchronized the entire globe in a single sporting calendar. Because of the hard, rule-bound nature of sport, records and victories become independent of the context in which they are produced; they are symbolic tokens exchangeable across space, time, and cultural barriers.[4] The world of sport was built on a fundamental dualism: based on the principle of national representation, it nevertheless claimed a universalism that transcended nationalism. All people of the world, grouped into nations, were to be united in the world of sport. Through international sport, belonging to the world was mediated by belonging to a nation.

This book charts the development of the imagined world of international sport during the 1930s. This decade was a critical period in the expansion of sport, for it was during these years that older competitions, such as the Olympic Games, and new ones, such as soccer's World Cup, attained a level of popularity and worldwide significance that set them apart from what came before and that crystallized the attributes that would shape the enormous sport extravaganzas of the second half of the twentieth century. The Olympic Games of 1932 and 1936 marked a new stage in the decades-old festival, shifting it from a European-based pageant for the elite to mass entertainment on a global scale. The World Cup, first held in 1930, quickly became an event of similar global popularity and import. Everywhere sport exchanges rose rapidly in number and scope. From U.S. basketball teams touring Latin America to Soviet soccer teams in Paris and Japanese swimmers in Europe, the once lightly trod routes of international contact in sport now became highways for the exchange of ideas and expertise.

It was also at this time that modern sport displaced its major European rivals—workers' sport and traditional gymnastics—securing for itself a position as the leading form of physical culture in Europe. The socialist brand of workers' sport and the nationalist-oriented gymnastics systems were powerful movements in the interwar years that represented alternatives to modern sport, collectivist rather than competitive, mass-based rather than elitist, underpinned by different philosophical conceptions of the modern body. Sport's victory over its antagonists in Europe in turn presaged its postwar success in supplanting or marginalizing traditional forms of physical recreation in the rest of the world. Like an invasive species, modern sport would outcompete its rivals, infiltrating every corner of the globe by the end of the century. Sport is now a global culture.[5]

The stunning growth of international sport was achieved despite the extraordinary economic dislocation, ideological conflict, and nationalist extremism that stunted so many of the rich and vibrant cultural connections that had arisen in the 1920s. It was, after all, a decade that began with the collapse of the global economy, an event that stifled international trade and sent many economies into tailspins characterized by massive unemployment and drastic cutbacks in production and consumption. It was a decade of violence and popular discontent, when democracy stumbled and dictatorships of left and right seemed to many observers to offer salvation. It was a decade of aggression, as Mussolini's Italy attacked Ethiopia, a dictatorial regime in Japan invaded Manchuria and then the rest of China, and Hitler's Germany set out to conquer Europe, first remilitarizing the Rhineland, then annexing Austria and—with the short-sighted collusion of Western powers that would make "appeasement" a dirty word for the rest of the century—part of Czechoslovakia, before annexing the rest and then moving on to Poland. It was a decade that ended in humanity's most destructive war ever, a conflagration of barbarity, death, and ruin.

The rapid growth of international ties in such an apparently inhospitable environment, this book argues, lies in sport's peculiar potency as a means of mediating between national and international identities. The

growth of nationalist rivalry and international community in sport pro-
ceeded in tandem, each reinforcing the other. International sport acted
as a forum for nationalist rivalry, but nationalist impulses increased the
internationalist power of sport. Much has been made of the way dictatorships manipulated international sport, but international sport also
constituted a dictatorship of sorts, and its rule extended even to the dic-
tators. Participation in the world of sport entailed acceptance of and
adaptation to norms and values, including the primary standards of
competition, hierarchy, high achievement, individualism, and universalism, that sometimes acted to subvert nationalist ideologies and that
shaped the form and content of nationalism in important ways.

The rapid internationalization of modern sport was propelled by its mass
appeal, and particularly by its capacity to consolidate group identity at local and national levels. Governments and political elites also promoted
sport as a modernizing force. Competitive and achievement-oriented, sport
offered a means of inculcating disciplinary norms and providing physical
conditioning that was highly suited to preparing better soldiers and more
productive workers. But sport's existence as an international system—
its constitution as what political scientists would call an "international
regime"—was also critical. The strength of sport as an international system
is precisely what made it appealing as a stage for nationalist competition.
Sport organizations with global ambitions sought to create a universalistic
framework for sport, one that provided uniform rules and conditions for
the practice of sport across time and place. This uniformity and universalism made sport appear to offer a uniquely objective and quantifiable means
to compare national strength. Sport contests offered an unambiguous nu-
merical outcome in the form of points, times, or distances. Rising nationalism, mass-based and ideologically driven, thus entwined with the
formation of an internationalist mentality in sport to create a mutually reinforcing cycle. Sport became a useful arena for governments eager to display the virtues of their national systems for the increasingly sought-after
judgments of a new force in international affairs: world opinion. Just as the
nationalization of politics in interwar Europe was dependent on a transnational organization of finances and resources, so, too, was the nationalization of a mass sport culture fostered by transnational links.[6]

This book traces the role of key actors and events in the consolidation
of the international sport world. The community of sport was shaped, in
ways hidden to even the most avid readers of the sports pages, by the

largely unheralded control exerted by international organizations over-seeing individual sports and Olympic competitions. The most influential of these, the International Olympic Committee (IOC) and the international soccer federation, sought global control and universal standards and provided much of the content and symbolism for the world of sport. The two most important international sporting events of the decade were the Olympic Games of 1932 in Los Angeles, which gave an enormous boost to sport's commodification and commercialization, and the Games of 1936 in Berlin, which highlighted international sport's battle to balance nationalist extremism with idealistic universalism.

This book also examines the relationships of the United States, Nazi Germany, and the Soviet Union to the world of sport. Strongly isolationist and representing starkly antagonistic ideologies—liberal democracy, fascism, and communism—all three countries were nevertheless drawn into the globalizing world of sport. For those in the United States, sport offered the same opportunities to modernize and democratize the world found in other areas of politics, culture, and commerce. As the acknowledged leaders in many sports, they sought to mold international sport into forms consonant with the values and ideals of U.S.-style capitalism and democracy.

That the period's most xenophobic and illiberal states, Nazi Germany and the Soviet Union, both came to embrace a world so deeply embedded in the structures of liberal capitalism is perhaps one of the most surprising outcomes in the history of cultural internationalism. Both regimes were founded on rejection of the values and institutions of liberal civilization; both tried to isolate their populations from outside cultural influences; and both claimed exemption from the international norms governing relations among "bourgeois" states. On ideological grounds, both the Nazis and the Soviets initially disdained participation in the emerging world of international sport, instead favoring forms of physical culture that represented alternatives to modern sport. Both, however, were drawn into participation in Western international sport, with Nazi Germany becoming a leader in the international sport world and the Soviet Union moving haltingly toward a full-fledged membership that would be achieved immediately after the war.

In the popular mind, today's sports are variants of games that have been played for millennia and whose genealogies can be traced in a continuous line back to ancient Greece. This conception contains a kernel of truth.

Play is a universal element of human society, and games involving basic movements like kicking, throwing, and running, with implements like balls and sticks, have existed for thousands of years. What we know today as sport, however, is a uniquely modern and historically contingent form of physical activity that was born in eighteenth- and nineteenth-century Britain and from there was transmitted to the rest of the world. Defined as a competitive, rule-bound, autotelic physical contest, sport is only one of many possible varieties of "physical culture."[7]

It was the continuing reverberations of Britain's earlier industrial revolution that transformed leisure and produced modern sport. As German sociologist Henning Eichberg has argued, older games became modernized—that is, became sports—through a process of temporal and spatial disciplining that was also occurring in other areas of British society. Measurement became central. Participation was no longer an end in itself but was directed to the production of concrete, quantifiable results: goals, inches, seconds. Time, now conceived of as one-dimensional and absolute, measured in minute quantities by the stopwatch, created the boundaries within which games were played (quarters, periods) and provided a key means of measuring results. Space, too, was tightly controlled, as natural variations in the environment were replaced by the uniform geometries of the gymnasium and the stadium.[8] Even variations in weather were considered problematic and undesirable.[9] As the focus of sport became directed toward the production of records, the rationalization of body movements to maximize efficiency followed logically, culminating in the vision of the body as a machine, to be trained and manipulated according to scientific principles.[10]

During the course of the twentieth century, this brand of physical culture has become perhaps the most visible of the imagined worlds that together constitute our new globalized civilization. Modern, rule-bound, competitive sport has spread to nearly every country. Where a rich diversity of traditional games and contests based on varied body cultures once proliferated, modern sport now occupies a hegemonic position. Where traditional games survive, they have typically been marginalized or "sportified," and the dominant form of physical culture is shaped by a single, universal standard: rationalized, achievement-oriented sport, governed by oligarchic, Western-led international federations.[11] National variations—in the particular sports played in a given country, in their styles of play, and in their cultural significance—continue to exist and to play highly influential roles in shaping the popular imagination, but these variations are expressed within a set of limits that are much narrower than those that existed a century ago.

Today participation in the Olympic Games and major international competitions is a necessary marker of nationhood, and such contests are followed with enormous passion and interest by much of the world's population. The IOC has more members than the United Nations—and greater power to enforce its dictates. At the 2004 Summer Olympic Games in Athens, more than 10,000 athletes from 201 countries participated directly, and roughly half the world's population participated indirectly: an estimated 3.9 billion people in 220 countries and territories watched part of the 35,000 hours of Olympic coverage broadcast worldwide on television.[12] Soccer's quadrennial World Cup, the largest international sports contest outside the Olympics, is also followed by billions of people across the globe and excites levels of emotion unmatched by any other cultural medium.

The widespread popularity of sport has made it a potent political tool, used by governments domestically to promote national identity, public health, and social values, and in diplomacy to support foreign-policy goals. Both the Nazi and the Soviet dictatorships, where the state controlled international sports contacts, directed such contacts toward concrete political ends, such as reinforcing alliances and encouraging friendly relations with neighboring countries. By indirectly representing national power, sport competitions were intended to demonstrate a nation's value as an ally and mettle as a foe. In the United States it was not the state but rather private groups that oversaw foreign sport contacts, but they, too, used sport to promote good relations with countries in Europe, Asia, and South America and to spread national values. In general, sport tended to be an instrument of foreign policy rather than a variable that affected policy, but it nonetheless had important effects on public opinion and attitudes.

During the Cold War sport took on a highly politicized role in the international system. Entry into the IOC and international sport federations became an important avenue for nations seeking recognition and legitimacy. Victories in sporting competitions were compulsively tallied for use as propaganda to demonstrate the superiority of political and ideological systems, and boycotts were deployed as international sanctions against military actions and racial policies. The German Democratic Republic, for example, turned to international sports as a vehicle for achieving recognition as an independent country when it was unable to use more orthodox means such as trade, diplomacy, or war; South Africa was excluded from international competition because of apartheid; and representation in international sport bodies has been an issue of contention in the rivalry between Taiwan and the People's Republic of China.[13] More recently, sport has become a central element in a global, U.S.-dominated commercial and media empire.[14]

Sport's popularity is a function of the inherent unpredictability of every contest, which produces genuine drama, and of its capacity to create a uniquely powerful emotional bond between spectators and participants. In a world fraught with ambiguities and complexities, sports contests produce a simple, clear-cut outcome: there are winners and there are losers. Yet sport also offers the continual prospect of change. Records fall, rankings change, today's victors become tomorrow's losers. In an unjust world, sport offers an idealized space where rules are observed and effort and merit appear to be rewarded.[15] Countless observers have noted that sport functions like a religion, providing collective symbolism and ritual that help modern civilization ward off alienation and anomie.[16]

Among elements of mass culture, where cross-national exchanges are typically informal, sport is unique in having a powerful system of transnational governance, mirroring the international political structures that have sprung up alongside national governments in the twentieth century. Membership in the international sport community entails submission to the dictates of global authorities in matters of eligibility, rules, and adjudication, as well as acculturation to the philosophical and moral values that underpin modern sport, including the primacy of competition, individualism, an emphasis on quantifiable achievement, and notions of egalitarianism and fair play.

Advocates of modern sport have often argued that it is an inherently liberal and democratic form of popular leisure. Authoritarian tendencies are deeply embedded in sport, however, and the global hegemony of sport has produced a near-monopoly on discourse about the body and physical culture. Modern sport, to use terminology suggested by Arjun Appadurai, is a "hard" cultural form, one that comes with "a set of links between value, meaning, and embodied practice that are difficult to break and hard to transform" and that therefore "changes those who are socialized into it more readily than it is itself changed."[17] The hard quality of sport is reinforced by the institutionalization of international sport—its control by international organizations that place narrow constraints on the outward forms of particular sports. Both participation and spectatorship in sports are significant ways that people "learn" their bodies, and body knowledge shapes the way people regard both the self and the outside world. In the words of one sociologist, the way we experience our bodies "directly influences what and how things can be meaningful for us, the ways in which these meanings can be developed and articulated, the ways we are able to comprehend and reason about our experience, and the actions we take."[18] Jacques Ellul's claim that "[sport's] mechanisms reach into the individual's innermost life, working a transformation of his body and its motions" is not far from the mark.[19]

Sport's global hegemony, then, exerts powerful but largely unseen influences on the lives of much of the world's population. It has influenced leisure and consumption patterns, moral values, aesthetics, ideas about the body, race, and gender, and conceptions of time and space, work and play, individual and society. Yet because modern sport has cloaked itself as a natural activity, one that is rooted in thousands of years of human tradition and expresses inalterable human characteristics like conflict and aggression, its role in our lives is often unexamined and unchallenged.

The major focus of this book is the intersection of the national and the transnational in the realm of sport culture. The relationship between transnational influences, globalizing processes, and foreign cultural products, on the one hand, and countervailing pressures to assert national, local, and particularist identities, on the other, is one of the central questions of our era. Some scholars argue that foreign cultural influences (sometimes characterized as "cultural imperialism") act to powerfully reshape cultures and societies on the receiving end, ultimately leading to cultural homogenization.[20] Others stress resistance and modification by receiving societies, arguing that societies "indigenize" foreign cultural imports to suit their own traditions and tastes, without significantly altering values or patterns of behavior.[21]

Sport has clearly proven spectacularly amenable to indigenization. Even as a foreign import, sport has an unusual capacity to create powerful bonds of identification within groups, a capacity that has made it a potent tool of nationalism. Cricket, for example, despite its British origins, has become an integral part of the national identities of former colonies like India. Historians and sociologists have devoted much attention to this phenomenon, and the historical literature on sport has focused overwhelmingly on sport within national borders and on the role of particular sports in the formation of class, gender, and national identities. The emphasis has been on the ways sport is appropriated, indigenized, and nationalized, rather than on transnational origins and connections.

The transnational elements of modern sport deserve more attention.[22] Major sports such as soccer, boxing, and track and field are no longer identified as products of any one national culture; instead they have been subject to complex currents of internationalization, becoming in the process transnational and deterritorialized. International sport is therefore much like environmental problems, migration and refugee flows, terrorism, and other phenomena that cross national boundaries and that can be fruitfully studied with transnational approaches.[23] In my own field—the history of international relations—state-centered approaches to the study of diplomacy have given way to a broader vision of what constitutes international affairs and international actors. Studies of topics such as the social construction of gender, ideologies of race, cultural elements like film and tourism, and nonstate actors like missionaries have enriched our understanding of international relations.[24]

Though sport has elicited more passionate interest from greater numbers of people than other aspects of culture, historians of international relations have devoted little attention to it.[25] Yet sport has much in common with the new subjects of international history. It has important connections to film, tourism, and consumer culture. Sport is unique among elements of popular culture in having a powerful international institutional apparatus, but sport organizations are broadly similar to other prewar international organizations with moral agendas, including the League of Nations, the Boy Scouts, the Red Cross, the Nobel Prize Committee, and the Young Men's Christian Association (YMCA).[26] And in its mixing of nationalism and internationalism in spectacular festivals, sport can be compared to the expositions and world's fairs that did so much to shape the international imagination in the century before World War II. The study of sport, then, has implications for how we conceive of the role of nonstate actors, cultural transfer, perceptions, mega-events in the construction of a world community, ideologies of race and gender, and the incorporation of the developing world into the international system.

In tackling a subject as broad and varied as international sport, this book necessarily leaves out a great deal. Sport was well on its way to becoming truly global in the 1930s. The first World Cup in 1930 was played in Uruguay, and the 1940 Olympics, canceled due to war, would have been held in Tokyo.[27] The territorial focus of this book, however, is primarily on Europe and North America, where the key battles over the content and character of an international "physical culture" regime were being waged. The focus is also on those sports with transnational mass appeal, such as soccer, swimming, boxing, and track and field, which experienced the highest levels of internationalization.

International exchange in the 1930s occurred in both mass-participation and high-achievement spectator sport. Governments, educators, and reformers heavily promoted mass participation in sport and physical recreation after World War I to increase health and fitness levels. They studied the physical education programs, paramilitary training regimes, and mass leisure pursuits of other countries, often borrowing or emulating those deemed useful. Educators held international conferences on physical education; public and private bodies sent representatives on fact-finding tours of recreational facilities in other countries; doctors and scientists exchanged views on athletic training and sports physiology; and international organizations like the YMCA took up physical education as part of their reformist mission.[28]

The most significant internationalization occurred, however, in the realm of elite, high-achievement sport. Here a truly transnational culture was established, one that attained an existence independent of the countries participating in it. Elite sport did not exist in an entirely separate sphere from mass sport. Sport officials believed, justifiably, that only by cultivating a wide base of athletes could the few with high potential be found and nurtured. Elite sport was seen as an extension of mass efforts, the tip of a vast pyramid. In most cases a single national association governed both mass and elite sport, overseeing a network of clubs and teams that operated at all levels of the pyramid and abided by similar rules and regulations. The two realms nevertheless increasingly diverged as the distance from the top to the bottom of the pyramid widened and as spectator sport developed into a mass leisure pursuit in its own right. While mass sport was still defined in significant respects within the confines of a national culture, top athletes competed more and more in a system constrained by international norms and standards. Their fans, their training regimens, the rules that governed their sports, and the competitors against whom they measured themselves were part of an increasingly global culture.

Another key split, similar to but not congruent with the mass versus elite divide, was the one between amateur and professional sport—a distinction that constituted an almost obsessive preoccupation for most sport officials in the interwar years. Although the concept of amateurism arose in the context of the British class system and was regarded with puzzlement by many Europeans, it insinuated itself so deeply into the ideology of sport that it became an entrenched part of the entire international sport system from its beginnings, enduring even as the fundamental dynamic of achievement sport rendered it obsolete. That amateurism also drew on a deeply rooted Western dichotomy between work and play helps explain the otherwise puzzling fact that both Nazi Germany and the Soviet Union in the 1930s strongly disdained professionalism in sport. The distinction became truly important only at elite levels, because only the best athletes were likely to receive some form of remuneration. Here the issue of spectator appeal was the critical factor: soccer, with millions of fans, went professional early on, whereas sports with a more limited fan base, such as weight lifting, adhered more strictly to pure amateurism. Track and field fell somewhere in between, in a gray zone between putative amateurism and outright professionalism. At the top levels, however, both amateur and professional sport exhibited broad similarities in the dynamic of internationalization.

The world of international sport before World War II was overwhelmingly a male domain. The values sport was assumed to promote, such as physical strength, courage, and willpower, were associated with masculinity. Sport, it was often said, taught the virtues of manliness. As the "manly sport" of early Victorian England spread decades later to Tokyo and Bombay and Rio de Janeiro, the precise definitions of "manliness" naturally varied, but the assumption almost everywhere was that sport was fundamentally entwined with manhood. Participation and spectatorship formed an important part of male socialization in many societies. Sport's ties to paramilitary training and its emphasis on physical strength reinforced notions of sport as a man's domain.

For women the rise of sport presented a mixed picture. On the one hand, their participation in sports and physical education programs offered an entry into the public sphere and sometimes worked to subvert notions of feminine frailty and dependence. On the other hand, their participation was limited, marginalized, and often framed within dominant notions of women's physical and mental inferiority. Many educators, both male and female, saw sport as useful for women only insofar as it promoted healthy and physically robust mothers. Experts disagreed vigorously about the amounts and types of exercises they deemed appropriate for women, but virtually all concurred that such exercise should be moderated lest it damage women's health or reproductive capacity.[29] In the interwar years a vigorous international network of women's groups pressed, with some success, for greater access to international competitions, but governments and the major international and national sport federations construed sport as an inherently male activity, and their preoccupation was with sport by and for men. There was universal sport, which meant men's sport, and then there was "women's sport," and to the extent that the men who played the leading roles in shaping the international sport community thought about the latter, it was as an adjunct of peripheral interest and importance.

Not surprisingly, given its origins in the era of high imperialism, modern international sport also had racist overtones. The organizations that oversaw rule-setting and competitions were heavily dominated by wealthy white European men, and international contests were limited to those countries where sports were played. For many years the result was that international sport was a matter for Europe and the Americas and very little beyond. For colonized peoples and for racial minorities in countries where sport was widespread, such as the United States and Brazil, institutionalized racism sharply limited opportunities to participate in sports. But the imagined world of sport was a global one, not defined by race, and the doors to major international competitions were open to all races and nations. As modern sport spread, nonwhite athletes—and non-European countries—gained prominence in the world arena. By the 1930s African American and Japanese athletes stood so frequently on the victory platforms at Olympic Games that the racial universalism of sport was becoming a reality. Such victories did not necessarily constitute a step toward genuine equality, because often enough whites explained the athletic success of nonwhites in racist terms, referring to their innate savagery, their closer connection to the life of the jungle, and other such nonsense.

Sport's adherents, moreover, tended to see it as a manifestation of the superiority of Western civilization and an embodiment of Western values. Yet the ideal of universalism meant that much of the racist underpinning of sport would gradually be undermined.

The imagined world of modern sport, then, was based on a fraternity of elites, among both the athletes who garnered public adulation and the officials who wielded power behind the scenes. It was composed of men and imbued with the "masculine" attributes of Western civilization: competition, strength, hierarchy, "playing by the rules." The Olympic Village, inaugurated in 1932, was the symbolic home of the global citizens of this sporting fraternity, a place where the world's youth gathered in peaceful competition. It was a world oddly poised between modernity and tradition, embracing technology, quantification, and progress even while grasping outdated ideals of amateurism and the purity of play. It mediated between nationalism and internationalism, strengthening both simultaneously.

In tracing the development of this imagined world in the 1930s, Chapter 1 outlines the global obsession with physical fitness of the late nineteenth and early twentieth centuries that helped propel the spread of sport, along with other forms of physical recreation. Manifestations of the idea that sport performances were linked to national prestige appeared early in the twentieth century as international competitions first appeared. At the same time, European sport enthusiasts began to form international organizations to standardize rules and eligibility requirements, a process examined in Chapter 2. In the years before World War II these organizations took on a critical role in shaping international sport events, creating a framework that would prove enormously successful at harnessing the twin forces of nationalism and internationalism.

In explaining the transformation of international sport in the 1930s, Chapter 3 turns to the role of the United States. As the world's foremost "sporting nation," the United States was an international leader in sport just as it was in other areas of culture and commerce. Despite the indifference foreign publics showed toward baseball and football, Americans had a deep and abiding influence on global sport. In the 1930s the United States was a model in amateur and individual sports like track and field and swimming, as well as in the creation of a commercialized sport industry based on mass spectatorship. The United States played a key role in commercializing and democratizing international sport, in imbuing it with moral and technocratic impulses, and in expanding its connections to the worlds of entertainment and mass culture. Despite strong feelings of isolationism, many in the United States were committed internationalists in the cultural sphere, convinced that spreading sport abroad was a means to spread peace and democracy. For much of the public, U.S. sports victories helped affirm beliefs in the country's benevolent role in the world and in the superiority of democracy as a political and social system.

How Americans helped to popularize international sport is examined in Chapter 4, which covers the 1932 Los Angeles Olympic Games, the single most important contribution of the United States to international sport before World War II and a milestone in the creation of the mass-entertainment Olympic spectacle so familiar today. The U.S. organizers' adept staging of the Games, careful cultivation of press relations, and shrewd use of the Hollywood connection did much to expand the global popularity of international sport and had lasting effects on the character of the Olympic Games.

Chapter 5 begins with the now-legendary boxing matches of 1936 and 1938 between the great African American boxer Joe Louis and his German rival, Max Schmeling. Depicted as a struggle between two ideological systems, the 1938 heavyweight bout that resulted in a victory for Louis was hailed by Americans as a victory for democracy itself. The chapter also examines the very different perspective held by the Nazis, who scrambled after Schmeling's ignominious knockout to distance themselves from a boxer they had claimed as a German hero. The question of why the Nazi regime staked so much on a boxing match between an "Aryan" and an African American leads to a broader exploration of the relationship between international sport and dictatorship, as the chapter goes on to untangle the reasons for the puzzling participation of Nazi Germany in the globalizing world of sport. The Nazi Party's racist and nationalist ideology was fundamentally hostile to the universalizing and democratic vision embodied in modern sport. As a result the Nazis initially favored the indigenous German gymnastics movement known as *Turnen,* with its long tradition of opposition to "English sport." Yet despite early condemnations of sport, the Nazis quickly became eager adherents of the new global sport structure—and indeed were highly successful at manipulating it for their own purposes, although adherence to international norms worked in small ways to subvert Nazi ideology.

The dynamics of this process as they played out in one venue are the subject of Chapter 6, which covers the greatest sporting feat of the Nazi regime and the single biggest sporting event of the decade: the infamous 1936 Berlin Olympic Games, on which Hitler lavished resources and attention. Much has been written about the "Nazi Olympics," and much of this literature justly condemns the world for turning a blind eye to Nazi abuses and allowing an evil regime to gain prestige and legitimacy by hosting such a major event. The Olympics were only a partial success for Hitler's propaganda machine, however, a success qualified by small but perceptible gains for the universalist and egalitarian ideals of international sport.

Did Stalin, too, grasp the opportunities presented by international sport? Chapter 7 looks at the other end of the ideological spectrum, finding that Stalin's Soviet Union had a complex relationship with the fundamentally capitalist-based world of sport well before the USSR's emergence as a sport superpower during the Cold War. Like Germany's efforts to cultivate a uniquely German sport culture, the Soviet Union's attempts in the 1920s to develop a "proletarian" brand of sport were ultimately unsuccessful. Despite efforts to promote a communist alternative to sport, and despite the Soviet regime's strenuous efforts to seal itself off from Western culture, by the 1930s the regime was avidly emulating Western sport, a process that had significant domestic consequences. The chapter details the Soviets' tentative rapprochement with the capitalist sport world—with particular emphasis on soccer, which underwent a rapid global expansion in the 1930s—and the social repercussions of this partial opening to Western culture.

When the Soviet Union became a full member of the international club after 1945, international sport was already well on its way to becoming a worldwide community. Major changes were yet to come—the advent of television, rampant professionalism, pervasive politicization—but the outlines of the imagined community of sport were already clear. The foundations of what would become one of the most significant elements of globalization had been cemented in the era of Hitler and Stalin.

Sport, the State, and International Politics

One of the forces driving the internationalization of sport was the establishment of sport as an essential practice of a modern state. "Today the people of the world pay more and more attention to the question of physical education," the British Board of Education noted approvingly in 1936. "They are beginning to grasp that healthy physical training is of decisive importance for the health and welfare of the nation."[1] By the late twentieth century participation in international sports competitions like the Olympic Games had become a necessary marker of nationhood, a standard means of representing national identity to both domestic and foreign audiences.[2] Almost everywhere in the twentieth century sports became an important way to instill a sense of belonging to a nation, to solidify loyalty, to create a bond of attachment to an abstract entity. At the same time participation in international sport competitions became a statement of membership in a community of nations.

For the great powers it became a matter of urgency to win more medals or more championships than rival powers. For the smaller nations it became critical not so much to win but to show up, to perform respectably, and to be seen as a member of the club. Sport, with its readily quantifiable results, proved especially hospitable for the new currents of competition in the emerging international system based on national representation. Like participation in world's fairs, the possession of a flag and anthem, and the sending of diplomatic representatives abroad, sport became one of the practices that shaped the form and image of nations as they entered the international order.

The origins of the close relationship between sport and nationhood lie in a confluence of factors in late–nineteenth-century Europe. Rising standards of living, increased amounts of leisure time, technological innovations like telegraphy and steam-powered printing, and the commodification and commercialization of entertainment created the preconditions for the rise of mass sports and physical education. These factors intersected with fears of degeneration, Social Darwinism, and state intervention in matters of public health to produce new physical recreation movements that represented the state's strength in terms of its population's health. Across Europe the conviction grew that physical recreation could produce morally upright, economically productive, and militarily useful (male) citizens. As a result, fitness became a matter of state importance. National wealth was not just a matter of gold reserves, industrial output, or natural resources, but also of human resources. A healthy nation, vigorous enough to produce economic growth and maintain its stature in the world, depended on a healthy population.

These new views of health and leisure helped propel a tremendous upsurge in programs of physical exercise in the late nineteenth and early twentieth centuries. In Europe, the United States, and in many parts of Asia, Latin America, and the Middle East, politicians and reformers turned to physical exercise programs as a panacea for social ills and as a tool to increase national power. Private clubs mushroomed, factories introduced recreation programs, schools introduced physical-education classes, and governments began to spend public funds on playgrounds, stadiums, and gymnasiums.

Although the vogue for what was then called "physical culture" manifested itself in various forms, from bodybuilding to bicycling fads, the most important development of the nineteenth century was the creation of modern sport. Spurred by urbanization, the rise of mass media, and improvements in transportation, modern competitive sports (most significantly, track and field and team sports like soccer) were codified and standardized in Britain, then spread to other countries, and by the second half of the twentieth century had established global supremacy in the realm of physical culture.

In the interwar years, however, competitive sport represented only one strain of the physical-culture movement. In Europe, gymnastics was sport's main rival. In philosophy and practice, gymnastics represented a starkly different model of physical recreation. Unlike sport, gymnastics was primarily noncompetitive; instead of quantifiable achievement, it emphasized process and posture. "Gymnastics and sport," a Belgian gymnast noted in 1894, "are *diametrically opposed* activities and [we have] always fought against the latter as *incompatible* with [the] principles [of gymnastics]."[3] From the late nineteenth century until World War II, gymnastics and sport were antagonists in a battle for supremacy in the field of popular recreation. On much of the European continent and elsewhere gymnastics was the dominant form of physical culture until at least World War I, with sport merely "an ambitious younger brother."[4]

A thriving workers'-sport movement posed a similar challenge to modern sport in interwar Europe. As with gymnastics, workers' sport emphasized cooperation and group solidarity over individual competition. Unlike gymnastics, workers' sport was predicated on internationalism, a transnational proletarian identity. Workers' sport was dealt a serious blow by Nazi repression, but the experience of the Soviet Union, where a Soviet version of worker's sport was introduced but then replaced by competitive Western sport, suggests that the competitive advantages of the mainstream international sport system would have relegated the European workers' sport movement to the margins even had it not been actively repressed.

Across the rest of the world traditional pastimes and recreations predominated. Sometimes these were resuscitated and modernized as part of broader reform agendas, but more often they were gradually pushed aside by Western imports. By definition, traditional recreations were uniquely local or regional. Gymnastics was essentially national, unique within each country and lacking a strong internationalist component. Workers' sport was class-based. Sport, however, was a universalist international system, and it was this characteristic that ultimately made it more appealing as a medium for nationalist impulses, helping to propel its meteoric rise to global supremacy.

The Rise of "Physical Culture"

Eugen Sandow was one of the best-known men in the world in 1900. The German émigré strongman and performer toured Britain, the United States, Australia, New Zealand, South Africa, India, Dutch Java, Burma, China, and Japan. He published a widely read magazine, sold thousands of photographs and postcards of himself in neoclassical poses that showcased his thickly muscled physique, and devised and marketed a system of physical training, centering on the use of dumbbells for muscular development. His body was widely heralded as an ideal; physicians proclaimed him the most perfect male alive.[5]

Sandow's rise to international fame was the product of a craze for physical culture that swept much of Europe, the United States, and beyond in the second half of the nineteenth century, reflecting fundamental shifts in views of health, fitness, and bodily ideals. Like Sandow's fame, the vogue for physical culture was furthered by transnational currents. Wrestling and bodybuilding, the craze for cycling, and tennis are notable examples of phenomena whose turn-of-the-century popularity crossed national borders. As the convening of the first International Congress on Physical Education in 1889 indicates, there was also a lively international exchange of ideas and practices in physical education.

Physical culture movements of the nineteenth century were driven by a common set of concerns arising from modernization and industrialization. The conditions of modern life, many nineteenth-century thinkers worried, led to degeneration, emasculation, and decline. They looked around their societies and saw men sitting in offices pushing paper or standing in factories engaged in narrowly specialized, repetitive labor, becoming morally and physically weak. Social Darwinists who saw life as a struggle among races and nations argued that physical strength was key to the "survival of the fittest" for human societies. And in an era of mass conscription, the health and fitness of individual men was directly tied to military power.

The public hygiene movement of the nineteenth century regarded physical fitness as an important component of healthy living, and hygiene advocates pressed for public efforts to promote physical exercise. By the turn of the century new ideas about public health combined with widespread fears of physical degeneration and weakness among "civilized" societies to produce a biological model of society, which gave new urgency to the longstanding idea that the health of the "body politic" depended on the health of individual bodies that constituted it.[6]

Recreation was also heralded as a remedy for social ills. The growth in leisure time spurred by industrialization meant that governments and reformers were eager to foster socially beneficial forms of recreation, ones that would not only promote good health, but also instill moral virtues and divert the working class from such vices as gambling. In a sharp reversal, physical recreations once condemned as dissolute now came to be seen as character-building. In Britain, for example, the authorities had long battled against popular recreations, which they considered harmful, inhumane, and unproductive, but by mid-century many social and religious leaders came to see some of these pastimes not as hindrances but as aids to moral development. Politicians and social reformers now believed that proper physical activities could instill discipline, morality, courage, and other valued character traits.[7] One nineteenth-century American reformer even argued that "naturally stupid" people could be made "comparatively intelligent, by prevailing on them to take gymnastic exercise."[8] Proponents of "muscular Christianity," a doctrine that originated in Britain in the early nineteenth century, believed that perfection of the body through physical exercise was an essential part of Christian morality and personal salvation. By the end of the nineteenth century, the idea that "character" could be shaped by physical exercise had gained broad currency. Pierre de Coubertin, founder of the modern Olympic Games, went so far as to declare in 1894 that "character is not formed by the mind, but primarily by the body."[9]

Gymnastics versus Sports

In Britain the mania for physical exercise was expressed mainly through sports, especially team sports, which developed into their modern forms in the second half of the nineteenth century. The rise of competitive sports in Britain was driven by broader processes lumped under the general heading of "modernization." Bureaucratization, standardization, specialization of roles, and quantification marked new features that separated modern sports from traditional predecessors. Urbanization provided one essential precondition for the development of modern sport: large numbers of people living in proximity and hence able to participate in common pastimes. Railroads provided cheap and efficient transportation that brought distant teams in competition against each other; rising literacy, the mass press, and telegraphy helped to communicate results across regions. Games that were local became sports that were national.

The main incubator for modern team sports was the English public school, where educators promoted and codified games for their male pupils as a way to instill the virtues of "manliness": courage, self-discipline, respect for rules, and fair play. By the 1850s elite education was dominated by the culture of athleticism, as Thomas Hughes memorably described in his 1857 novel of life at Rugby School, *Tom Brown's School Days*.[10] Students at Eton, whose battlefield victories were later famously attributed to their experiences on the school's playing fields, were obliged to play soccer once a day or be "fined half a crown and kicked."[11]

Originally the preserve of the upper class, sport became a middle-class craze in Britain in the last decades of the nineteenth century. It spread as well to the working class, spurred by technological advancements, more leisure time for workers, and a growing appreciation among social and religious leaders for sport's moral benefits. Upper-class reformers in Britain deliberately promoted certain sports as a means to divert potentially dangerous working-class energies into "civilized" channels. One British parliamentary committee opined that "if you provided [working people] with footballs and made them kick footballs, they would not be so inclined to kick policemen in the street."[12] Some sports remained the preserve of the wealthy (golf, yachting) as others (soccer) became associated with the working class. Social distinctions were maintained through the moral code of amateurism, which initially prescribed not only playing without material reward but also a "gentlemanly" style, effortless and scrupulously fair.[13] With few exceptions, sports were a male domain, celebrated as a quintessential expression of masculinity.

Originally introduced by English émigrés, sport also found a fertile home in the United States, where it was nurtured by the same conditions of industrialization, urbanization, and middle-class formation that had spurred its growth in Britain. Transforming English games into baseball and football, the United States claimed the title of world's foremost "sporting nation" by the end of the nineteenth century. What Mark Dyreson has called a "sporting republic" emerged in the period from 1880 to 1920, centered around the idea "that modern nations should employ the regulation and training of body and mind through organized athletics for the production of civic virtue and national vitality." Advocates of the "strenuous life," including Theodore Roosevelt, vigorously proclaimed that sports produced the type of citizen required for individual and national success.[14]

The European continent, however, proved far less hospitable to modern sport. Here indigenous gymnastics movements like *Turnen* in Germany and the Ling system in Sweden were deeply entrenched as the primary form of physical education and recreation. Though these systems were similar to sport in aiming to instill moral and patriotic values, they differed in key respects: they were noncompetitive, stressed group cohesion rather than individual effort, and valued process and posture over quantifiable achievement.

Often triggered by military defeat, gymnastics movements designed to rebuild national power and honor swept the Continent in the nineteenth century. It was first in the German states, after the Napoleonic occupation, that physical culture and fitness became political matters, when Friedrich Jahn devised *Turnen* as a way to strengthen physical and moral resources in the patriotic drive for national revival.[15] Jahn's exercise program centered on equipment he invented, such as the parallel bars, and was designed to promote both health and moral qualities. Also in the first decades of the nineteenth century (and also prompted by military defeats), Per Henrik Ling in Sweden pioneered what became known as Swedish gymnastics. Judging Jahn's approach too complicated, Ling devised instead a system based on slow, limited, and systematic movements.[16] As one historian describes it, the Ling system "relied largely on deliberate calisthenics and on the tonic effects of group or dual counterbalancing routines where individuals could aid one another by providing light resistance to muscular effort."[17] The German and Swedish brands of gymnastics were influential in physical education programs abroad, from the United States to Japan. Unlike sport, however, gymnastics lacked an internationalist ideology, an institutionalized framework, and an ethos of quantitatively based competition, which meant that the spread of gymnastics programs did not create the kind of cohesive community that the spread of sport facilitated.

In France exercise and fitness regimes were important elements of a military and nationalist revival. Defeat in the 1870–1871 Franco-Prussian War and fear of biological degeneration produced an obsession with physical culture. French thinkers at the end of the nineteenth century began to measure national decline in biological and medical terms. Hygienic concerns in turn gave rise to physical culture movements that aimed to resuscitate what many observers saw as a tired and effete civilization. By the 1880s prominent right-wing nationalist groups were agitating for mass participation in physical exercise programs. Rather than embracing sport, however, many French hygienists favored Swedish gymnastics. Proponents of this form ridiculed what they described as the "violent gestures so dear to English brutality and American barbarism" as well as the "harsh and automatic movements cherished by German militarists." Sport and German gymnastics both had their advocates, but the Swedish method predominated in military training and in public schools before World War I.[18] The military in particular was hostile to competitive sport, believing that it fostered individualism and could endanger the cohesion of the group.[19]

Most English observers were naturally convinced that their system of competitive sports produced far superior results, both physical and moral, than the gymnastics systems that dominated the Continent. One educator wrote in 1870 that the graduate of the French lycée, who was offered nothing but the regulated exercises of gymnastics, is "pale and worn, his limbs badly formed, his body without proper development, either elongated and thin, or stunted and obese, weak in either case. Mentally he is without decision, feels himself lost in the wide world, and detests law and order." In contrast, the English youth, given time for voluntary athletic sport, "usually possesses a clear complexion and well-proportioned figure; is able to shift for himself should circumstances compel him to do so; and is proverbially a law and order loving member of society." Some foreign observers agreed: one French journalist opined in 1862 that cricket had made the Englishman "a magnificent specimen of human kind."[20]

Despite the dominance of gymnastics in many parts of Europe, the English version of sport gained a foothold abroad in the last decades of the nineteenth century. This diffusion occurred less through proselytism than by a spontaneous process of imitation and adaptation. The British government made few active efforts to spread sports to other countries, and it was instead British merchants, students, sailors, and engineers, based wherever British power, commerce, or industry had penetrated, who formed sport clubs for recreation that then drew in locals to fill out teams or to provide competition.[21] The slow diffusion, hardly noticeable at first, would over time make sports of British origin nearly ubiquitous across the globe.

Sport and the State in the Interwar Years

The catalyst that transformed sport into a mass phenomenon of great social significance was World War I. During the war, military officials in many countries included sport in training programs to increase fitness and in recreational activities to keep recruits from less savory diversions.

At war's end the YMCA organized, for the American Expeditionary Force, an extensive series of athletic competitions that led to the Inter-Allied Games in France in 1919, a huge festival that drew about half a million spectators over two weeks. As a result of their military experience, millions of men were introduced to sport, significantly increasing its popularity and legitimacy.[22]

As sport became more widely popular around the world, the rise of a mass consumer culture in the years after the war provided a fertile home for its growth. The consumption of sport as spectacle—that is, spectator sport—grew even more rapidly than did participation in sport. Stadiums accommodating crowds in the tens of thousands were built; new forms—leagues, cups, championships—were devised to govern competition. Athletes, like the icons of other new forms of popular culture, became national stars with cult followings. Newspapers expanded their sport sections, and new dailies devoted exclusively to sport sprang up.

With sport's meteoric rise in popularity, government interest in sport expanded. As state regulation of populations increased sharply in areas such as managing the reproductive capacities and procreative practices of citizens, so, too, did state involvement in the promotion of recreation expand.[23] Many governments, dismayed by the poor fitness levels of their wartime recruits, turned to physical education and sport as key tools in raising military strength. In the twin tasks of preparing men for labor and war, the military aspect now assumed more importance. Most spectacularly in the dictatorships but by no means limited to them, sport in the interwar years took on a distinctly militarist flavor.

For the first time in many countries, governments were willing to devote substantial public resources to sports facilities and programs. Around the world educators and government officials adopted the view that physical education deserved a place in school alongside math, science, and literature. Many governments now formed ministries for sport or other specialized state agencies to oversee the promotion of physical recreation. In most cases the selection and preparation of teams for international competitions was left to private bodies, but these groups now often had government support. The French government, for example, in 1919 formed a Tourism and Sport Department in the Ministry of Foreign Affairs to promote France's image abroad, and in 1920 granted a small allowance to sports bodies preparing for the Olympic Games.[24]

Although it was a foreign import outside of Britain, modern sport proved to have an extraordinarily potent appeal to group sentiments, including those at the national level. Eric Hobsbawm has called sport "one of the most significant of the new social practices" directed toward nation-building in an age of mass politics.[25] As sports were adopted and became indigenized, they were appropriated for the construction and consolidation of national identities.[26] Cricket in India, rugby in France, soccer in Italy—all are examples of imported sports that became bound up with the creation of national traditions and the expression of perceived national characteristics.

The quest to build healthy, fit populations through physical education—which included both sport and gymnastics, but increasingly tilted toward sport—was a global phenomenon in the interwar years. The comments of one Iranian reformer reflected a view in common circulation: "In the thought of those who have investigated deeply the philosophy of the progress of nations and its secrets, [physical sport] is counted among the most prominent reasons for national power, for the nation's progress, independence, civilization, and survival."[27] Commenting in 1930 on the importance of participating in the Olympic Games, China's Foreign Minister Wang Zhengting expressed similar sentiments: "If a people wants to pursue freedom and equality in today's world, where the weak serve as meat on which the strong can dine, they must first train strong and fit bodies."[28]

Typically both social groups—often middle-class modernizers—and the state were involved in introducing and promoting physical education and sport programs with explicitly nationalist agendas. In Iran in the 1920s and 1930s, for example, an emerging, reform-minded middle class embraced sport as a beneficial use of free time at the same time that the monarchy adopted sport as part of its efforts to create a healthy and productive nation. Influenced by many of the same currents that had driven the physical culture movement in Europe—belief in the moral benefits of modern, disciplined sports practices, a desire to foster social cohesion and a national culture, and worries about the debilitating physical effects of modern lifestyles—Iranian social reformers and government officials spurred an upsurge in school sports programs and in private sports clubs. Although Iran would not send a team to the Olympic Games until 1948, by 1936 it had hundreds of clubs in sports like volleyball and soccer, and by 1939 the first national championships in athletics, football, and swimming were held.[29]

Perhaps the most avid emulator of Western practices, in sport as in so much else, was Japan. After the Meiji Restoration of 1867, physical education became part of modernizing efforts. Japan's Ministry of Education introduced calisthenics programs in schools as a way to build stronger bodies and instill obedience to the state. By the 1890s college educators and students turned to team sports and athletic clubs to foster stamina and self-discipline. Buoyed by what Donald Roden has called "the quest for national dignity," baseball surged in popularity. Like the ideologues of Victorian manliness in the West, Japanese student athletes paid homage to the "strenuous life" as a defense against the softening influences of industrial civilization. When a Japanese college team beat a team of U.S. residents in Yokohama in the first official U.S.-Japanese baseball game in 1896, Japanese proclaimed it as a "victory for the Japanese people" that would help accelerate Japan's rise to equal status among the world powers.[30] While some traditional activities like sumo, swordsmanship, and judo survived in modernized forms, Westernized sport was emphasized, as one U.S. writer put it, as a way "to gain the respect and admiration of the world."[31]

Many Japanese likewise saw participation in the Olympic Games as a way to secure international prestige. As early as 1911 the Japanese Amateur Athletic Association was organized to participate in international meets, and the country began sending teams to the Olympic Games in 1912. The state offered subsidies beginning in 1924, and by 1928 Japan had won its first medals. Remarking on the benefits Japan had accrued from that medal victory, one Japanese observer commented that it offered the first occasion for many foreigners to hear the Japanese anthem and see the Japanese flag. By 1936 Japan placed an impressive eighth in the unofficial national rankings at the Olympic Games and secured the right to be the first country outside Europe and the United States to host the event. As the 1930s wore on, sports and physical education were more overtly militarized, and Japan's expansionist projects eventually led to the abandonment of its plans to host the 1940 Games.[32]

In China, too, the promotion of modern physical culture was seen as an essential part of creating a modern state and citizens. In the first decades of the twentieth century both the Anglo-American model of sport, promoted by the YMCA, and European-style calisthenics and gymnastics made significant inroads in China. For Chinese modernizers, Andrew Morris has argued, these modern physical disciplines were not only a means to building a fit population; they would also "teach the values—competition, sportsmanship, confidence, awareness, discipline—that would create a new China." In the 1920s Republican China constructed what Morris calls a "liberal democratic physical culture" dominated by competitive sport and the values of sportsmanship and teamwork. This movement declined after 1928 as the Guomindang state introduced new fascist models of mass-based physical culture, though elite competitive sport persisted. The country's first participation in the Olympics came in 1932 and was seen, Morris concludes, "as a great step in establishing a foothold in the community of modern nations."[33]

Integration into the world of sport lagged in Africa. In sub-Saharan Africa, most of which was under colonial rule by European powers until the 1960s, missionaries and colonial administrators brought their sporting traditions with them, but before World War II organized sport for indigenous Africans was limited in many places to training programs for the army and the police and to a very small number of African schools.[34]

The Rise of International Sports Competitions

The same outward momentum that propelled sports competitions from city to region to nation also propelled competitions at the international level. International contests grew slowly before World War I, limited by sport's still narrow geographic base and by the high cost and slow pace of long-distance transportation. In the interwar years, the rapid expansion of sport and improvements in transportation led to an explosion in international meets of all kinds, from major multinational championships at the most elite level to informal competitions among weekend athletes.

The earliest international competitions were arranged informally between clubs, not between national organizations. For example, in 1885 the Paris Football Club and the English Civil Service Club arranged to play a rugby match in England; in 1887 a Southampton soccer club played at Le Havre; and in 1891 a delegation from the New York Athletic Club rowed against Racing Club in Paris, an event presided over by the U.S. ambassador to France.[35] In more elite circles such international meets began even earlier: the New York Cricket Club played a Toronto club in 1840; the America's Cup yachting race was founded in 1851; and Harvard met Oxford in a rowing match on the Thames in 1869.[36] By the 1890s national sports associations were becoming involved in arranging, sanctioning, and setting the terms of such competitions. In 1893, for example, the French sport union (the Union des sociétés françaises de sports athlétiques), with the help of the French Foreign Ministry, negotiated a convention on rowing with England's Committee of the Henley Royal Regattas to allow French rowers to participate in the English regattas.[37]

Although national rivalries made an appearance at such contests, these meetings were generally viewed as encounters between two groups of athletes. It was not until the first decade of the twentieth century that national sports associations began to field representative national teams for international matches, in which the team became synecdoche for the nation.[38] This development was in part a response to new ways of envisioning the nation. As Michael Budd has noted, "the tendency to envision nations as bodies helped to support notions that societies not only were dangerously susceptible to the forces of degeneration from within but also were organic entities that battled one another for survival on the outside."[39]

The founder of the modern Olympic Games justly noted that the creation of international championships was "the logical consequence of the great cosmopolitan tendencies of our times." Writing in 1896, Baron Pierre de Coubertin described the proliferation of international connections that were then arising:

> The great inventions of the age, railroads and telegraphs, have brought into communications people of all nationalities. Easier intercourse between men of all languages has naturally opened a wider sphere for common interests. Men have begun to lead less isolated existences, different races have learnt to know and understand each other better; they have compared their powers and achievements in the fields of art, industry and science, and a noble rivalry has sprung up amongst them, urging them on to greater accomplishments. Universal Exhibitions have collected together at one point of the globe the products of its remotest corners. In the domain of science and literature, assemblies and conferences have united the most distinguished intellectual laborers of all nations. Could it be otherwise, but that sportsmen also of divers nationalities should begin to meet each other on common ground?[40]

Coubertin, a French aristocrat who chose physical education as his life's work, is perhaps the single most influential individual in the history of modern international sport. A nationalist who was bitterly shaken by France's defeat in 1870–1871, the baron saw it as his primary mission to *rebronzer* (strengthen) France by implanting what he saw as the secret to English power and success: the moral and physical training produced by public-school sports. Sport, he believed, cultivated not only strong and healthy bodies but also moral qualities like patriotism and devotion to the common good. He scorned the German-style gymnastics that then predominated in French physical education as "nothing [but] ensemble movements, rigid discipline, and perpetual regimentation"; it was the competitive spirit bred by English athletics that he wanted to instill in French youth of all classes.[41] In the 1870s and 1880s his view of sport was not widely shared by other French reformers, for whom sport was both incompatible with the order and equilibrium they sought in physical exercise and, as a foreign import, an affront to nationalism.[42] For Coubertin, however, sport was a quintessentially modern practice, uniquely suited to the social and psychological demands of modern industrial society.[43]

With sport as yet little practiced in France, Coubertin hoped to popularize it through international competition, where French athletes could learn to emulate the exploits of champions. As he later reconstructed his reasoning: "Before 'popularizing' it would be necessary to 'internationalize.' . . . It would be necessary to organize contacts between our young French athleticism and the nations that had preceded us on the path of muscular culture. It would be necessary to give these contacts a periodicity and an indisputable prestige."[44]

In the 1890s Coubertin threw his personal, social, and financial resources into his campaign to further the spread of sport in France. He cultivated international contacts with like-minded men and traveled widely to examine conditions in other countries. In 1889 and 1893 he traveled to the United States to study the organization of sport and physical education in schools and universities. He was disappointed to find that German and Swedish gymnastics predominated in physical education programs, but found much to admire in the spectator sports that were becoming widely popular. According to biographer John MacAloon, Coubertin "saw sport as a dominant emblem and instrument of the vitality, democracy, and happy blending of tradition and modern innovation which he found distinctive of the United States."[45] During his 1889 visit he struck up friendships with Princeton historian William Morgan Sloane, who would play an important role in the founding of the International Olympic Committee, and with Theodore Roosevelt, an outspoken advocate of the "manly virtues" of sport and outdoor activities. When the Olympic Diploma was created in 1901, Coubertin made Roosevelt (by then president of the United States) its first recipient.[46]

In his quest to develop international sport competitions, Coubertin was influenced by a general European fascination with classical Greece and with ancient Olympia in particular. He was aware of the German excavations at Olympia in the 1870s and of local athletic festivals organized under the heading of Olympic Games.[47] Linking his athletic project to ancient Greece gave Coubertin's plan an aura of tradition and an ostensible link to a heroic past for what was otherwise a purely modern invention. The most salient difference, in his view, was that the ancient Games had been for Greeks only. The modern Games would be "international and universal."[48]

A central inspiration for Coubertin came from his visits to the world's fairs of 1889 in Paris and 1893 in Chicago. Beginning with the London Crystal Palace exhibition in 1851, world's fairs represented the largest international gatherings of the late nineteenth and early twentieth centuries, drawing tens of millions of visitors. Many of these exhibitions featured sports as part of the events, and the grounds of nearly every major exhibition in France, England, and the United States in the half-century before World War II were given over to sports after the fair ended. Beyond this close association, international sport competitions and exhibitions were structurally homologous: both brought representatives (or representations) of nations together. Sports events were less didactic, more explicitly competitive, and more temporally limited, and they offered much greater constraints in the means of representation. Like world's fairs, however, they offered arenas for the presentation of national achievements to international audiences and were major vehicles of worldwide cultural interaction.[49]

"Let us export rowers, runners and fencers," Coubertin declared when he first proposed a modern Olympic Games in 1892. "This is the free trade of the future, and on the day when it is introduced within the walls of old Europe, the cause of peace will have received a new and powerful support."[50] When this first insufficiently concrete proposal fell flat, he tried again. In 1894 he organized an International Athletic Congress at the Sorbonne, inviting dozens of individuals and officials of sport clubs to discuss harmonizing the rules of amateurism, which were subject then (and later) to widely varying standards. As he later admitted, the discussion of amateurism was a "screen" to ensure widespread participation. The meeting's real purpose was to "revive" the Olympic Games "on bases and in conditions suited to the needs of modern life."[51] Although Coubertin was the driving force behind the congress, he wanted to emphasize the broad international appeal of his ideas and, in particular, to ensure the involvement of the two countries most associated with modern sport. In the invitation and program, therefore, he listed England's C. Herbert and William Sloane of the United States as co-organizers.[52]

The Olympics' founding congress attracted seventy-eight official delegates, the majority from France, but twenty delegates from eight foreign countries (Belgium, Great Britain, Greece, Italy, Russia, Spain, Sweden, and the United States) were also present.[53] This time Coubertin's proposal was adopted almost without debate. The congress agreed to hold the Games in a different city every four years, with the honor of holding the first bestowed on Athens as a tribute to the Olympic Games of ancient Greece. "To emphasize the world character of the institution," as Coubertin put it, subsequent Games would be held in France (Paris, 1900) and the United States (St. Louis, Missouri, 1904).[54]

In Coubertin's formulation the Games were to include "all the forms of exercise in use in the modern world," but in fact his vision encompassed only modern Western recreations.[55] From the beginning, then, the Olympics embraced a narrow definition of the forms of physical contest suitable for the world stage. The initial program of events included not only "athletic" sports (track and field) but also gymnastics and recreations with aristocratic lineages—what Coubertin termed combat, equestrian, and nautical sports (for example, fencing, riding, and sailing). He tended to speak of all physical contests as "sports," despite the distinct genealogies of British athletic sports, elite pastimes, and European gymnastics, and although he included gymnastics in the programs of the Games, the Olympics from the outset emphasized the competition and individualism associated with the British model of competitive sport.[56] Coubertin himself wanted to include only individual sports, in keeping with the legacy of ancient Greece, but team sports gradually made their way onto the program.[57]

Although Coubertin himself was equivocal about the principle of amateurism, he accepted it as a deeply entrenched part of English sport.[58] In limiting participation in the Olympics to amateurs, the 1894 Congress adopted a relatively broad and flexible definition, excluding those athletes who had received money or prizes for competing or for work as sport teachers or coaches, but leaving open the question of reimbursement for expenses.[59] It was the first of many attempts to define a concept that would preoccupy the IOC for much of the next century. Enforcement of the definition was left to national bodies, but before 1912 there were few national Olympic committees that could enforce amateur rules consistently, resulting in frequent accusations that some countries were violating Olympic standards.[60]

The baron envisioned his great educational and athletic festival as a purely masculine endeavor. As the ancient Greeks had, he preferred to exclude women from the events altogether. The first Games were an all-male affair, but as early as 1900 women's events began to appear on the program in a handful of sports, such as tennis and archery, that many contemporaries regarded as suitably "feminine." Women's participation expanded slowly but steadily thereafter to track and field, swimming, and other events. Until late in the twentieth century, however, women represented only a small percentage of participants, and Olympic congresses were perpetual battlegrounds for debates about which events were appropriate for women.[61]

In Coubertin's vision the Olympic Games were deeply intertwined with pedagogical and moral aims. They were intended to be not just "ordinary world championships," but also "festival[s] of universal youth," combining the intellectual, moral, and religious bases of the ancient Games with the "democratic internationalism" of the modern world.[62] He explained:

> Our intention in reviving an institution that has lain forgotten for so many centuries, is as follows: Athletics are assuming growing importance every year. The part they play appears to be as important and as lasting in the modern world as it was in antiquity; they reappear moreover with new characteristics; they are international and democratic, suited therefore to the ideas and needs of the present day.[63]

He expected the Games to develop "nobility of sentiments, high regard for the virtues of unselfishness and honour, a spirit of chivalry, virile energy and peace."[64] To further his educational mission he added art competitions to the Olympic roster in 1912, awarding prizes for Olympic- or sport-themed entries in architecture, sculpture, music, painting, and literature.

The symbolic and ceremonial aspects of the Olympic Games that Coubertin was careful to cultivate have done much to shape the appeal and influence of the event. He was powerfully influenced at the 1889 Paris world's fair by rites that he would later appropriate for the opening ceremony of the Games: entry procession, flag raising, national anthems, the declaration of opening by the host nation's head of state.[65] The symbols and rites of the Olympics were expanded in the interwar years to include the Olympic flag, the Olympic flame, the Olympic Village, and the torch relay.

In Coubertin's view, bringing the youth of the world together every four years for "a happy and brotherly encounter" would serve to "gradually efface the peoples' ignorance of things which concern them all, an ignorance that feeds hatreds, accumulates misunderstandings and hurtles events along a barbarous path towards a merciless conflict."[66] For Coubertin, the rhetoric of peaceful internationalism was not a façade but an expression of deeply held convictions. Coubertin had close ties to the fin de siècle European peace movement and was likely influenced by models of private international organizations like the one set up to administer the Nobel Prizes.[67] (Coubertin himself was nominated for a Nobel Peace Prize in the 1930s.) Promoting a French nationalist revival was one goal of the Olympics, but it was not incompatible, in Coubertin's view, with the promotion of international peace. "Wars break out," he wrote, "because nations misunderstand each other. We shall not have peace until the prejudices which now separate the different races shall have been outlived."[68] He was not so naive as to assert that merely bringing people together would overcome prejudices; he was all too aware that encounters with foreign peoples could simply confirm or exacerbate prejudices. As his biographer writes, a true internationalist, in Coubertin's view, celebrated national differences "as different ways of being human," and it was the recognition of such differences that would lead to peace and mutual respect. In ways he never clearly spelled out, Coubertin was convinced that Olympic athletes, officials, and spectators were true internationalists, drawn into deep and rich interaction with foreign cultures that produced genuine experiences of common humanity.[69]

This vision became deeply embedded in the self-understanding of promoters of international sports. It was most overt at the Olympic Games, but the sentiment was broadly used as a justification for international sport contests in general. Organizers of such contests frequently acclaimed sport as "the best League of Nations," arguing that international competition on the basis of sportsmanship and fair play produced mutual understanding, respect, and goodwill not only among the participating athletes but also among the broader public.[70] The idea that sport created a genuine fraternity that transcended national, religious, and racial barriers more effectively than traditional diplomacy or other forms of international communication pervaded the rhetoric of sports in the interwar years. It was an idea repeated in various guises across the world. Compare, for example, the remarks of a U.S. coach in 1935, who wrote that international athletic tours "create an atmosphere of friendship that cements the Nations into one large family. Diplomatic relations, tourist travel, and commerce are a great help, but the greatest good is derived from having our athletes compete on foreign soil," with the comment in a Malayan sports magazine in 1932 that "cricket knows no creed, religion, or politics. A well chosen cricket team is the best possible ambassador—as good as and certainly cheaper than any League of Nations."[71]

For his part, Coubertin intended the Games to inspire both patriotism and peaceful internationalism. He saw no conflict between love of one's country and respect, based on recognition of difference, for other countries. In the 1894 appeal that founded the Olympic movement, he called for "representatives of the nations" to meet face-to-face in "peaceful and chivalrous contests [that] constitute the best of internationalisms."[72] Athletes, in his view, would participate for the glory of their countries and at the same time develop a mutual understanding that could be "a potent, if indirect factor in securing universal peace."[73] From the beginning, however, there were those who saw in international sport the exact opposite tendencies.

Nationalism and the Politics of International Sports

When Coubertin first floated his idea of instituting a modern version of the Olympic Games in 1894, Charles Maurras was among the plan's most vigorous opponents. An extreme right-wing nationalist, a monarchist, and founder of the political movement l'Action française, Maurras regarded the growth of international sporting competitions with disdain. He was repulsed by the "mixing" of different nationalities at such events. In his view such events produced "the worst disorders of cosmopolitanism." Still, when the first Games were held in Athens in 1896, he packed his bags and went to see for himself. To his surprise and delight, he saw none of the international understanding and goodwill promised by the organizers. "Far from suppressing patriotic passion, all this false cosmopolitanism in the stadium serves only to inflame it," he wrote in *La Gazette de France*. "In the past, nations dealt with each other through ambassadors . . . Now peoples will confront each other directly, insulting each other face-to-face." Coubertin and his supporters claimed that bringing people together would promote peace, but Maurras was convinced the opposite was true. The contact engendered at events like the Olympic Games, he gleefully concluded, would propel rather than propitiate the forces of international enmity and mistrust.[74]

Centering the Olympic revival on the principle of competition among "representatives of the nations," rather than among individuals, inevitably led to the use of the Games for nationalist and chauvinist purposes. In the years before World War I, each successive Olympiad saw an increase in expressions of nationalism. Genuine national teams, selected by national organizations as the best representatives in particular sports, made an appearance at the 1908 Games in London. At the same time, several European governments began to provide small subsidies to cover the expenses of their teams.[75] In 1912, at the Stockholm Olympics, public opinion began to see in the Games "a measure of national prowess as well as a test of individual ability."[76] As preparations for the 1916 Berlin Games got under way, president of the American Olympic Committee Robert Thompson noted approvingly that "the nations [are] entering into the spirit of competition with a whole-heartedness that has been missing in past Olympic games. Instead of the individual athlete being the first consideration, the nation now directs the actions of the athletes, and this . . . will result in better competition, world-wide interest, and add to the importance of the games."[77]

These rather tentative signs of sporting nationalism paled beside the excesses that would come to characterize the interwar period. As sport's domestic popularity increased, so did its international significance. Governments began to actively promote international competitions as a way to publicize national achievements. The outcome of these contests was interpreted by governments and by the general public not just as an indication of the athletic abilities of individuals or teams, but also as a reflection of the quality of a country's sociopolitical system. Victories became a barometer of a nation's overall power and prestige, in part because sport seemed to offer a universal and easily quantifiable standard of achievement. In the Olympic Games, for example, a point total (computed in various ways) quickly became a standard way to measure the overall performance of a national team. Like steel output or export of manufactures, then, performance in international competitions produced a number that, in the view of many observers, correlated with national strength.

The embrace by governments of international sport as a medium for promoting national prestige can be attributed in part to one of sport's most unique characteristics. Unlike other forms of culture, which can be judged by different standards, sport offers a single, universally accepted standard of achievement. By its nature, any sporting event is bounded by rules accepted by all parties, and the result of the event is therefore determined (at least in theory) only by merit: the best man wins. As with any other form of communication, different cultures may attribute different meanings to the same event, but there is a core set of rules and assumptions that frame the acceptable bounds of interpretation.

It was the relative latecomers to sport in Europe that were most likely to link sports achievements with national power and to devote government subsidies to secure them. The British government steadfastly adhered to the view that sport was a private, nonpolitical matter. When the Foreign Office briefly departed from this position in 1929, quietly suggesting to the Football Association that perhaps it ought to send only its strongest teams for competitions in Europe, the press immediately ridiculed the idea that international sport competition should be linked with "abstract considerations" of "British prowess." "The view of the Whitehall mandarins," one article scathingly remarked, "seems to be that unless our footballers were fairly certain of winning, British prestige would receive an irreparable blow, the peace of Europe would be endangered, and Sir Austen Chamberlain would have to do whatever Herr Stresemann told him."[78]

The U.S. government took a similarly hands-off approach toward international sport, as it did toward cultural relations in general, providing no subsidies for and evincing little interest until the Cold War made everything from ballet to space exploration a matter of urgent state importance in the struggle against communism.[79] Politicians, military leaders, and sports officials nonetheless commonly cited the defense of national honor as a central justification for international competition. In the words of one top sports official, every U.S. Olympic athlete should recognize that "he will compete not for himself alone, but for all of his fellow countrymen . . . If American life produces better men and women, we should be able to prove it by comparative performances in the Olympic Games."[80]

As athletes came to be viewed as "ambassadors" for their respective countries, sport was increasingly subject to the vicissitudes of international relations. Although international sport organizations in principle adamantly insisted on the separation of sport and politics, in practice sport was inherently politicized and politics often forcefully intruded on sport relations. One striking example of this phenomenon was the ostracism of Germany by the victors' sport associations after World War I. The French, the British, and the Belgians refrained from sport competitions against German teams until political relations between the Allies and Germany were normalized in the mid-1920s. Representatives of the Entente powers also sought to remove German members from international sport federations, in many cases successfully. When the international soccer federation refused to institute an official ban on meetings with soccer clubs in Germany, the British withdrew from the organization. With the tacit agreement of the IOC, the organizers of the 1920 Olympic Games in Antwerp excluded the defeated Central Powers from the list of invitees. Austria and Hungary were allowed to participate in the 1924 Games in Paris, but Germany was barred until 1928.[81]

Who was right, Coubertin or Maurras? The debate has continued to rage to the present day. One side argues that global sport contests inflame nationalist passions and incite international hostility. As George Orwell put it, sport is just "war without the shooting." The other side argues with equal conviction that international contests, by bringing people of different races and nationalities face-to-face in friendly competition, leads both competitors and fans to a deeper understanding of other groups, an understanding that naturally serves to promote peace.

The experience of the twentieth century has in many respects borne out Maurras's predictions. The sport system can be, and often has been, a vessel of nationalist hostility, and on at least one occasion an international sport event has been a contributing factor in triggering war.[82] Yet sports competitions also subsume nationalism in an internationalist structure and can foment not only hostility but also cooperation—sometimes both at the same time. Coubertin was partly correct, too.[83]

The story of the Olympic Games and other international contests is not simply one of nationalist urges masquerading in humanitarian guise.

What Maurras failed to see is that Olympic claims to promote mutual understanding and respect among different national groups have a legitimate foundation: a genuinely internationalist element underpins the practice of international sport. Simply to play the same game on the same field according to the same rules is to acknowledge an essential equality, a common humanity, among competitors. The competitive spirit of modern sport thrusts it in a universalist direction. (Significantly, this universalism has been coded as "male," and the world of sport in the twentieth century was a masculine domain into which women were permitted only partially and often reluctantly.) Sport's competitive, hierarchical dynamic means that the best competitor in one region is naturally driven to test his skills against ever-widening circles of competitors. Physical contests were once unique expressions of a local community, ipso facto restricted to members of that community, with outcomes of purely local significance. Now, physical contests are global and their results become part of the permanent record of human achievement. Athletes compete not just against their immediate competitors, but also against all of humanity—past, present, and future. Measurement, quantification, and the pursuit of records inexorably further the view that an athlete, though he or she may act in one sense as a representative of his or her nation, is also fundamentally part of a universal human endeavor.

Unlike sport, gymnastics staked its appeal on a purely national level. German gymnastics, for example, zealously protected and celebrated its uniquely German character, disdaining any internationalism beyond pan-Germanism. Global *Turnen* was an oxymoron. Especially in Europe, gymnastics remained a central, often preeminent element of physical culture through the interwar years. By the end of the 1920s, modern sport had established itself as a major form of popular culture alongside gymnastics in many parts of Europe, and was a mass phenomenon in Japan and in many parts of Latin America. Yet gymnastics systems and traditional games and contests continued to thrive, and the outcome— that sport would become the dominant form of physical recreation throughout the world—was not predetermined. The onset of a worldwide Depression and the turn toward isolationism and autarky in many countries might suggest that modern sport's internationalizing momentum would have been halted in the 1930s. Instead, it accelerated.

2

The Rise of International Sports Organizations

As the nineteenth century's burst of nationalism and imperialism pushed the world toward an integrated system of nation-states, it also spawned new forms of internationalism. The half-century before World War I saw a striking proliferation of international organizations, both private and governmental, devoted to endeavors as diverse as standardizing weights and measures, promoting a universal language, humanizing the conditions of war, and safeguarding public health. In the 1890s a new form of organization appeared, whose mission in some senses touched on all of these fields: the international sport organization. By 1914 about a dozen such groups had been formed to regulate individual sports and international competitions. As their power and influence grew, they would come to play a critical role in shaping the "imaginary world" of global sport. These bodies, as structures that disseminated ideas and practices to virtually every country aspiring to membership in international society, helped to channel and shape the explosion of nationalist movements in the twentieth century.

As was true of the international system more generally, the world of sport was fundamentally a European creation. Though claiming universal relevance, international sport was run at the outset almost exclusively by white, Christian, aristocratic or upper-middle-class European men. Like the international political system, the sport system was framed as a means of making the world more humane, orderly, and peaceful. Idealistic internationalism, a movement that sought to promote peace through international contact, was a powerful current in the period when the first international sports organizations were founded, and the imprint of their birth in the milieu of peaceful internationalism is visible in these organizations' continued adherence to the idea that sport promotes peace as a central element in their claims to legitimacy.

International nongovernmental organizations, as sociologists John Boli and George Thomas have suggested, "seek, in a general sense, to spread 'progress' throughout the world: to encourage safer and more efficient technical systems, more powerful knowledge structures, better care of the body, friendly competition and fair play." Sport organizations fit clearly within these parameters, with one major exception. While most international nongovernmental organizations are characterized by strong norms of open membership and democratic decision making, sport organizations are typically governed autocratically, with self-appointed memberships and often with closed voting procedures.[1] This difference, rooted in the historical circumstances of their foundings, would come to have profound implications for the world of sport.

International organizations were central to the creation of a global sport culture. Themselves global bodies, they were instrumental in endowing sport with a cultural autonomy separate from local and national contexts—or, to put it more simply, in allowing the same games to be played all over the world. As sociologist Norbert Elias has explained: "At the level of traditional local outdoor contests without hard and fast rules, the game and the players were still largely identical. An impromptu move, the whim of a player which pleased the others, might alter the traditional pattern of the game. The higher organizational level of a regulating and supervising club endowed the game with a measure of autonomy in relation to the players. And that autonomy grew as supervisory agencies at a higher level of integration took over the effective control of the game."[2] Sports never became entirely divorced from the contexts in which they were played or from the influence of the athletes who played them. Local cultures continued to interpret the meaning and significance of games in different ways, and games continued to be played with local styles and inflections. Nevertheless, as Elias points out, the relative autonomy of a sport—the degree to which its form and content were determined outside the local context—increased as the power of national and international federations grew.

Despite the formative role these organizations played in disseminating and shaping global sport, their role in global affairs, like the role of international organizations more generally, is little understood.[3] Today sport organizations are global behemoths, with control over worldwide events that generate billions of dollars in revenue and that capture the attention and imagination of billions of people. It is a power undreamed of by the men who, a century ago, founded the tiny organizations that for years foundered on the edge of obscurity and bankruptcy. During the interwar years these organizations transformed themselves from marginal, unstable groups into powerful global bodies, asserting sharp control over the shaping of an international sport regime. Weak and poorly organized at the outset, sport organizations in the long term demonstrated greater longevity and more widespread appeal than many similar organizations founded before World War I.[4]

By the 1930s a sea change in the international sport world was under way. With the success of the 1932 Games in Los Angeles, the IOC found itself in charge of a festival that had grown from a rather marginal curiosity to an event of great public, commercial, and diplomatic significance. This position gave the IOC greater leverage in its dealings with other sports organizations and with national governments, even while leaving it increasingly susceptible to the vicissitudes of international politics. The Olympics also raised the profile of the various sports on its program, and the IOC's reliance on international sport federations to set the technical regulations of the Games enhanced the power and legitimacy of these federations. Other events, most notably the World Cup staged by the international soccer federation beginning in 1930, generated sizable revenues from gate receipts and later from new sources like radio broadcasting, producing a measure of financial stability for some international federations that allowed them to develop a permanent and salaried bureaucratic apparatus. Whereas previously such federations had been weak associations in which national bodies retained primary control over domestic affairs, the balance of power now began to shift in favor of a centralized administration.

When sport surged in popularity after World War I, these organizations were able to channel the international dimension of the sport craze to their advantage. How they did so can be seen by examining the development of the two most significant sport organizations: the IOC, which claimed authority over the world's largest amateur sport festival, and the Fédération internationale de football association (FIFA), the international federation that oversaw the world's most popular team sport, Association football (known in the United States as soccer).[5] Although the two represent divergent trends in the 1920s and 1930s—the IOC adhered tightly to amateurism even as FIFA moved to embrace professionalism, often bringing the two into conflict—their development followed similar patterns. Each succeeded in establishing monopolistic control over its sphere of interest, allowing it to constrict the parameters of sporting life around a narrowly defined conception of sport. Initially composed only of European and North American members, each organization had universalist pretensions and pursued global expansion as a way to achieve this end. Each came to center its membership on the principle of nationalism and provided a major forum for the expression of nationalism on a global stage. Each channeled that nationalism in internationalist directions, shaping an emerging conception of a global community that claimed to transcend race, class, and national divisions.

Sport Organizations before World War I

Bureaucratization and standardization were preconditions for the nationalization of modern sport, because for a sport to be truly national, it had to be played under the same rules throughout the country. Efforts to create a single, nationwide set of rules were spurred by improvements in communication and transportation, especially the railroad, that made it possible for teams and individuals from different regions to compete against one another. The quantitative focus of modern sport also furthered the movement for standardization because records set at different times and places could be compared if they had been made under uniform conditions. Bureaucratization and standardization naturally occurred first in England, the birthplace of modern sport. The twin processes channeled the vast spectrum of games that centered on the kicking of balls, for example, into two distinct sports—rugby and soccer—whose rules were codified in the 1860s by national organizations created for that purpose.

Such national organizations usually claimed jurisdiction over a single sport, with the right to set standard rules and eligibility requirements. (In most cases, eligibility rules meant enforcing the moral code of amateurism.) In Britain, for example, the Football Association was formed in 1863, the Rugby Football Union in 1871, and the Amateur Athletic Association in 1880. The decades before World War I saw a similar flowering of organizations in Europe. In Germany between 1883 and 1902 associations were organized for rowing, bicycling, track and field, soccer, and tennis.[6]

Such organizations often began by controlling a few clubs in one local-
ity and then gradually expanded their powers over other clubs and other
areas, often struggling against rival authorities, until they became truly
national bodies with monopolistic or near-monopolistic control over a
single sport or a group of related sports. Their spheres of competence expanded to include organizing competitions and championships, certifying the validity of records and results, disseminating information, and
creating increasingly detailed standards to ensure uniformity. When the
English Football Association was formed in 1863, for example, it had
only ten member clubs and was one of many associations that had codified a set of rules. During the next fifteen years, it established a position
as the leading national soccer body, gaining a permanent office, a salaried
secretary, and one thousand members. In addition to establishing a uniform set of rules and eligibility requirements, it organized national
championships, beginning in 1871 with the Challenge Cup.[7] Eventually
national multisport unions acting as umbrella organizations for bodies
governing individual sports were formed. Like the Amateur Athletic
Union of the United States (AAU), these organizations often organized
international meets and enforced amateur standards.

In similar fashion the growth of international competitions spurred
the establishment of international sport federations. The increasing frequency and growing prestige attached to these meets created pressures
for guidelines on rules, refereeing, and eligibility. The impetus for establishing federations often came from European countries, whose proximity to one another and late entry into sport made international authority
more desirable than it was for the pioneers, Britain and the United
States. Britain's national associations proved reluctant to initiate or to encourage the formation of international authorities in the sports they had
invented or standardized. FIFA, for example, which governed Britain's
most popular sport, was formed in 1904 at French initiative, without
British support; before 1946 it received only intermittent British participation. It was often the leaders of European national associations who
took the lead in forming international federations, and because these
men were naturally intent on maintaining their prerogatives within their
national fiefdoms, these federations were initially quite weak. At first
they had no powers over the domestic affairs of the national bodies that
comprised them, many of which continued to maintain their own rules
and standards for domestic matches. Indeed, national associations saw

international federations as a way to protect and enhance their own powers against rival organizations that might arise in their own countries. One of the major functions of the international federations, then, was to support each national association's monopoly position over the sport in question in its country. International federations also formed before many countries had created national organizations, so that it was often international bodies that prompted the formation of domestic ones.[8]

By 1914 fourteen international federations had sprung up, governing popular sports with significant levels of international competitions, including rowing, skating, cycling, soccer, weight lifting, swimming, tennis, and track and field. In the interwar period additional federations for archery, field hockey, skiing, canoeing, basketball, and equestrian sports were formed.[9] At first these organizations wielded limited authority and rested on precarious financial bases.[10] Only a few developed into significantly powerful institutions before 1945, but all succeeded in imposing greater standardization of rules and norms and in facilitating the internationalization of sport.

Federations were relatively slow to create world championships, in part because the Olympic Games offered many sports the equivalent of a championship and in part because costs were prohibitively high; long-distance travel was still time-consuming and expensive. World championships nevertheless slowly became a part of the sport landscape, appearing in ice skating in 1896, shooting in 1897, tennis in 1900, gymnastics in 1903, fencing and cycling in 1921, bobsleigh and ice hockey in 1924, wrestling in 1929, soccer in 1930, and skiing in 1937. In many cases these were primarily, if not exclusively, European events, and it was only gradually that their geographic reach came to justify the "world" label. Other major international competitions, staged on a regular basis but not under the auspices of the federations, were begun in these years, such as the enormously popular Tour de France, the cycling race created by the French sport newspaper *L'Auto* in 1903.[11]

The International Olympic Committee

The IOC, as we have seen, was founded in 1894 by Pierre de Coubertin to oversee the staging of a modern quadrennial Olympic festival. At the outset its membership was handpicked by Coubertin. As he noted, he deliberately chose "almost exclusively absentee members," mostly aristocrats and directors of educational institutions who would lend the committee credibility while leaving him a free hand in its direction. He was also careful, however, to cement the international character of the organization by choosing men from eleven countries.[12] The committee was nevertheless overwhelmingly European. Before World War I, it included only a handful of representatives from North and South America and one each from New Zealand, Australia, Japan, Turkey, Egypt, and South Africa.[13] Its official languages were French and English, and it required its members to speak one or both of these languages. Its annual decision-making sessions (the plenary meetings of members) were almost invariably held in Europe, further discouraging the participation of non-European members, who had to pay their own travel and hotel expenses.

The IOC was undemocratic as well as Eurocentric. In a move that would have lasting repercussions, Coubertin chose to structure the IOC not along the lines of nineteenth-century middle-class sport "associations," which were based on open admittance and governed by democratically elected committees, but instead on the model of an eighteenth-century aristocratic, self-appointed "club": the Henley Royal Regatta. Members were co-opted for life terms and were supposed to represent the IOC to their countries, rather than being representatives of their countries to the IOC.[14] First as general secretary and then as president, Coubertin had autocratic powers and ran the committee almost single-handedly, with the advice of an inner circle of Olympic enthusiasts, including William Sloane of the United States, Jiri Guth-Jarkovsky of Austria-Hungary, and Victor Balck of Sweden.[15] The high proportion of aristocrats on the committee would gradually decline, but it would for decades continue to be heavily dominated by rich European men.

In its structure the committee was not based on equality of members. It did not (and still does not) adhere to a one-country, one-vote system, nor are countries that participate in the Olympics entitled to de jure representation: some countries had two or even three representatives on the IOC, while others had none. Because selection was made on the basis of personal connections among IOC members, rather than by national organizations selecting representatives to send to the committee, the organization had a very clubby, "old-boy" character. It had no black members until 1963 and no women in its ranks until 1981.[16]

One of the major focuses of IOC efforts in the early years was to encourage standardization of rules. Coubertin lamented in 1898 that "every country has its own rules" and "discord reigns supreme from one end to the other" in the world of sport.[17] At a 1901 IOC meeting some members pressed for internationally binding rules. The AAU, in anticipation of organizing the 1904 St. Louis Games, proposed that the IOC reach an agreement on standard rules with international sport federations, and in 1902 the IOC sent a questionnaire on the matter to all national and international federations involved. The small number of replies received suggested that international federations were as yet too weak to impose uniform standards.[18] At a 1905 IOC meeting Coubertin again advocated the standardization of rules for international competitions, but without practical effect.[19] Thus, for lack of a better alternative, technical regulations at the early Olympics were left largely in the hands of the local organizers, which led to frequent disputes between host and visitors.[20]

The early Olympic Games were rather haphazard and unremarkable affairs. The first, held in Athens in 1896, was poorly advertised, attracted relatively few athletes, and garnered little notice in the European press.[21]

At the 1930 Berlin Congress of the International Olympic Committee, a well-connected group of aristocrats and the wealthy; from left: Reichstag President Paul Löbe, German IOC member Theodor Lewald, IOC President Count Henri de Baillet-Latour, and Interior Minister Josef Wirth. *Source:* © Bildarchiv Preussischer Kulturbesitz, Berlin.

The 1900 Games in Paris and the 1904 Games in St. Louis were mere sideshows to the world's fairs they were staged alongside. Some of the athletes did not even know they were participating in the Olympics.[22] The relative insignificance of the early Olympic Games was a reflection of sport's marginal status in much of Europe, where sport was still often viewed with suspicion as the "English disease." As Coubertin remarked, it was difficult to attract spectators to sporting events, and most politicians saw sport as "something quite unimportant, only to be appreciated to a minor degree like any other healthy amusement."[23]

The IOC's financial situation was precarious and would remain so in most respects until television revenues became a significant source of income in the 1960s. Until then, income was derived from voluntary contributions and small annual subscriptions.[24] The expenses of organizing the Games were borne by the organizing committee in the host country, and even when the Games achieved a surplus, as they did in Los Angeles in 1932, the IOC did not seek a percentage. Although office expenses were small—Coubertin paid for them out of his own pocket—the president was also expected to assume the costs of festivities associated with IOC meetings, which especially in the early years were high-society gatherings filled with garden parties, costumed riding displays, and diplomatic receptions. Even though Coubertin received a large inheritance in 1905, the costs of his Olympic and other pedagogical ventures left him nearly bankrupt by the time he died in 1937.[25]

By the outbreak of World War I, however, the Games were on a relatively firm footing. Still marginal in comparison to the heights of popularity reached in the 1930s, they were nevertheless well-enough established that their continuation even after four years of war was not seriously in doubt. (To safeguard the principle of Olympic neutrality during the war, Coubertin moved his headquarters from Paris to Lausanne, Switzerland, in 1915.)[26] At the outset a body that existed only on paper, the IOC had developed by the 1920s the trappings of an established institution: a charter, annual sessions, periodic congresses, a publication, and administrative headquarters.[27] It did not, however, have any official legal status until much later.[28]

In the years after the war, international sport federations became better organized and more powerful and began to demand a greater role in the staging of the Olympics. As a result, the 1920s saw escalating conflict between the federations and the IOC. While the IOC wished to have the federations assume responsibility for the technical rules at the Games, it was reluctant to share authority in determining the program of events. It also tried to discourage federations from staging world championships that could serve as rivals to the Olympic Games and rebuffed federation efforts to gain official representation on the IOC. Disputes over the power to set and enforce definitions of amateurism also sharpened, as federations like FIFA (for soccer), which controlled the most popular event at the Olympics and was thus a critical source of revenue for Games organizers in the 1920s, pushed for looser restrictions on payments to players.[29] As national Olympic committees began to form as permanent bodies, they, too, demanded a greater role in the staging of the Games.[30] Despite these disputes, however, a division of labor was established that contributed to the consolidation of the Games. The IOC determined the program, location, and general philosophy governing the Games, the national committees oversaw participation; and the international federations set the technical regulations and made final judgments on the eligibility of athletes.

In the 1920s the IOC became an institution with a life of its own, no longer subject to the autocratic control of its founder. In 1921, as Coubertin prepared for a trip to South America, he formed an executive committee within the IOC to handle affairs in his absence, and it quickly transformed the IOC from an autocracy to an oligarchy.[31] Dissatisfied both with the direction of international sport, which he felt was moving away from his central pedagogical concerns, and with the usurpation of power by the executive committee, Coubertin resigned from the IOC in 1925, though he continued to lend his support to Olympism. Count Henri de Baillet-Latour of Belgium, a passionate equestrian who had served as IOC member for Belgium since 1903 and as vice chairman of the executive committee since 1921, was elected as the new president.[32] Until his death in 1942, Baillet-Latour steered the Olympic movement to new heights of popularity and growth.

The Fédération Internationale de Football Association

International sport federations had a complicated relationship with the Olympic Games, partly antagonistic and partly cooperative. The tremendous rise in sport spectatorship after World War I meant that federations controlling sports with potential profitability (such as soccer, skating, and boxing) had significant opportunities outside the Olympics to exercise power and generate revenue. Federations governing these sports were pulled in the direction of professionalism. Typically they continued to oversee amateur-level competition but soon came to devote much of their attention to the professionals who generated major revenues and especially to championship events for professionals. Federations supervising less-popular sports (such as fencing, rowing, and weight lifting) wielded less autonomy because they relied on the Olympic Games to provide publicity and recognition they would not have been able to achieve on their own. In some cases these sports staged annual amateur championships of their own. In others federations relied on the Olympics every four years to serve as the pinnacle sporting event.

The federations benefited from the growing popularity of sport that the Olympics helped to foster, but they were also driven by independent concerns. Whereas the IOC's mandate was limited to staging a quadrennial festival, federations were responsible for a wide range of day-to-day activities involved in sport governance. In the interwar years many federations vastly increased their powers and expanded their activities to new realms. Few did so as boldly and as successfully as did FIFA, which initiated a quadrennial professional championship that quickly established itself as a rival to the Olympics.[33] FIFA's control of the period's most widely popular sport gave it access to more power and resources than other federations, but the dynamics of FIFA's growth are broadly similar to those of other federations that sprang up in the first years of the twentieth century.[34]

The soccer federation was founded by wealthy Europeans who were involved in sports at the local level and sought greater control at the national level. Dutch and French soccer club owners founded FIFA in 1904 after being rebuffed by the British, who had invented the game but showed little interest in sharing international governance with others. (Then, as now, Britons have tended to regard with suspicion schemes from other parts of Europe to create transnational bureaucracies.) FIFA counted seven members at its founding: the football federations of France, Belgium, Denmark, the Netherlands, Spain, Sweden, and Switzerland. Within a few years, FIFA membership had expanded to include almost every country with a significant football constituency.[35]

The major aims of the federation were to secure and enhance the powers of its member associations, and in this task it quickly demonstrated success. As the initial statutes indicated, FIFA's goals were "to regulate and develop international soccer and to take to heart the interests of its affiliated associations." Thus, the very first article in the statutes required reciprocal and exclusive recognition of member associations "as the sole associations governing the sport of Association football in their respective countries and as the sole competent authorities to engage in international relations."[36] By requiring that only one association be recognized in each country, FIFA legitimized each association's monopoly control of soccer within its country. (Britain was a key exception to this rule; it was allowed to have separate member associations for England, Wales, Scotland, and Northern Ireland.) As an official later described, membership in FIFA was "an insurance premium for the authority of each national association in its own area." In its first decade FIFA's support helped member associations in England, Belgium, and the United States ward off challenges from rival organizations.[37]

FIFA also promoted its own monopolistic aspirations in the international sphere by requiring that matches be played only among member associations.[38] By 1908, the rule was strengthened to prohibit any matches against nonmembers, whether deemed international or not.[39] It thus ensured that any country aspiring to play top-level football had to become a member or languish in isolation. It also claimed for itself the sole right to stage an international championship, though it would not choose to exercise that prerogative until 1930. For the moment, soccer's inclusion on the program of the Olympic Games, beginning in 1908, was enough.

In its early years the new soccer body made little effort to establish uniform standards for international competitions. It did not occupy itself with the rules of the game, instead using the British rules set by Britain's International Football Association Board as the international standard. In 1913 FIFA was granted representation on the international board, but effectively without power, as the British members reserved the right to implement changes even over FIFA's veto. Germany's national soccer association objected that "FIFA must become the unrestrained governing body in International Football." As FIFA's secretary-treasurer noted, the new arrangement put FIFA in a "peculiar position." Now "the whole"—the multinational organization—"would be represented in a part"—a national body. It was, he said, as if the central government of a country was offered representation in the municipal administration of that country's capital. The objections were voted down, however, and FIFA's Congress recognized the board's authority to determine the laws of the game, biding its time before attempting to assert control in this sphere.[40]

In the years after World War I the activities and powers of the federation grew rapidly, in tandem with the striking rise in popular interest in soccer and in international competitions. FIFA began to assert more authority over its member associations, particularly in enforcing standards of amateurism, which produced some grumbling in the 1920s.[41] The federation also began to assert more independence in relation to the IOC and voted at last to run its own world championship.

President Jules Rimet and Secretary Henry Delaunay, two Frenchmen long involved in French soccer who were now at FIFA's helm, persuaded FIFA's 1928 Congress to set up a world soccer championship. They recognized that the preconditions for such an event were in place. The organization was now large and stable, and its long-running efforts to promote uniform international rules had achieved success.[42] But the World Cup was, above all, a reflection of the fact that soccer had outgrown the Olympics. By 1928 soccer events were the major draw at the Olympics, bringing in about a quarter million spectators, and were key to the financial success of the Games. Yet the boom in soccer's popularity after the war had also pushed the sport toward professionalization, putting it on a collision course with IOC standards of amateurism.

Long established in Britain, professional leagues appeared in Hungary, Austria, Czechoslovakia, and Spain by the late 1920s; in much of the rest of Europe and in Argentina, Brazil, and Uruguay semiprofessionalism was rampant.[43] With amateurism defined in narrow terms, many forms of remuneration were construed as professionalism, including payments for broken time (salary lost during training or competitions), prizes, benefits like meals and equipment, jobs as physical education instructors, and commercial endorsements. Professionalization was fraught with controversy, within FIFA and without. Some FIFA leaders viewed professionals as "artists" who tarnished the ideals of sport and should remain outside the frames of football organizations.[44] But market realities proved an irresistible force. Spectator demand and pressures to win at international competitions pushed inexorably toward professionalization, and by the mid-1920s the IOC was threatening to exclude soccer from the Olympic program if stricter rules were not implemented. Only the sharp protests of the Dutch organizers, who were depending on soccer revenues to make the Games financially viable, prevented the exclusion of the game in 1928.[45] Popular demand also created pressures for a championship among the best players, more and more of whom were now professionals.[46]

The result was a world championship from its beginnings open to professionals. It was also a championship for national teams. When FIFA executives had first floated the idea in the early 1900s, they had envisioned having clubs, not countries, contest the championship. By 1928 the principle of national representation and the example of the Olympics made a contest along national lines the only viable option.[47] In contrast to the Olympics, the World Cup was devised from the beginning as a money-making enterprise, with revenue from spectators paying traveling expenses of the teams, and the remaining profits divided between FIFA and the national associations.

Tiny Uruguay won the honor of staging the competition by virtue of its strong football tradition, its gold-medal victories in the two previous Olympic Games, and its willingness to cover any deficit should revenue fall short of expenses. Although 100,000 spectators thronged the stadium in Montevideo at the final match to see Uruguay beat Argentina 4–2, the first World Cup was a disappointment in that only four teams from Europe had been willing to take the long voyage to South America. Subsequent World Cups in Italy in 1934 and France in 1938, however, would more than bear out the event's potential for financial and popular success.

The disappointments of the first World Cup led to criticism and calls for reform within FIFA.[48] Some members, led by the German representative F. Linnemann, argued that FIFA should remain a group of associations with shared interests, not a superordinate or commanding authority. Linnemann, unhappy with FIFA's growth and the consequent dilution of power of its once-dominant European members, also argued that voting should not be on the basis of one vote per national association, but rather should be weighted in favor of national associations with larger numbers of member clubs and longer histories of membership in FIFA. It was, however, the advocates of a stronger federation who won. This side, led by the Italian and Austrian members, argued that FIFA must "assert its authority, either in accord with all countries or through coercive measures that are inevitably essential to assure the common interest, as well as to ensure that constitutional norms are respected by all."[49]

The changes that were voted into place at the 1932 Congress in Stockholm, after considerable debate, created a stronger central apparatus, although in one significant area more power was delegated to the national associations. Instead of trying to regulate amateurism, FIFA delegated that authority to the national associations. The complex and lengthy qualifications detailed in the first thirteen articles of its regulations were eliminated, leaving it up to each national association to determine on its own what constituted an amateur. This move was primarily a ploy to placate the IOC and to reinstate soccer on the Olympic program after its removal at the 1932 Games in Los Angeles. The World Cup, after all, had been carefully timed to meet during the lull between Olympiads and thus serve as a supplement to rather than a replacement for the Olympics. The reforms also increased the powers of the executive committee, a small body headed by the president and elected by the congresses, which handled day-to-day administrative affairs.[50] Finally, the discovery in 1931 that FIFA's part-time, unpaid secretary-treasurer had embezzled the entirety of its funds prompted one additional reform: the Congress voted to establish a permanent secretariat, and Zurich narrowly defeated Paris as the seat of the new headquarters.[51]

The establishment of a permanent bureaucratic apparatus in 1932 was a watershed in FIFA's history, a symbol of its transformation from a tiny, marginalized body that was largely a tool of national associations into a large, financially secure institution that wielded real power over its members. Its new "bricks and mortar" presence in a small, modern building on Zurich's elegant Bahnhofstrasse and its two new full-time, salaried employees signified its stature as the governing body of the world's most popular sport.[52] Ivo Schricker, an official from the German football federation, became the new salaried, permanent secretary in Zurich, a position he held until 1951.

The reorganization succeeded in strengthening FIFA and setting it on a path toward greater power and influence over world soccer. It did not quite succeed, however, in another of its key goals, which was to entice the British football associations back into membership. These associations had only briefly joined before quitting in protest over loose definitions of amateurism. Their continued absence was a perpetual source of irritation and concern to FIFA officials, who naturally felt their aspirations to be a truly global body could not be realized without the participation of the game's inventors, especially at a time when British teams were still the best in the world. After the adoption of the 1932 reforms, Rimet optimistically stated that the British "no longer have any reason to stay outside a global organization that expresses in the spirit of its statutes that it does not think to meddle in the private affairs of each association, but that it is in their own interest to join such an organization, which guarantees order internationally and respect for laws."[53] His hopes were only partially fulfilled. Although the British associations continued to shy away from submitting to FIFA's authority until after World War II, relations with FIFA substantially improved in the 1930s, becoming so cordial and cooperative that one historian has referred to Britain's "virtual membership."[54]

Along with its growing authority, FIFA's financial position improved during the interwar years. In its early years FIFA's income was derived almost entirely from the annual membership fee charged to each national association. This fee rose from $10 in 1923 to $50 in 1926. With the scope of its activities growing, FIFA instituted a new fee in 1923. Now a host country had to pay a percentage of the gross receipts from every international match held on its territory. Originally set at 0.1 percent of net receipts, the levy was raised to 0.75 percent in 1924 and to 1 percent in 1932. As the number of international matches rose, FIFA's income from these fees grew, and by the 1930s they constituted the main source of the organization's regular income. Income from the World Cup provided substantial additional revenues.[55]

An international match was defined, with minor variations during the years, as a contest "between two National Associations, members of the Federation, and in which each team bears the name of its country. The players must be selected by the National Associations concerned." International matches were distinguished from interassociation, interleague, and interclub matches, which, though played between teams of different nationalities, were exempt from levies.[56] In the early years national associations were required to schedule international matches at FIFA's annual congress. As the number of international matches rose after the war, the regulations were changed to allow matches to be arranged at any time as long as FIFA was notified prior to the meet.[57] In 1924 Rimet tried to require that international matches be subject to authorization by FIFA, but the move was voted down.[58]

As an organization that came to be devoted largely to professional sport, FIFA's purpose and mission were defined significantly in terms of commercial and entertainment value. The rhetoric of peaceful internationalism was not as pervasive in FIFA's public pronouncements as it was in the IOC's, but it nevertheless played an important role in FIFA's self-conception and self-presentation. FIFA officials and members generally accepted the views that sport was morally valuable and that international sport contacts promoted peace, and they expressed these views with some frequency to support the idea that the organization played a benevolent and useful role in world affairs. They considered FIFA to be part of a cohort of international organizations devoted to the pursuit of peace. As one member said in 1907, "the cause of the progress of soccer is a cause of civilization, it is a work for peace."[59]

FIFA officials were particularly interested in gaining recognition by the League of Nations for the social importance of soccer and hoped to establish "an international center for sports activities in the League of Nations." In 1931 two members of the executive committee traveled to Geneva for discussions with the League of Nation's Hygiene Commission.[60] In addition, when setting up the new secretariat in Zurich, the executive committee consulted a legal expert at the League of Nations on the question of how to establish a legal existence as an international organization. The expert suggested the solution that had been adopted by the International Committee of the Red Cross—that is, investing juridical personality in a separate committee—but FIFA members evidently dropped the matter after deciding it was too complex.[61]

The Principle of National Representation

At the first Olympic Games in 1896, an Englishman and a German teamed up to win the doubles competition in tennis, marking the first and last time an international team has been represented at the Games.[62] In conception and practice the Olympic Games and other world championships have brought together not athletes as individuals but athletes as representatives of particular nations. In this respect sport meets shared the same form as other international gatherings and contacts that arose in the context of a developing international system based on national representation. The Nobel Prizes, instituted in 1901, were entwined with nationalism, and the Boy Scouts (founded in 1908), the

YMCA (1844), and the Red Cross (1863) were international movements based on associations of national bodies.[63]

The principle that "countries" rather than individuals are represented at the Olympic Games and world championships like the World Cup in soccer is firmly entrenched, but it is a principle that was not always easy to implement in an era before the nation-state became the standard unit of political organization. The IOC and the international federations arose at a time when empires still dominated Europe and when European imperialism in the rest of the world was at its apogee. Until the burst of decolonization after World War II ended, the IOC frequently recognized political entities that did not meet formal criteria as sovereign states, and even today the IOC grants membership not only to nations but also to "independent territories, commonwealths, protectorates and geographical areas," including (controversially) nonstate entities such as the Palestinian Authority.[64] Yet all such entities participate on an equal footing, marching under a national flag at the opening ceremony—with the notable recent exception of East Timor, which, while under UN transitional rule, was permitted to send four athletes to the 2000 Olympic Games in Sydney as individuals competing under the Olympic flag.[65]

In the early decades the IOC interpreted the principle of national representation without regard to firmly defined standards, preferring to rely on an ill-defined "sports geography" and to settle disputes on a case-by-case basis. (As Coubertin remarked, "rough and ready compromises had to be made.") The question of territorial jurisdiction was, in Coubertin's words, "extremely complex"; solutions, he argued, should take into account "sporting realities" above all, "irrespective of international law but without contradicting its principles too much."[66] The IOC's 1920 rules stated that the Games "assemble amateurs of all nations under conditions as equal as possible" and that to participate "one must be a native of a country or naturalized subject of that country."[67] By 1932, international federations had adopted (within the context of a definition of amateur) a more essentialist construction of nationality, excluding from eligibility "those who have already competed in the Olympic Games for another nation . . . except in the case of conquest or the creation of a new state ratified by treaty."[68]

At FIFA's formation in 1904, the organization required that member associations be the sole authorities governing soccer in the regions under their control, but there was no definite requirement that such a region correspond to a national unit. Both Finland, then part of the Russian Empire, and Bohemia, then part of the Austro-Hungarian Empire, formed independent soccer associations that were accorded FIFA membership. At the 1907 FIFA Congress Austria objected to recognizing the Czech organization as an independent association, arguing that Bohemia was a province of Austria. Germany supported Austria, but England's proposal to extend the Bohemians' provisional affiliation for another year was accepted in a close vote.[69] The following year the Czech association was excluded on the basis that the Austrian association was the controlling body for that territory, but a Finnish association was admitted provisionally until a Russian association could be formed.[70]

The IOC grappled similarly with "the Bohemian question" before World War I. In 1896 Guth-Jarkovsky, a Czech nationalist, a close colleague of Coubertin's, and a founding member of the IOC, used his position on the IOC to push through a proposal to allow the various nationalities in the Austro-Hungarian Empire to constitute their own national Olympic committees. He anticipated that the right would be accorded not just to the Czechs, but to the Germans, Poles, Slovaks, Slovenes, and Croats in the empire. A Czech Olympic Committee was formed in 1903 and was not disbanded until 1916, and a separate Bohemian delegation competed in the 1912 Olympics. Austrian objections were overruled by Coubertin, who also thwarted Austrian efforts in 1905 and 1911 to remove Guth-Jarkovsky from the IOC. It was Coubertin's view that "the sporting importance" and relative autonomy of the Czechs entitled them to separate representation.[71] In 1912, however, an IOC Congress refused to allow Bohemia further independent rights, voting to require the Czechs to compete in the 1916 Games under the Austrian flag.[72]

Colonies posed similar dilemmas. According to FIFA's statutes, a colony could either "remain a subordinate part" of the colonizer's national association or create its own national association and affiliate directly with FIFA, depending on the wishes of the colonial power.[73] On several occasions associations became members and then were excluded when the colonial power objected.[74] Australia, Canada, and South Africa posed their own set of problems for the IOC. As dominions, or self-governing states, of the British Empire, their participation in the Olympics from the beginning as independent states irked U.S. representatives, who, Coubertin recalled, "were quite indignant at Britain's 'privileges.'"[75]

National representation inevitably fostered expressions of nationalism. Indeed the structure of the Olympic Games was explicitly designed to accentuate nationalism. In its early years the IOC had an official ranking system based on the number of medals each nation won. Although such official rankings were eventually abolished, they continued to be widely used. Other official manifestations of nationalism (such as flags and anthems) persisted and new ones arose (such as the victory ceremony introduced in 1932).[76] For Coubertin, the "wise and peaceful internationalism" the Olympics were supposed to promote were premised not on cosmopolitanism—the extirpation of national distinctions—but on respect for and celebration of national and cultural differences.[77]

Global Expansion

The history of the IOC and of international federations is one of steady growth, culminating by the late twentieth century in global domination. Although they began as organizations of almost exclusively European and North American members, they—unlike other regional sports bodies—claimed global aspirations from the beginning. In 1900 nineteen countries participated in the Olympic Games. By 1936 the number was forty-nine.[78] At FIFA's founding in 1904 it counted seven members. In 1914 the number had risen to twenty-four; by 1939 it was fifty-one.[79] Other sport federations followed similar trajectories. The international swimming federation, for example, grew from ten members at its creation in 1908 to fifty-three in 1939.[80] Still geographically centered in the West, the international sport community was slowly extending its reach to include countries—some independent and some still under the control of European powers—such as Afghanistan, China, Egypt, India, Japan, and the Philippines.

In the early years the global aspirations of sport organizations were constrained by limits on communications and transportation technology, and by the fact that sport was weakly developed in much of the non-Western world. As those constraints diminished in the years after World War I, these organizations developed strategies to draw in members from outside Europe and North America. Many sport officials and enthusiasts saw sport as an element of Western civilization that could educate and uplift all people. Not surprisingly, European and U.S. sport officials shared the prejudices of many of their contemporaries in regarding Asians and Africans as backward people in need of tutelage in the ways of civilization. Yet it was significant that they believed that sport was suitable for all. As Coubertin wrote in 1931, "sport is the apanage of all races." He scoffed at the idea, which he characterized as prevalent until recently, that Asians were "excluded by nature" from sport, recounting that "last year, in Geneva, one of the Japanese delegates at the League of Nations said to me: 'It is impossible to imagine to what extent the revival of the Olympic Games has transformed my country. Since we have been taking part in the Games, our youth have taken on a fresh lease of life.'" Delegates from India and China conveyed similar sentiments, he noted.[81]

From the beginning it was Coubertin's wish to see the Games established on a global scale with universal male participation. Contests that limited participation based on regional, ethnic, political, or religious criteria sent the wrong message, in his view; competition should transcend such divides and embrace the entire world. On the occasion of the IOC's twentieth anniversary in 1914, he introduced what is today one of the world's most widely recognized symbols: the Olympic flag. Its five intertwined circles of blue, yellow, black, green, and red were supposed to include "the colors of all nations of the universe without exception," the IOC press release proclaimed, with each ring symbolizing one of the continents of the world. "Never," the IOC report offered, "has an emblem had such a completely international character."[82]

Eager to facilitate the expansion of sport, Coubertin and the IOC cultivated relationships with newcomers to sport. Coubertin and Baillet-Latour toured South America in the early 1920s specifically to "spread Olympism."[83] The IOC also recruited members in Asia. Jigoro Kano of Japan served from 1909 to 1938, Dorabji Tata of India was a member from 1920 to 1930, and Dr. C. T. Wang of China became a member in 1922.[84] As a clear testament to its commitment to globalize, the IOC awarded the 1940 Games to Tokyo, capital of the most sport-minded non-Western nation, one that had demonstrated its prowess with impressive Olympic performances in 1932 and 1936. After touring Japan to examine the preparations for the Games, Baillet-Latour praised "the complete disappearance of certain xenophobic tendencies" and their replacement with "a sincere desire for international collaboration," especially in sport.[85] His assessment was off the mark, for in 1938 the Japanese government renounced the Games to focus on war.

In much of Asia and Africa, however, sport was still unknown or largely limited to Westernized elites. The first task, then, was to introduce sport on a wider scale. The IOC did not undertake to spread sport, but it did lend its support to the efforts of groups like the YMCA-sponsored Philippine Amateur Athletic Federation, which established the Far Eastern Athletic Association that began staging Far Eastern Championship Games in 1913. Organizers described the championships as an "Olympic kindergarten" whose aim was "to bring every country in the Orient into competition."[86] In the 1920s Coubertin supported similar, though unsuccessful, efforts to introduce a regional African Games as a means of "speeding up the march of civilization" there.[87]

Although it was an overwhelmingly European organization preoccupied with European affairs, FIFA, too, had clearly global ambitions.[88] These ambitions were forcefully signaled when Rimet chose Uruguay to host the first World Cup in 1930, and in 1928 when FIFA's emblem was revised to include a drawing of the world's two hemispheres, symbolic of its global empire.[89] It tried in small ways to encourage the spread of soccer outside Europe, including reducing dues for non-European countries where associations and revenues were small.[90] Soccer in South America was enormously popular, and although South American national federations were technically members of FIFA, FIFA's influence was limited. Instead, the South American football confederation, the Confederacion Sud-Americana de football, played the major governing role. Rimet's move to hold the first World Cup in Uruguay was partly a bid to bring the South American federations more firmly into the fold, and Rimet traveled to South America again in 1939 to improve relations. Eager to extend power, FIFA officials were less willing to share it, and it was only after years of dithering that the FIFA Executive Committee admitted a delegate of the South American confederation into its inner circle in 1938.[91]

The IOC and federations like FIFA vigorously presented themselves as above politics, guardians of sport's "moral purity." Sometimes this stance meant turning a blind eye to abuses of Olympic ideals—which in itself, of course, is a political statement. Even outright aggression was not enough to warrant exclusion from the "Olympic family." Japan's invasion of Manchuria in 1931 did not deter the award of the 1940 Games to Tokyo, nor did Japan's war against mainland China after 1937, including widely publicized atrocities in Nanking, lead to a revocation. With aspirations to encompass the globe, international sports organizations sought to include countries irrespective of political ideology. They showed no inclination to exclude Nazi Germany, even when the actions of the Nazi regime contradicted their principles and rules. Even the Soviet Union, the pariah state of the interwar years, could have been a member of the club. Coubertin regarded workers' sport in a positive light, believing that sport was for all classes and that the spread of sport among workers was "an undeniable guarantee for the survival of Olympism," regardless of the outcome of the struggle between communism and liberal democracy.[92] Under Baillet-Latour, a staunch anticommunist, the IOC was more hostile to the idea of Soviet membership (though the Soviets did not attempt to participate in the Olympics). FIFA and other international federations did pursue relations with the USSR and, despite political difficulties, sought to facilitate the country's entry into their organizations, ultimately unsuccessfully.

International competition in sport began at the very end of the nineteenth century, but like modern sport itself, such competitions did not become common or widely popular until after World War I. As sport increased in popularity in the interwar years, there was a striking proliferation of events, including international competitions, world championships like soccer's World Cup, and regional events like the British Empire Games. The Olympic Games, begun in 1896, gained in visibility and popularity, and by 1932 they were significant international events, measured by levels of participation, media coverage, popular following, and government interest. International sport organizations gradually came to play key roles in staging and governing these events. These organizations had begun to form in the 1890s but were at first very weak. Initially they were little more than places where national bodies gathered to discuss common problems. As the visibility and demand for international sport increased, tensions developed over the proper role of the organizations. National associations wanted to retain a substantial degree of autonomy, both in setting their own rules internally and in negotiating the rules and conditions that would apply to international competitions, but ultimately federations came to develop an institutional identity apart from their national members and asserted claims to control a wide range of conditions relating to international sport.

The result of this conflict was that, during the 1930s, international federations came to dominate international sport in a variety of ways. On the one hand, the institutional system governing international sport greatly reinforced nationalism, by predicating participation on the concept of national representation. On the other hand, the system was also based on a vision of an explicitly global sport, in which all countries and all regions participated. To pursue this goal international organizations centered their efforts on the promotion of standardization and uniformity in the rules and conditions of play—on creating regulations so specific and so detailed that sports become universalized, at least on a certain plane; they were played everywhere according to the same rules and standards, even if the cultural meanings attributed to these games continued to vary. The importance of this mission was underlined by the secretary of the international boxing association, who wrote in 1937: "The greatest trouble in boxing is that sporting rules are not understood and carried out in uniformity all over the world. I devoted my whole work to make our rules to be uniform in the whole world."[93]

As Rimet wrote, "When a referee crosses the globe to direct a soccer match in a country about which he knows nothing, between two teams whose members have never seen each other and who do not speak the same language, he need only appear on the field for his decisions to be intelligible to all."[94] The situation was not quite as clear-cut as he depicted it, for disagreements about different ways to interpret the rules and language barriers among referees and players were a frequent cause of friction in international matches.[95] Yet in the interwar years FIFA and its fellow sport federations succeeded in endowing sport with a genuine autonomy. More successfully than many other international groups in the interwar years, sport organizations shaped a new vision of a global community.

The result of the drive for universalism was the creation of a transnational sport culture, particularly at the elite level, where top athletes crossed borders in search of opportunities; rated their achievements in comparison with international as well as local or national results; performed within the context of uniform international rules and practices; and commanded multinational popular followings. Noting the dense and detailed panoply of rules and regulations instituted by the international swimming federation in the interwar years, one historian has accurately described the result as "a relative cultural homogenization" of elite sport.[96] As subsequent chapters will explore, the nationalism and internationalism of sport operated in tandem, as nationalist aspirations served to propel the internationalization of sport culture.

3

Democracy and International Sport: The United States

What role did the United States, the twentieth century's dominant power, play in the globalizing culture of sport? The rise of U.S. power, particularly cultural power, and the spread of modern sport across the globe are major developments of the last century that appear to traverse distinct and unrelated paths. During the course of the "American century," and despite the vehement objections of foreign elites, foreign publics exhibited an often voracious appetite for U.S. popular culture, as the farthest reaches of the globe gobbled up fast food, jeans, Hollywood movies, jazz, and American slang. The one striking exception in this otherwise clear story of U.S. cultural dominance seems to be sport: it is the one element of U.S. popular culture that foreign publics seemed to find unpalatable. With important exceptions, the world has greeted baseball and American football—the team sports that dominated the U.S. landscape for most of the twentieth century—with a level of boredom and indifference fully reciprocated by the disdain most in the United States displayed toward "the world's game," soccer. The result was that the United States had a largely insular and self-contained sport culture for much of the twentieth century, as compared to those countries embedded in the interconnected and internationalized world of soccer (or rugby or cricket).[1] Yet this divergence, important though it is, is limited to professional team sports, and generalizations about U.S. sport isolationism obscure a more complex picture when amateur and individual sports are taken into account.

The most popular team sports in the United States were unique, but in many amateur sports Americans were very much a part of the international sport world. As the world leader in key amateur sports for most of the century, the United States played a central role in the internationalization of modern sport. And when "sport culture" is construed broadly to include training methods, moral and pedagogical issues, attitudes toward competition, the cult of celebrity, connections to advertising and mass consumption, and the commodification of sport as entertainment, then U.S. sport culture appears far more a part of, rather than an exception to, the broader currents of cultural influence exercised by the United States.

The importance of the United States in global sport is evident in the 1930s, when despite an isolationist mood and the economic catastrophe of the Depression, Americans extended their influence on international sport, shaping its form and content in key ways. The United States was a major power in many of the amateur sports on the program of the early Olympic Games, consistently winning large numbers of medals and often gaining first place in the unofficial point totals. In track and field and swimming, sports with wide popular appeal before World War II, Americans reigned supreme. The country's dominance at the Olympic Games and its reputation as a leading sport nation made it a model for many countries seeking to improve public health and fitness through sports and physical education programs.

As the world embraced sport, demand for U.S. expertise increased. During the 1930s ever-greater numbers of international sport tours facilitated exchanges of ideas and techniques between U.S. and foreign athletes. At the same time U.S. sport officials became more involved in the European-based international sport organizations that were wielding increasing power over sport practices. Although these Americans opposed foreign political entanglements, many of them were eager internationalists in the realm of sport—indeed, for these Americans, political isolationism went hand in hand with an aggressive, idealistic internationalism in the cultural sphere.[2] They were convinced that the popularization of sport was an effective way to spread their own values and ideas, and they framed their participation in global sport as a moral crusade to spread peace and democracy. Their relentless didacticism did much to embed a strongly moralistic element in international sport. The major "democratizing" effect of U.S. influence, however, was to hasten the transformation of international sport from an elite cultural pursuit to a mass cultural phenomenon based on commercialism and the new consumer culture.

The United States, then, did not export its major team sports but it did export training techniques, a competitive, high-achievement ethos, and a moral underpinning that helped cement a remarkably durable legitimization for international sports contests. As U.S. participation in international sports events grew in number and in visibility, it helped to shape foreign views of the United States and the "American way of life" and influenced Americans' perceptions of their country's power and place in the world. At the same time, involvement in sport affairs abroad pulled Americans into a multinational network, inculcating an internationalist outlook and to some extent enmeshing them in a web of international rules and norms not of their own making.

U.S. Sport "Exceptionalism" and Cultural Expansion

If U.S. cultural dominance has been so profound during the twentieth century, why doesn't the world play American sports? The uniqueness of major professional team sports in the United States is a paradoxical result of the country's early embrace of British sports. British games arrived in the United States before they had evolved into fixed and standardized forms, and the evolution of these varied games toward modern, codified forms occurred on parallel but separate lines in each country. Among kicking games, for example, rules and practices fluctuated within wide parameters in the mid-nineteenth century. In England debate over the key issues of handling and tackling eventually led to the development of two distinct sports in England, rugby and soccer. Kicking games underwent a similar evolution in the United States in the same period, but with a divergent result, as the push and pull between handling and kicking variants produced American football by the end of the century. Nationalist desires to differentiate the young republic from its former colonial master also played a role in the creation of distinct U.S. variations of English sports, as was certainly the case with baseball, first developed in the 1840s and 1850s as a spin-off from the English children's game of rounders and the English sport of cricket.[3]

Timing, then, was the primary determinant of global sport geography. The emergence of team sports in Britain in modern, codified, and standardized form at the end of the nineteenth century coincided precisely with the peak of the British Empire's reach. Carried by the builders of empire, British soccer, rugby, and cricket established toeholds in many areas of the world by the turn of the century. The variants of these sports that Americans had developed earlier, notably baseball, spread only to areas such as the Caribbean and Japan where U.S. influence was strongest. For reasons persuasively articulated by Andrei Markovits, team sports are difficult to dislodge once they have staked a claim to a country's "sports space," so that by the time the United States and its seductive popular culture had become a major global presence, the early toeholds established by British sports had become strangleholds.[4]

That much of the world ignored baseball and American football was rarely a source of much concern for most Americans. College and major-league baseball players occasionally made exhibition tours of Latin America and Japan, but there were few sustained attempts to win converts to the "national pastime" and virtually no efforts before World War II to spread the U.S. version of football beyond the continent. Americans also showed little interest in soccer even as the game underwent a remarkable global expansion in the interwar years. The United States had a national soccer federation that was a member of FIFA and that participated in World Cup competitions, reaching the semifinals in 1930. On the whole, however, the game's popularity was limited mainly to recent immigrants; the sport never achieved mainstream appeal.[5]

Though sports fans may be loathe to admit it, these team sports share important underlying similarities. Baseball, American football, and soccer share central characteristics of modern sports, play similar social and cultural roles, and are situated within professionalized, mass-entertainment sport industries that are broadly similar across national boundaries. Even so, the discontinuities between U.S. and global team sports have had profound consequences. This is especially true because whereas most forms of cultural exchange are informal and decentralized, sports such as soccer are governed by international organizations that require strict adherence to rules and norms. As a result participation in soccer has knit much of the world into a global community that encourages an internationalist outlook among millions—even billions—of the world's people. Soccer players have been traded across national borders since the inception of professional leagues in Europe in the 1920s, and frequent international meets and championships have given soccer fans high exposure to foreign teams and players. The mental map of a soccer fan in the twentieth century was international in a way that U.S. baseball and football fans (despite the occasional foreign player and despite the misnomer "World" Series) would never have imagined. Thus, while soccer has internationalized much of the world's population, U.S. isolation from the global network in professional team sports has arguably reinforced, in daily lives and attitudes, the general isolationism and retreat from international engagement that often prevails in American thought.[6]

Outside of these major team sports, however, the United States has been a key player in the global spread of modern sport. Its recreational, physical education, and playground movements were influential in many parts of the world beginning in the late nineteenth century. In professional individual sports, in amateur sports, and more broadly in approaches to training, the United States began to exert significant influence abroad early in the twentieth century. In 1902 William Stead included sport as part of "how America Americanises" in his examination of what he presciently labeled *The Americanization of the World*.[7] Although modern competitive sport is a British invention, by the interwar years it was increasingly identified with the United States.[8] At many levels the sporting cultures of the United States and the rest of the world, particularly in Europe, were deeply interconnected. In the elite worlds of tennis and golf, Americans and Europeans played by the same rules and in the same championships at both amateur and professional levels. In the working-class arena of professional boxing, Americans held a clear supremacy in what was an increasingly global sport. Boxers Joe Louis and Jack Dempsey were international stars, and major stars abroad, including Germany's Max Schmeling, came to the United States to compete for the title of "world" champion. In track and field, widely regarded as the most important sport at the Olympic Games, Americans were consistent leaders, and track and swimming provided the major impetus for America's assumption of a leading role in international amateur sport during the 1920s and especially in the 1930s.

American influence in these areas of sport paralleled the powerful inroads that U.S. culture, technology, and goods made in many parts of the world during the interwar period. In sport, as in other areas of culture and society, many observers in other countries saw the United States as the exemplar of modernity, technology, and progress. Writing in 1930 Bertolt Brecht explained why Europeans had chosen to imitate Americans: "What men people were! Their boxers the strongest! Their inventors the most practical! Their trains the fastest!"[9] Many of the hallmarks of "Americanism"—materialism, efficiency, largeness, mechanization, standardization, mass production, mass consumption, mass democracy, technocracy, uniformity, pragmatism, reformism, optimism—were as relevant to the world of sport as they were to automobile production. Like jazz, Hollywood movies, and Ford's mass-production techniques, U.S. sport techniques and styles inspired emulation and envy (as well as distaste). U.S. cultural influence had interlocking effects: the prominence of prizefights in Hollywood films, for example, helped popularize boxing in Europe, and the successes of America's athletic champions spurred demand for American products.[10] In the 1930s the Depression did much to tarnish the image of the United States as a beacon of modernity and progress, but in sport the "American way" continued to command respect.

Sport Exchanges

As it did elsewhere, the carnage of World War I led in the United States to a renewed emphasis on recreation, physical education, and sport as ways to develop healthy populations and promote public welfare. Physical-education courses became a standard part of school curricula, and local governments appropriated public funds to build parks, playgrounds, stadiums, and swimming pools. The postwar years saw the almost universal adoption of physical-education programs in schools, and by the 1930s gymnastics and physical training, formerly the staples of physical education, were supplanted by sports programs. Though the effort was primarily directed at males, physical-education programs for girls and women also expanded.[11]

Male-oriented spectator sport, already popular before the war, became a central part of national life, as the cinema, radio, and the mass press fanned public interest. The sports page, which first appeared in U.S. newspapers at the end of the nineteenth century, became a standard feature in large dailies in the 1920s. Major prizefights and the World Series were front-page news, and radio broadcasts of major sports events drew millions of listeners. Athletes like Babe Ruth became national heroes on a par with such icons as aviator Charles Lindbergh and actor Rudolph Valentino. Like other celebrities, star athletes were tapped by advertisers to endorse products, vividly symbolizing sport's integration into the new mass consumer culture.[12]

If American sport experienced a Golden Age in the 1920s, the onset of the Depression in 1929 dulled some of its luster. Attendance at spectator events fell, private clubs folded, and sales of sport equipment slumped. Professional baseball was especially hard hit, as gate receipts dropped from $17 million in 1929 to $11 million in 1933. College football receipts suffered a comparable decline, leading to cuts in athletic budgets and scholarships. Yet inexpensive participant sports flourished, and spectator sports continued to shape American life in important ways.[13] The Depression spurred federal spending on sport and recreation, in part because the Roosevelt administration revived Progressive ideas about the use of sport and recreation to promote social welfare. Between 1935 and 1941, the Works Projects Administration spent $229 million on recreational programs and $941 million on construction of recreational facilities, including 5,898 athletic fields and playgrounds and 770 swimming pools.[14] In the realm of international sport, the Depression had surprisingly little effect. Fund-raising difficulties led to cutbacks in the Olympic team in 1932, but the economic catastrophe did not prevent a dramatic increase in sporting tours abroad later in the decade.

Whereas many countries formed government agencies for sport to centralize the promotion of sport and physical education and to finance participation in international competitions, in the United States the federal government took a hands-off approach.[15] State and local governments promoted sports by legalizing prizefighting, repealing laws restricting amusements on Sundays, requiring physical education in schools, and indirectly subsidizing college athletic programs. The U.S. Department of Commerce did not hesitate to assist sporting goods manufacturers in the same way it helped other companies, but the State Department, unlike foreign ministries in other countries, did little to encourage or assist private initiatives in "sport diplomacy," such as informal sports tours abroad. Its policy with regard to sport was entirely in keeping with its view of cultural relations in general as an arena for private, not governmental, intervention.[16] A notable exception was the Office of the Coordinator of Inter-American Affairs, a government agency created in 1940 to further friendly relations with Latin America, which was prescient enough to see sports as a useful tool; it formed a (tiny) sports section, which tried to encourage "interchange of athletes, teams, coaches, and demonstration groups" between the United States and Latin American countries.[17] Such efforts were cut short by U.S. entry into the war, and it was only after 1945 that the U.S.

government began in earnest to take an interest in the political and diplomatic ramifications of international sport.

Until the Cold War the State Department remained mostly oblivious to the growing public significance of the Olympic Games, and the federal government played no direct role in selecting, financing, or promoting U.S. participation in the Olympics. Although some other countries began providing subsidies to their Olympic teams even before World War I, U.S. teams have relied almost exclusively on private financing.[18] The State Department took an interest in monitoring private sports contacts and expressed general approval of their aims; however, it offered little proactive support. It frequently assisted international cultural conferences when such events were deemed of high educational value, but officials were surprisingly reluctant to offer basic assistance for the 1932 Olympic Games in Los Angeles.[19]

The military played a much more active role in international sport. U.S. Olympic teams before World War II, filled mostly by college students, also included significant numbers of military personnel. High-ranking officials in the War and Navy Departments participated in the American Olympic Committee (AOC) and the Amateur Athletic Union (AAU). General Douglas MacArthur, for example, served as president of the AOC in 1928 and accompanied the U.S. team to the Amsterdam Olympic Games that year. The military also frequently used polo meets and informal competitions to reinforce military ties with other nations.[20] Beyond the military's interest in sponsoring the participation of its own athletes, leaders of the armed forces had a perceived interest in the health and physical fitness of the general (preconscription) population and for this reason took on public roles as propagandists for sport.[21]

Politicians and government officials were often sports fans. The attendees at the now-legendary Louis-Schmeling boxing match in 1938, for example, included a "who's who" of New York politics. Politicians also saw sports events as part of their cultural-patronage duties. President Herbert Hoover, for example, threw out the first pitch at baseball games and officiated at tennis's Davis Cup draw.[22] With athletes enjoying unprecedented levels of public idolization, politicians sidled into the stars' limelight hoping that some of the luster of public approval would rub off on them. Aiming at the "Negro vote," both presidential nominees in the 1936 election sought the endorsement of Jesse Owens, the African

American sprinter whose dazzling performances at the 1936 Olympics made him a national hero.[23]

Business interests, of course, played an important role in encouraging contacts between U.S. and foreign athletes and in promoting American sports abroad. The brief frenzy provoked by a 1931 report that Italy was adopting baseball as the national sport provides one indication of how sporting goods manufacturers hoped that the spread of U.S. sports and sports techniques would increase demand for their products.[24] The report was false, but the successes of U.S. athletic champions did spur demand for American goods. As the National Geographic Society noted in 1928:

> American movies, automobiles, dental schools, typewriters, phono-graphs, and even its prize fights lead in spreading American fashions and customs throughout the world . . . Millions won by [boxers Jack] Dempsey and [Gene] Tunney prompt young men, white, yellow, brown, black, or red, with two good fists to try them out, and incidentally equip themselves with the necessary "gym" shoes and boxing gloves from the "land of champions."[25]

Other businesses also saw profit potential in sport exchanges. U.S. busi-nessmen with commercial interests in Latin America were major backers of various schemes for Pan-American Games hatched in the second half of the 1930s, and newspaper publishers here and abroad were among the most eager internationalizers in sport, as was the case for the Los Ange-les Olympics and baseball tours of Japan.[26]

The primary overseers of U.S. international sport contacts were pri-vately run organizations that took on foreign meets as part of their man-dates. In the interwar years the two key organizations were the AOC, which selected and funded U.S. Olympic teams, and the AAU, a consor-tium of national bodies overseeing about a dozen sports.[27] Though the two groups often clashed over issues of power and control, together they oversaw a rapid expansion in U.S. sport ties abroad before World War II, in the process helping to shape the way Americans viewed international sport and the image the United States projected abroad.

As sport became more international and demand rose for U.S. athletes to compete abroad, the AAU became a clearinghouse for accepting and issuing invitations to international competitions. As the body that con-ferred or denied amateur status, the AAU controlled which invitations were accepted and issued and which athletes were permitted to compete here or abroad in many amateur sports. Any athlete in one of the sports under the AAU's control had to secure the organization's approval before participating in international competition.[28] In 1924 the AAU established a Foreign Relations Committee to oversee this task, and it became one of the organization's busiest organs. As international meets became routine, the AAU began to levy fees on them, collecting a small percentage of the gross receipts.[29]

Avery Brundage and William Gus Kirby exemplify the attitudes and assumptions that guided the U.S.'s increasingly assertive role in international sport. Brundage and Kirby were successful businessmen who pursued leadership positions in amateur sport as a sideline. As the two dominant figures in U.S. amateur sport in the interwar years, both held top positions in the AOC and the AAU. They were indefatigable publicists for sport, giving hundreds of lectures, radio addresses, and interviews, publishing hundreds of articles, attending dozens of national and international conferences, and helping to organize countless athletic events. Brundage, who built his wealth in the Chicago construction industry, was a passionate devotee of amateur sport who competed in the 1912 Olympic Games in the pentathlon (and dropped out of the heptathlon competition won by U.S. athlete Jim Thorpe). He was president of the AAU from 1928 to 1934 and headed the AOC throughout the 1930s. He was a member of the IOC's Executive Board from 1936 on, held positions in several international sport federations, and was vice president in the track and field federation (IAAF) from 1930 to 1952. He traveled widely, making frequent trips to Europe to attend sport organization meetings, and visiting Russia, Latin America, and Asia in the years before World War II. He had many friends and acquaintances in the world of international sport and carried on an extensive international correspondence. After the war he became president of the IOC (1952–1972), where his most memorable (or infamous) act was to declare at the 1972 Munich Olympics that "the games must go on" despite a terrorist attack that left eleven Israeli athletes and officials dead.[30]

If Kirby failed to achieve similar international prominence—he, too, coveted membership in the IOC—it was not for lack of trying. He was a tireless and dedicated proponent of amateur sport for more than half a century, claiming for himself (falsely) a role in the founding of the modern Olympic Games and trumpeting (justly) his attendance at every Olympic Games from 1896 until his death, when the *New York Times* hailed him as one of the last great "elder statesmen of amateur sport."[31] He was a New York lawyer and an early member of the AAU and the Intercollegiate Association of Amateur Athletes of America (IC4A). He served as president of the AOC from 1919 to 1922 and as its treasurer throughout the 1930s. Despite a lack of tact that alienated many of his colleagues, Kirby's boundless energy made him indispensable to amateur sport. He published and lectured widely, helped to organize and referee countless athletic matches, and helped to invent the photoelectric camera for timing race finishes.[32]

Brundage and Kirby were both conservative Republicans, sympathetic to Nazi Germany and fascist Italy and strongly anticommunist.[33] Brundage described communism as "the arch-enemy of all that is democratic," "diametrically opposed to Americanism," and (in 1936) "perhaps the greatest menace in the world today." These, he suggested, were the reasons why the USSR did not participate in the Olympic Games.[34] For both men sport was an essentially masculine activity that inculcated "manly" virtues. Brundage even claimed that sport, not New Deal social spending, was the best remedy for the Depression. Sport, he said in 1936, inculcates self-reliance and discipline and makes charity and public aid unnecessary. "I have never heard of an athlete on relief," he declared.[35] Both men saw sport as inherently "democratic" and as an embodiment of American virtues, and both were tireless exponents of the view that international sports contacts promoted peace and mutual understanding.

Brundage, Kirby, and their colleagues in the AAU and the AOC oversaw a tremendous expansion of foreign sports contacts in the 1930s. As outspoken public advocates for international sport and as the point men for U.S. amateur sport's foreign relations, these men were the architects of the United States' imprint on global sport before World War II. This imprint was constructed through sport exchanges involving coaches, athletes, trainers, and managers, as well as ideas, techniques, and training methods. Thousands of athletes traveled abroad in the 1930s, playing on every continent and reaching literally millions of spectators directly and millions more through news accounts. These included professionals such as baseball great Babe Ruth and hundreds of amateur (mostly collegiate) athletes.

The explosion in U.S. sport tours was made possible by an eagerness to establish ties abroad but was driven above all by the clamor from abroad for contact with U.S. athletes. As more and more countries sought to build sports programs, they turned to the United States as a model. Many foreigners admired U.S. success and attributed it to rigorous and extensive training and careful attention to technical efficiency.[36] Film analysis of technique, the use of wind tunnels to study motion, and laboratory studies of physiology and diet were among the ways Americans pioneered the "science" of sport.[37] American techniques and training methods in sports like track and field, swimming, and boxing were widely emulated. Other nations, eager to learn the secrets of American success, sought to encourage cultural transfer through direct contact with American athletes, the study of American training manuals, and the hiring of American coaches and trainers.

Despite the global economic downturn and mounting international tensions, the 1930s saw a dramatic increase both in international sport exchanges and in Americans' participation in them. Foreign athletes competed in growing numbers in the United States, and foreign coaches and athletic officials toured the country, inspecting facilities and studying coaching techniques. Like their counterparts in business and engineering, U.S. coaches were hired to train foreign teams. Princeton University's coach, for example, worked with Poland's national swim team for six months in 1937, introducing "real discipline," "modern technique," and "sound training methods."[38] Other coaches and former athletes were hired by Austria, Germany, Czechoslovakia, Hungary, Italy, New Zealand, the Philippines, and several Latin American countries—to offer only a partial list.[39] Dozens of sport organizations across Europe and Latin America subscribed to U.S. sports and physical-education periodicals.[40]

Other countries sometimes hoped to copy the commercial success of U.S. sports, as Babe Ruth's 1934 tour of Japan illustrates. Sponsored by a Japanese newspaper, the *Yomiuri Shimbun,* a team of American League stars led by Ruth competed against college and industry teams, drawing more than half a million spectators in eighteen games across the country.[41] Despite rising tensions between the United States and Japan, the visit was a great success. Ruth, who was a household name in Japan, was greeted as a hero; Ambassador Joseph Grew acclaimed the famed hitter as worth a hundred ambassadors. Ruth's image was plastered everywhere, from the front pages of newspapers to milk chocolate advertisements.[42]

Describing the welcome the Americans received in Tokyo, where a hundred thousand Japanese waved flags and threw confetti, the *New York Times* remarked that "the Babe's big bulk today blotted out such unimportant things as international squabbles over oil and navies."[43] When not playing baseball the Americans were shuttled to luncheons, garden parties, and dinner dances, often attended by leading Japanese businessmen, officials, and royalty. The visit led directly to the establishment of Japan's first professional baseball league—and to the attempted assassination of the tour's main backer, *Yomiuri* head Matsutoro Shoriki, by nationalist extremists angry about the tour.[44]

The most extensive channel of cultural exchange occurred as U.S. amateur athletes traveled abroad. What had been in previous decades a steady trickle of Americans competing abroad became a torrent in the 1930s, as the number, size, and scope of sport tours rose sharply. U.S. track and field athletes toured Europe nearly every summer, and boxers, wrestlers, weight lifters, swimmers, speed skaters, bobsledders, and ice

Babe Ruth being greeted by 100,000 fans in Tokyo during the 1934 tour of Japan by major league stars. *Source: The Asahi Shimbun.*

hockey, water polo, basketball, and baseball teams traveled to Europe, Asia, South Africa, and South America.[45]

Bidding farewell in 1934 to what was then the largest delegation of track and field stars that had ever left the United States for non-Olympic competition, the AAU's *Amateur Athlete* declared that "for once the sun will not set on an A.A.U. athlete."[46] Three separate track and field teams set off for Europe, a women's basketball team set sail for the world championship in London, a group of Polish-Americans went to the Polish Olympics at Warsaw, and Japan welcomed a track team, a group of swimmers, and the Harvard baseball team, as well as Babe Ruth and his major-league colleagues. Four years later the AAU sponsored tours for more than 150 athletes, again breaking the record for "the greatest non-Olympic invasion in history" and dispersing its athletic emissaries to almost every continent on the globe. Swimmers, basketball players (men and women), boxers, wrestlers, bobsledders, and water polo players competed in Europe, South America, Japan, Mexico, Bermuda, and Canada. Six weight lifters competed in the world championship in Vienna. An ice hockey team competed in the world championship in Prague and then toured France, Switzerland, England, and Germany. Forty track and field athletes, divided into three divisions, competed in ten European countries, drawing crowds of up to 100,000 at the principal events.[47]

Athletes traveling abroad, like film stars and other cultural icons, were treated as emissaries of the American way of life both by foreign government officials and by U.S. diplomats. On AAU-sponsored tours, athletes were exhorted to present themselves as American representatives. Team managers peppered their charges with speeches on good sportsmanship and fair play, on graciousness in victory and in defeat, and on courteous behavior off the field.[48] Athletes were selected for tours based not only on their sporting performances but also on the basis of officials' judgments about their tact, courtesy, and ability to get along with one another.[49] Sometimes such efforts meant that top African American athletes were excluded for fear that white teammates would object to traveling with them.[50] Most participants were men, though some female basketball players, swimmers, and track and field athletes toured Europe, South America, and Japan. Bound by the stringent requirements imposed on amateurs, most participants were college students of independent means.[51]

Competitions featuring U.S. athletes, even at the amateur level, drew tens of thousands of spectators, and in any one tour a million foreigners might view these U.S. representatives. Commenting with approbation on one European tour, a U.S. diplomat in Norway reported that every country visited had shown "enthusiastic admiration" for the U.S. athletes, whose accomplishments "had made a valuable contribution to international accord and friendship."[52] Contacts with foreign cultures extended far beyond the playing field to myriad cultural activities such as receptions, luncheons, dinners, theater parties, sightseeing trips, and meetings with foreign athletes and prominent state officials. Diplomats, politicians, and businessmen increasingly found attendance at international sports events de rigueur, and heads of state and top political leaders commonly hosted awards ceremonies and banquets. In 1935, for example, the Japanese prime minister and the minister of foreign affairs signaled the political importance attached to sport exchanges by holding receptions for visiting U.S. swimmers.[53] The scene at the 1932 Davis Cup match in Paris, where the president of France and the U.S. ambassador together watched the French-American matchup, was increasingly typical and highlighted the burgeoning popularity and political significance of major sports events.[54]

From the U.S. perspective, most of these tours were unqualified successes that reaffirmed the country's superiority, occasions for self-congratulation about the benevolent and uplifting influence Americans were exercising on the world. The patronizing tone of one report is typical: "Swimming throughout the world has made rapid advances during the past few years, largely due to the influence of our leadership."[55] The "tremendous advance in amateur sport throughout the world" in the interwar years was, according to Brundage, largely the result of "the general adoption of American methods."[56] Yet the purported effects of these tours were not limited to advancing sport but also included promoting international harmony and creating favorable impressions of the United States. Even as the level of foreign sport achievements rose, U.S. athletes and officials remained confident that American methods and techniques would continue to be the world standard.

Foreigners, of course, had a different view. Many sports enthusiasts abroad admired U.S. achievements and sought to replicate them, but they also expressed reservations about some of the ways these successes were achieved. The semiprofessionalism of college sport, excessive specialization, an overemphasis on competition, the public's glorification of sport heroes "far above their true value," and high levels of commercialism were among the ills frequently criticized by Europeans.[57] The influential critique of American society by French thinker Georges Duhamel included a caustic portrait of the brutality of American football and the mindlessness of mass spectatorship.[58]

Although U.S. sports leaders believed that the exchange was heavily one-sided, the flow was not unidirectional. As the rest of the world made rapid advances in sport performances, Americans recognized that keeping on top meant keeping track of the competition, something best done firsthand. As one team manager put it, foreign tours allowed officials and athletes "to keep in touch with the world situation" in an environment where "constant check-up" against competitors was necessary.[59]

Participation in international sport had important effects at home. U.S. rules in particular sports, which had been written by and for Americans only, were modified to conform to standards laid down by international sport federations that were typically governed by Europeans. The most striking example of this process was the adoption of the metric system in track and field in 1932. Worried that Americans "were not getting the glory and the credit due them" because their records were set in yards and miles while the rest of the world used meters, Kirby and colleague A. C. Gilbert pushed the AAU to adopt the metric system in 1932, over the objections of many of its affiliates. With the exception of the British Empire, the AAU was the last member of the international track and field federation to do so. Until then, records made in the United States were recognized only in the English-speaking world, while the rest of the world had its own set of records; only at the Olympic Games did U.S. athletes compete in meters.[60]

The switch to meters, though reversed in 1940, was significant as an indicator of global pressures on U.S. sport. The metric system's defenders adamantly insisted that the country's global role in track and field required conversion to the universal standard. Gilbert argued that "a prescription written by a doctor of the modern school of medicine can be filled in any country of the world, because it is written in the metric system . . . [and] so it should be in sport." In similar terms, Kirby defended the metric system by stressing the need for a "common denominator." It was not enough, he emphasized, for American athletes to compete against one another, ignoring the world at large. "What we want," he wrote, "is not alone athletes who will become the champions of the United States . . . but athletes who will become champions of the world and have their records recorded here and everywhere."[61]

Kirby's explanation is indicative of the way that for many Americans involved, participation in international sport helped cement a sense of the interconnectedness of the world and of the growing role of foreign public opinion in an age of mass politics. As Kirby observed in 1939, "nations can no longer be isolated, self-determining or governed by policies independent of the standards, practices and desires of the rest of the world."[62] For Americans like Kirby, international sport was knitting the world into a single global society, and even Americans had to conform to its rules and norms.

The "Mission" of American Sport

In 1935 Hollywood released a film, *Fighting Youth,* about a college football star distracted from his athletic pursuits by his girlfriend, who turns out to be a spy for a political organization trying to destroy the U.S. Constitution by breaking up college football.[63] The improbable plot highlights the extraordinarily tight link between sport and "Americanism" in the United States in this period. During the previous half-century, sport had become integral to conceptions of national identity in many countries, perhaps nowhere more so than in the United States. In the interwar years, as Warren Susman has observed, Americans became preoccupied with defining the United States as a culture and with illuminating the characteristics of an "American way of life," a term that became increasingly common in the 1930s.[64] Sport was unquestionably a significant component of what Americans saw as essential to their way of life, embodying for many the qualities that made the United States a great nation— democracy, fairness, and honesty foremost among them.

Popularized in such books as John Tunis's *Democracy and Sport* and in countless articles and speeches, the notion that sport was inherently democratic and intrinsically suited to the American character became a staple of public discourse.[65] Although these connections were more often asserted than examined or explained, the "democratic" nature of sport was held to derive from the equality of opportunity it supposedly offered. As Brundage explained to a visiting British Empire track team in 1930, "Wealth, social standing, religion or political creed make no distinction on the field of sport, where, so long as games are played cleanly and honestly, the athlete who can run the fastest or who can jump the highest will win the prize. This is perhaps the nearest approach to true democracy that we have."[66]

Public figures cited U.S. athletic supremacy as proof of the country's greatness. General MacArthur wrote, "Nothing has been more characteristic of the genius of the American people than is their genius for athletics. Nothing is more synonymous of our national success than is our national success in athletics." In 1938 Assistant Secretary of War Louis Johnson echoed the rhetoric of American exceptionalism in attributing the nation's unique freedom to its embrace of sportsmanship. "Why is there such a contrast between the Old World and the New?" he asked. "Why do we enjoy such a great freedom, and why do European countries impose so many restrictions?" The answer, he said, was that Europe and Asia had yet to comprehend the true spirit of amateurism and sportsmanship. "Fair play on the athletic field," he declared, "breeds fair citizens and just nations."[67]

Despite the lofty rhetoric of democracy, egalitarianism, and fairness, sport authorities in the 1930s placed narrow limits around their definitions of what constituted appropriate, truly "American" sport. These limits are sharply apparent in the contemporary discourse about race, gender, and amateurism (a cover, in many ways, for class) in sport. The "democracy of sport" was confined to white males: sport leaders did not hold up the presence in sport of African Americans and women—still subject to heavy discrimination—as reason to celebrate the egalitarianism of sport, nor were African American and female champions often celebrated as genuinely national icons. Americans were briefly elated by the four gold medals Jesse Owens won in 1936, but when he returned home his efforts to capitalize financially on his astounding success failed.[68] After defeating Max Schmeling in 1938, Joe Louis was embraced as a national hero, arguably to a degree even in the white South, but as was true of other black athletes, he often found his talent explained by references to the innate savagery of blacks. Even when he was a major star, white establishments in the North sometimes turned away his business.[69]

Women of all races remained on the fringes of sport. With sport coded as a masculine activity, the existence of female athletes—strong, competitive, aggressive—produced anxiety among many Americans. While the male-dominated sport establishment tolerated female athletes in a limited number of sports deemed acceptable for women, it expected

them to adhere to moral standards that did not apply to men and to social mores about femininity. The AAU, for example, required compulsory chaperones for female competitors.[70] When Eleanor Holm Jarrett, a
gold-medalist in swimming in 1932, danced and drank on the voyage to
Europe to compete in the 1936 Olympics, Brundage and the AOC expelled her from the team. Press coverage of female athletes at the 1932
Olympics highlighted their favorite recipes, sewing skills, and attractive-
ness while downplaying their athletic achievements.[71]

For the public the term "American sport" would have conjured up
professional baseball and semiprofessional college football. In the international context, however, the "American sport" projected abroad was
largely amateur. The AAU and the AOC applied strict rules for the establishment of amateur status, not only requiring would-be amateurs to
forfeit potential income from playing sport but also to abjure commercial endorsements, film roles, book contracts, and other opportunities
that could be construed as financial rewards for athletic performance.
Kirby offered "dishonesty" as one of the reasons why product endorsements should be banned for amateurs. Because athletes rarely used the
products they advertised, Kirby argued, endorsements undermined the
moral character required of amateurs. The underlying assumption was
that a true sportsman played only for the sake of the game, not for recognition or reward. But the impossibility of such a standard is evident from
the fact that hammering out what it meant in practice dominated the
agenda of amateur organizations for decades. The complexity of the issue can be gleaned from the questionnaire the AOC sent out in 1934 to
two thousand educators and officials. It ran to 18 pages and included
126 questions, among them: whether the spouses and children of professionals could be amateurs, whether anyone who receives money in one
sport is a professional in all sports, whether writing a magazine article
about one's experiences must lead to amateur disqualification, and
whether playing in any competition in which professionals also competed should automatically lead to disqualification.[72]

Like other emblems of the American way of life, U.S. sport—embodying
values such as courage, honesty, and democracy—became part of a moral
crusade to spread "Americanism" throughout the world. Brundage, Kirby,
and other sport enthusiasts believed that by disseminating their vision of
sport and sportsmanship, they were implanting a moral code that would

bring other nations toward democracy and peace. These men encouraged international sport contests not for their entertainment value, but above all for their educational value, not as a distraction from the ills of the world but as a remedy for them. Sport officials almost never spoke of "fun" (when they did, it was usually "good, clean fun") and they believed deeply that participation in sport was a solution to many problems, from unemployment at home to conflict abroad.[73]

By the 1930s the idea that sport contests promote mutual understanding was accepted as a truism by much of the U.S. public. A typical variant was expressed in the widely read *Literary Digest* in 1934. Admitting that contests often engender disputes and ridiculing the claim that international sport could prevent war, the article nonetheless concluded that "as a means of dispelling provincial ignorance, of multiplying and spreading the various forms of sport and even of promoting the mutual respect of the different peoples for one another's prowess and virtues," contests like the Olympic Games did far more good than harm.[74] In another common formulation, sport was described as "the language of the world . . . [and] the universal meeting ground of common understanding."[75]

The idea of a "civilizing mission" for sport was also widely held by civic and political leaders in the United States. In 1923 a group of New York men founded the Sportsmanship Brotherhood to foster and spread sportsmanship throughout the world. Matthew Woll of the American Federation of Labor served as president, and its board of directors included Franklin D. Roosevelt (out of whose Broadway offices the group initially worked) and Owen Young, the chairman of General Electric. During the 1920s and 1930s the group gradually expanded its activities, setting up college chapters and establishing ties with England, Hungary, and Japan. Linking sport not just to Americanism but to Christianity, the group saw sportsmanship as a manifestation of Christian brotherly love and a "bridge of understanding between the nations of the world." Defining sportsmanship as "truthfulness, courage, Spartan endurance, self-control, self-respect, scorn of luxury, consideration one for another's opinions and rights, courtesy, and above all fairness," the organization's leaders hoped to create "a better world" by encouraging nations to enter friendly sporting contests where sportsmanship would prevail. Sport, the group believed, offered the most potent means to train minds and characters in the spirit of democracy; it was "a medium for reaching the hearts and minds of hundreds of millions of the human race . . . a medium which establishes a direct contact between young and old, the wise and the simple, the right and the poor, both sexes and all nations." Once introduced on the playing fields, the spirit of sportsmanship would infiltrate other areas of life and become the governing principle in political and international relationships. The process was virtually guaranteed to be effective, Brotherhood members believed, because sportsmanship was an automatic product of playing according to the rules, and its principles were readily and unconsciously absorbed.[76]

Politics and Sport

International relations in the 1930s, of course, provided little basis for the kind of optimistic assessments presented by Brundage, the Brotherhood, and other groups. As U.S. influence in international sport increased, international hostility and militarism rose in tandem. Yet, just as the Depression had done little to inhibit the growth of international sport, political tensions had little effect on the growth of sport contacts. Officials like Brundage and Kirby had no qualms about pursuing close sport relations with dictatorships in Germany, Italy, and Japan. They generally saw as commendable these regimes' efforts to promote healthy populations through sports programs.[77] The success with which these dictatorships pursued high-level achievements in sport caused surprisingly few Americans to question their ingrained belief in the inextricability of democracy and sport. Brundage, Kirby, and others hardly stopped to notice or question the contradiction. Those who recognized that the successful appropriation of sport by dictatorships represented a challenge to their belief in the democracy of sport shrugged it off as an example of the perversion of sport. Sportswriter John Tunis, for example, saw the dictatorships' (mis)use of sport for propaganda, indoctrination, and military training as simply one of a host of distortions of sport's "pure" nature, albeit more egregious than the others he often denounced (such as professionalism, racism, and poor sportsmanship).[78]

Even in the face of open German and Japanese aggression in the late 1930s, U.S. sport officials did little to protest. In 1937 the AAU—then led by Jeremiah Mahoney, a former New York State Supreme Court judge, a leading Democrat, and an outspoken critic of Nazi Germany—prohibited U.S. participation in a track tour of Germany, in what the press labeled "the first rebuff to a foreign nation in the half century of [the AAU's] existence." Mahoney explained, "I do not believe that our American athletes should go to a country where freedom of speech, religion and action have been abolished . . . Nazi ideology cannot conform with American democracy." With a new president in charge the next year, however, tours resumed despite the March 1938 *Anschluss,* as the AAU sent its largest-ever contingent of track and field athletes to compete in Hamburg, Dortmund, Berlin, Dresden, Hanover, Munich, and Stuttgart, and a group of swimmers toured seven German cities.[79] In 1937 public outcry against Japanese atrocities in China led to a campaign to move the 1940 Games from Tokyo, but such sentiment did not derail AAU-sponsored American-Japanese wrestling meets in 1938. U.S.-Japanese sport contacts did drop off sharply after 1937, but the decline was probably due to lack of interest on the Japanese side as attention was diverted to the more pressing needs occasioned by the invasion of China.[80]

One issue that did generate an enormous amount of public controversy and soul-searching was the question of participation in the 1936 Berlin Olympics.[81] Some sections of the U.S. sport world and the general public could not reconcile the purported values of sport—namely equality of opportunity and the promotion of goodwill among people—with the staging of a major sport festival in the capital city of a regime based on race hatred, and they advocated boycotting the Games. As the *Christian Century* argued: "Move the Olympic games to some other country, and no twisting of the news in the controlled press could conceal from all the people of Germany—and especially from the Nazis themselves—a realization of the way in which the rest of humanity regards what is going on in that country."[82] From a narrower standpoint, some sport officials supported a boycott on the basis that the Nazi regime's obvious exclusion of Jews from its Olympic team violated Olympic principles. As Brundage wrote in a statement of principle he would later flout, "[the] very foundation of the modern Olympic revival will be undermined if individual countries are allowed to restrict participation by reason of class, creed, or race."[83]

A group led by AAU president Mahoney campaigned strongly in favor of a boycott on the basis that Germany's discrimination against Jews and other religious groups violated Olympic principles. "Under its present leadership," Mahoney wrote in a public letter to the German Olympic Committee, "your country not only is not observing but cannot observe the principles of democracy and of equality upon which the Olympic Games are based. The Olympic code, which recognizes in the realm of sports the absolute equality of all races and of all faiths, is the direct antithesis of Nazi ideology, which has as its cornerstone the dogma of racial inequality."[84] Brundage, as head of the AOC, forcefully advocated participation. Privately branding his opponents Jews and communists, Brundage countered that the Olympics should not be derailed by what he dismissed as "the present Jew-Nazi altercation."[85] Others, like Kirby, suggested that participation offered the best way to spur positive reforms in Germany. "Desirable social changes," Kirby wrote, "come by the intercommunication of ideas, [and] the highways between nations, intellectual and spiritual, must be kept open."[86]

The debate reached far beyond the world of sport. Businessmen, intellectuals, and Catholic, Jewish, and other religious groups joined the fray. An avalanche of pamphlets, radio interviews, rallies, demonstrations, congressional resolutions, letter-writing campaigns, petitions, and newspaper editorials descended on the public, as each side presented its case and castigated opponents. The *Nation* and the *New Republic* joined the boycott forces; the *New York Times* alone ran hundreds of stories on the issue; and the question was the subject of one of the earliest Gallup polls, which showed 43 percent of Americans in favor of a boycott in early 1935.[87]

Political leaders also weighed in on the issue. In Los Angeles, host of the previous Olympics, a handful of strongly anti-Nazi members of the city council killed a measure to appropriate a small sum to transfer the Olympic Games flag to Berlin, and IOC member William May Garland was left to do it out of his own pocket.[88] At least eight state governors and an equal number of U.S. senators and representatives publicly expressed reservations about participation or advocated a boycott.[89] New York Representative Emanuel Celler introduced a congressional resolution denouncing Nazi religious and racial discrimination and discouraging participation.[90] Two senators urged the State Department to give "serious consideration" to the question of withdrawing from the Games.[91]

Despite the public uproar, the State Department took the position that the matter was entirely a private affair. George Messersmith, first as U.S. consul general in Berlin and after 1934 as minister in Vienna, waged a vigorous one-man campaign to push the State Department into action. At his own initiative, he sent more than half a dozen reports on the

Olympics to various superiors, detailing Nazi discrimination against Jews in both sports and broader social life. Asserting that the Berlin Olympics "will play an important part in determining political developments in Europe," he argued that the United States "should refrain from participation" because involvement would further Nazi "aims for political expansion and prestige."[92] His aim was to convince the department to communicate confidentially with the AAU and its member groups, which, he felt, would surely come to their senses if they knew the true situation in Germany.[93]

Messersmith's appeals fell on deaf ears. The department refused to try to influence the AAU or to take a side in the public debate. Both President Roosevelt and Secretary of State Cordell Hull refused to take a position, as they did with regard to Nazi persecution of the Jews in general. Keeping well clear of the matter, the White House refrained from offering a farewell message both to the U.S. Olympic team and to another group going to Barcelona for an anti-Nazi counter-Olympics.[94] Forced to defend earlier acceptance of honorary positions on the AOC after that body sent out fund-raising letters with Roosevelt administration names in the letterhead, Hull explained that such patronage carried "no international political implication."[95]

The final decision was taken at the AAU convention in December 1935. By sheer force of will and clever manipulation of voting procedures, Brundage ensured that the delegates voted, by a razor-thin margin, in favor of sending a team.[96] By the time the Olympics were held the controversy had receded, and U.S. press reports of the Games struck a mostly celebratory tone, lauding the Nazis for their organizational achievements. The U.S. presence in Berlin has often been retrospectively, and justifiably, condemned as hypocritical, allowing the Nazi regime to score a major propaganda coup. There is no question that a U.S. boycott would have undermined Nazi Germany's quest for international standing and that participation implicitly sanctioned an evil regime. Kirby's self-serving argument, however, was not entirely without foundation. By threatening to boycott the Games—and, given U.S. dominance at the Olympics, such a boycott would have seriously diminished the stature of the Games— Americans cajoled the Nazi regime into small but significant concessions, including the inclusion of two athletes of mixed ancestry on the German team. American attitudes were a factor in forcing the Nazi regime to remove anti-Jewish placards near Olympic venues. Above all,

U.S. participation meant that a black athlete, Jesse Owens, became the hero of the Games and the darling of the Berlin crowds, vividly disproving Nazi racial theory in Hitler's own capital.[97]

The U.S. presence in Berlin in 1936, like American participation in international sport more generally, was premised on a deeply held belief that sport, American-style, could transform other ideologies and social systems. Those in the United States saw no contradiction in asserting sport's uniquely American qualities while at the same time offering it as a panacea to other nations. As Morrell Heald and Lawrence Kaplan have noted of U.S. cultural diplomacy in general, "what was considered most American was also considered universal."[98] Like other elements of popular culture that sometimes conveyed materialistic, shallow, or otherwise unflattering images of Americanism, sport was not an unproblematic medium. Unsportsmanlike behavior, questionable judging, violations of amateur rules, the quest for victory at all costs—these were some of the ways sport exchanges could spread negative impressions. And, as skeptics pointed out, U.S. supremacy had a downside in that it could leave other countries frustrated by their inability to win. For enthusiasts, however, sport was one of the most potent vehicles in the American mission to raise the moral and material condition of the rest of the world. Nations pursuing modernization and Westernization could adopt the material trappings of the West without adopting its spiritual values, but in the view of advocates for sport, the physical contests they championed would effortlessly and inevitably inculcate habits of mind and internalize democratic practices.

In 1935 the AAU's publicity director elaborated on the connection between the growth of sport and the spread of U.S. ideology. Noting that American athletes "have always triumphed" over rivals from "aristocratic, monarchic and despotic nations," Clarence Bush found the explanation for American success in "our competitive system of life," which was being imitated by the rest of the world. Bush was sanguine about the fact that imperialist and nationalist nations like Japan were exploiting sport for militarization. Such nations, he claimed, were "playing with forces whose effect they do not appreciate, forces which will eventually change their national concepts. What are these forces? We call them the forces of Americanism." Foreign athletes were copying American techniques but in the process were also "absorbing unwittingly our ideology, which is indispensable in exercising our technique and making it effective in breaking records and winning championships." As a result of using American techniques, other nations might soon challenge America's athletic supremacy, but because they were attaining success by adopting American ideology, Bush argued, "Americanism will still be triumphant."[99]

Bush was partly right. Sport is a carrier of values, and even if those values are modified when they are transplanted to foreign soils, they do alter the landscape. The growth of U.S. influence in international sport was part of broader currents of Americanization. At the same time, participation in this global society integrated part of the U.S. sport community into a larger world order and inculcated an internationalist perspective among a significant segment of the American population, despite prevailing isolationist sentiment. By garbing their participation in international sport in heavy layers of moralizing rhetoric, the nation's self-designated sport ambassadors influenced the way Americans perceived their country's role in the world, reaffirming deeply rooted convictions that the United States was a model for the rest of the world and a force for peace in international affairs. In an ironic twist of fate, however, U.S. leadership was perhaps most decisive in propelling the commercialization and commodification of sport in the international sphere. With one hand, U.S. officials clung tenaciously to an archaic amateur ideal; with the other, they ushered in changes—rigorous training, an achievement-oriented ethos, and the celebration of individual heroes—that inevitably drove competitive sport into professionalized and commercialized channels.

The U.S. case highlights the synergistic dynamic of nationalism and internationalism that underlay sport's expansion. The country's influence worked to standardize and homogenize sport, especially at the most competitive levels, helping to create in modern sports competitions a venue for apparently universal and fair comparisons. In tying sport to mass culture, entertainment, and leisure, the American influence also helped propel sport's global spread. Americans pushed for greater involvement in international sport for nationalist reasons, both ideological (to spread Americanism and democracy) and economic (to sell products and to create a more prosperous, purchase-hungry world). Yet the effects were not so much to create an Americanized world pliant to U.S. control but to create an internationalized sport system with an independence of its own, part of a global society whose internationalism could at times channel and redirect its constituent nationalisms.

4

"Americanizing" the Olympic Games: Los Angeles, 1932

On July 30, 1932, after years of preparation and millions of dollars spent, Los Angeles was ready to play host to what famed sportswriter Grantland Rice would dub, with typical oversell, the "greatest sporting pageant in world history."[1] By plane, train, ship, and car, U.S. and foreign visitors poured into the city in what the *New York Times* heralded as "the biggest migration to California since the [Gold Rush]."[2] Traffic jams clogged the city's long, straight boulevards, lined with eucalyptus and palm trees, and pedestrians crowded the downtown streets. Instead of the "here and there" decorations put up by previous Olympic hosts, the Los Angeles city center looked like the site of a huge party. Streets were gaily decorated with hundreds of colorful flags, streamers, and banners; buildings everywhere were bedecked with bunting. In Pershing Square, in the center of the city, an enormous poster hung over the street, inscribed with the words "X. Olympiad, Los Angeles 1932." Further along a huge emblem with the Olympic motto *Citius Altius Fortius* (faster, higher, stronger) was strung above a crossing. Shop windows throughout the downtown area showcased the official Olympic poster of a young champion draped with laurels. Hotel lobbies, streetcars, and taxis displayed the Olympic shield. Streetlights were festooned with the flags of forty nations, with maps underneath showing the location of each country whose flag was flown.

Foreign athletes in bright dress uniforms wandered about the town taking in the sights. Foreign tourists filled the city's hotels; at the posh Biltmore visitors from twenty-one foreign countries rubbed elbows. Lines of people hoping to buy tickets snaked in front of authorized ticket outlets. News of the forthcoming events filled the newspapers and formed the principal topic of conversation. Vendors hawked bronze pins and colorful ribbons, and everywhere white Olympic banners, with five varicolored circles symbolizing the linking of the continents, fluttered in the light ocean breeze.[3]

The 1932 Olympic Games seemed far removed from the soup kitchens and unemployment lines of the Depression, and Los Angeles was a long way from the capitals of Europe that had constituted the fulcrum of the Olympic movement to date. The setting of these Games on the far side of the New World symbolized in geographic terms the leap these Games represented in other terms, toward a more global, more competitive, more commercialized, and more Americanized version of international sport. A milestone in the internationalization of modern sport, with broad and wide-ranging effects on the Olympics and on the world of sport, the 1932 Games displayed in microcosm the broader tensions that beset the globalizing sport world before World War II. Although racial, class, and gen-

Downtown Los Angeles gaily decked out for the 1932 Olympic Games, which were used as a global advertisement for Southern California. *Source:* 1932 Olympic Games Official Report.

der prejudices that undercut universalist ideals were visible at these Olympics, internationalism gained ground at the Games. At the same time Los Angeles clearly tipped the balance toward commerce in the contest between the ludic and the lucrative.

American nationalism was, of course, on display in Los Angeles. Many Americans saw the Olympics as a venue for showcasing the nation's achievements, and U.S. athletes took home the lion's share of the laurels. There was, however, a price to be paid for the spread of the country's sport expertise. Already other countries, especially Japan, were proving adept pupils, successfully wresting spots on the victory podium. Much more so than in other sporting contexts, the U.S. public was forced to acknowledge the achievements of foreigners.

The 1932 Games marked the metamorphosis of the Olympics from a relatively marginal and elitist event into an entertainment extravaganza with wide popular appeal. As such, the staging of the 1932 Games represents the single greatest contribution of the United States to the development of international sport before World War II. At a time when the host city's organizing committee was largely responsible for the success of the Games, the Los Angeles organizers put a distinctively American imprint on the international festival, greatly expanding international sport's connections to the world of entertainment, consumerism, and mass media. Despite inauspicious timing in the midst of a global Depression, the Los Angeles organizers staged an enormous and highly successful event that boosted the worldwide popularity of the Olympics and stamped the Games as a globally significant festival whose meaning extended far beyond the sporting feats it showcased.

"Gosh, What a Spectacle!"[4]

Already in the 1920s the Games were becoming major events, their growth fueled by the explosion of mass spectator sport. The Games had established a reputation as the pinnacle of amateur sporting achievement, and the terms "Olympic champion" and "Olympic record" were filtering into everyday vocabulary. At Antwerp in 1920, Paris in 1924, and Amsterdam in 1928, each quadrennial festival sought to be bigger and better than the last. To some observers the program of events was reaching unmanageable proportions, with nearly twenty sports represented in about a hundred separate events that lasted weeks or months beyond the recommended two-week core. The competitions were drawing about three thousand participants from roughly forty countries, though only a handful came from countries outside the European and North American orbit.[5] Organizing committees, not always with the support of local or national governments, spent years preparing for the costly event, raising large sums of money to build new state-of-the-art facilities and to revamp older ones.[6] They also undertook extensive publicity efforts, printing hundreds of thousands of posters, stamps, postcards, announcements, programs, and travel brochures for international dissemination in several languages.[7] Hundreds of thousands of spectators—in 1928 the total was more than half a million—thronged the events, and with the advent of sport tourism, tens of thousands of visitors flooded hotels in Olympic cities.

Americans had been central and enthusiastic backers of the Olympic movement since its inception in 1896. Historian Sloane was a member of Coubertin's inner circle and a key player in the establishment of the IOC, and U.S. athletes had garnered a large share of medals at every Olympic Games. (Despite a common misperception, the United States did not win the overall medal count at every Olympics before World War II.) As a reward for U.S. support and to buttress his global aspirations for the Olympics, Coubertin wanted to see the Games hosted not only in the capitals of Western Europe but also in the United States, a country he liked and admired. He had already sent the 1904 Games to St. Louis, unfortunately before the Games had established a secure footing, so that the sporting events turned out to be little more than a minor adjunct to the concurrent world's fair. After World War I, he was ready to try the New World again.

In the early 1920s a group of Southern California boosters tapped William May Garland to head a campaign that would eventually succeed in snaring the second North American Games for the West Coast. While attending the 1920 Games in Antwerp, Garland made an impressive pitch to the IOC on behalf of Los Angeles, buttressed with invitations from state, county, and city officials and from local civic and athletic organizations. Coubertin already had plans for the 1924 and 1928 Games, but he made Garland a member of the IOC and encouraged him to try again. Garland did, in 1923, and this time Coubertin agreed to give Los Angeles the 1932 Games.[8]

Host cities were technically awarded by IOC vote, but in those days

Coubertin's wishes always prevailed. At a time when personal connections mattered a great deal, Coubertin took a liking to Garland. The IOC president had been to California and saw its distance from Europe as an asset: it was far removed from the political turmoil that he feared could endanger the Games. He was also swayed by Los Angeles's new 75,000-seat stadium, constructed by the nonprofit Community Development Association that Garland headed. For Coubertin these factors combined to promise a successful Olympiad.[9] The rest of the IOC simply followed Coubertin's lead—and not always on the most informed basis. Garland later recounted that one IOC member from Central Europe said to him after the vote, "Billy, I voted for Los Angeles because I like you personally, but where is Los Angeles? Is it anywhere near Hollywood?"[10]

If the rest of the world knew relatively little about Los Angeles, the city was nevertheless a perspicacious choice. The European press protested, of course, for entirely self-interested motives. Their athletes would be at a disadvantage after such a long journey, and the Americans, who already dominated so many sports, would have the further advantage of being on home turf.[11] But Los Angeles was a vibrant, booming city at the crossroads of East and West—an ideal setting for a Games bent on global expansion. Frank Lloyd Wright sniffed in 1940 that "it is as if you tipped the United States up so that all of the common people slid down into Southern California," and the city was indeed a magnet for migrants. Its population already surpassed a million in 1930, and the Depression only slightly slowed its growth through the rest of the decade. As the largest city in the country in terms of square miles subsumed in its relentless sprawl, with its car-centered culture, a climate that seemed to inspire optimism and energy, and the "open and cultivated hedonism" of its middle and upper classes, the city seemed to encapsulate the American dream.[12]

Coubertin later characterized the Los Angeles Olympics as "propaganda for tourism," and he was largely right.[13] Garland, who headed numerous community groups including the Los Angeles Athletic Club, was a well-connected, energetic, and savvy civic booster backed by key figures in Southern California's business elite. He and fellow Olympic promoters were less interested in sport than in what they presciently recognized as an advertising opportunity, a chance to raise the profile both at home and abroad of the fastest-growing city in the United States.[14] Olympic project supporters included the president of the famed movie studio

Metro-Goldwyn-Mayer, Louis B. Mayer, who was also a member of the California Olympiad Commission, and Harry Chandler, owner of the *Los Angeles Times,* who saw the Olympics as a way to boost tourism, to encourage migration to the area, and to promote business. The general public was also supportive, and both state and city voters approved million-dollar bond issues to fund new construction and renovation of facilities.[15] Critically for the success of the Games, the organizers secured funding for the Games before the Wall Street crash snuffed out the prosperity of the 1920s.

When the Depression hit and deepened into a prolonged crisis, prospects for the Olympics dimmed. Some Americans called for canceling the event, seeing it as inappropriate frivolity when more pressing needs—for food and shelter—were unmet. But the organizers pressed on, undeterred by disapproval at home and hesitancy abroad. Responses to the invitations were slow to come in, as many European countries weighed whether they could afford to participate when costly transatlantic and cross-country travel was factored in with new economic woes. Many countries sent reduced contingents, and even the U.S. team, with far lower travel expenses, suffered cutbacks. A few months before the opening, both ticket sales and guarantees of foreign participation were "near zero."[16] Funds were difficult to raise almost everywhere, but no team matched the Brazilian in entrepreneurial flair. Sailing on a ship filled with donated coffee beans, the athletes sold their cargo along the way to pay their expenses.[17]

Instead of scaling back their preparations, the organizers went to great lengths to mitigate expenses. They negotiated with steamship lines and railroad companies for fares that cut the costs for teams coming from Europe by two-thirds, and subsidized participation by promising to feed, house, entertain, and provide local transportation to every competitor for $2 a day (considerably less than cost) in an innovative "Olympic Village." In the end forty countries sent a total of 1,503 athletes—fewer than had participated in the 1928 Games but a respectable number.[18]

In the years of preparing for the event Garland's committee took on a broad array of tasks. It issued official invitations, transmitted by the U.S. State Department, to the sixty-two nations recognized as Olympic members. It printed and sent out official rulebooks for each sport, a total of 53,000 in four languages. It built and renovated facilities, including separate sites for swimming, fencing, boxing and wrestling, rowing, cycling, shooting, and equestrian events. It expanded the Coliseum to hold 105,000 seats, enlarged the press section, improved the dressing rooms, and built a scoreboard, a public-address system, and a 107-foot Olympic Torch. It procured and tested standardized equipment to ensure that events were staged under uniform and fair conditions. Only English boxing gloves approved by the International Boxing Federation could be used in Olympic boxing matches; springboards for the swimming competitions had to be approved by the international swimming body; special Swiss timing watches certified by the IAAF had to be used to time track races.[19]

The real feats of organizing, however, were devoted to the production of the Games as spectacle. Here the Americans drew on the skills that had made the United States the world leader in mass culture—organization, press and public relations, advertising, salesmanship, and promotion. Far surpassing the flawed efforts of the Dutch organizers of the 1928 Amsterdam Games, the Los Angeles group set up a sophisticated, well-designed system intended to maximize satisfaction for spectators and the press. Some measure of the system's complexity can be gleaned from equipment figures: two eighty-line switchboards were installed in the central executive office and at the Olympic Stadium; across all venues, 350 private lines with almost 500 telephones fielded more than 85,000 outgoing calls in 1932. Replacing the confusing and inconvenient mail-in procedure that had generated many complaints at the Amsterdam Games, Garland's staff handled ticket sales to the 117 individual events through an elaborate and highly efficient system of phone banks and new technologies staffed at its peak by sixty clerks. Twenty operators at an "information bureau" fielded queries from the public.[20]

Spurred by excellent marketing and relatively low prices—one or two dollars for most events—ticket sales soared despite the Depression. In 1928 paid attendance had numbered just over 660,000, over a third of which had been for the hugely popular soccer matches. Even without a major team sport (the IOC had removed soccer from the 1932 program due to disputes over amateurism), the Los Angeles Games drew twice as many paying spectators, setting a record at 1.25 million. These included as many as 325,000 out-of-town visitors, according to one projection. Most of those who came were Americans, but visitors from at least fifty other countries attended the events, bringing in gate money to the tune of $1.5 million and giving the Games a substantial surplus.[21]

As part of their efforts to popularize the Games, the organizers emphasized pageantry and entertainment in the production of the Olympic spectacle. The opening ceremony was no longer a stiff, formal affair but a dazzling show. The two-hour event drew a sell-out crowd of 105,000, more than four times the number that attended the opening in Amsterdam.[22] The spectators crowded into an immense stadium gaily decorated with what one ticket-holder described as "color, color everywhere." Flags of all the participating nations fluttered from the ramparts, and zeppelins and airplanes circled overhead in the clear blue sky.[23] The ceremony began when "The Star-Spangled Banner" welcomed U.S. Vice President Charles Curtis, who waved to the cheering crowd as he took his spot in the presidential loge. The centerpiece of the event, as always, was the Parade of Nations. Each nation's delegates entered the stadium in festive uniform, headed by a flag bearer and greeted by cheers and applause as they made their way around the stadium. When the athletes had assembled in front of the Tribune of Honor, the vice president declared the Games open with the prescribed formula: "I proclaim open the Olympic Games of Los Angeles, celebrating the Tenth Olympiad of the modern era." As a crashing ten-gun salute sounded, Curtis reached to the side of his chair and pressed a silver button to light the giant Olympic torch at the top of the peristyle at the stadium's main entrance. Thousands of white doves, released from the field, flew above the crowd as trumpets and cannon roared. A 1,200-voice chorus sang the Olympic hymn, followed by the swearing of the Olympic oath and the raising of the Olympic flag. It was, observers agreed, a magnificent pageant.[24]

Adroit management of publicity and press relations proved to be another of the organizers' fortes. Almost the first action taken by Garland's team was the formation in 1929 of a press department, which disseminated information to the world press through news releases in five languages and an official Olympic announcement bulletin. Billed as "the first systematic world news service during the preparatory period of an Olympiad," the department worked hard to increase worldwide interest in the years leading up to the Games, enlisting the aid of foreign consuls, steamship and railroad offices, and the U.S. Department of Commerce to compile a mailing list of six thousand foreign periodicals.[25] The motion-picture industry also helped to publicize the Games. Cinema idols Mary Pickford and Douglas Fairbanks, long fans of the Olympics who counted many star athletes as friends, broadcast a worldwide appeal to attend the

Games, and studios produced short subjects about the Games that helped stimulate public interest abroad.[26]

The advance publicity helped draw more than nine hundred journalists to cover the Games—half again as many as had covered the Amsterdam Games. During the Games these journalists were catered to and coddled far more adeptly than previous organizing committees had attempted. Vastly improving on the telephone booths and telegraph facilities that had been provided in Amsterdam, the Los Angeles committee put in place a highly sophisticated communications system with hundreds of telephones, capacious telegraph facilities, and teletype machines. To ensure that results were released as quickly and as accurately as possible, the committee devised a novel system based on the Dow-Jones electric writing machines that were used to disseminate stock market news. The

The press box at the main stadium in 1932. The American Organizing Committee's expert handling of press and public relations put the Olympics on a new footing. *Source:* 1932 Olympic Games Official Report.

overall result was what journalists reportedly called "the finest Press arrangements ever provided for any event of world magnitude," an achievement that undoubtedly helped increase news coverage abroad, further stimulating public interest in the Olympics.[27]

One local journalist claimed that the Games had produced "millions of special articles, descriptions, illustrations, editorials and cartoons in columns circling the globe."[28] The assessment was something of an overstatement, as coverage abroad varied widely. In Japan the events were covered heavily. In Italy, where Mussolini placed special importance on international sport victories as a way to achieve glory and whose team performed very well at the Games, press coverage was also extensive.[29] The French were markedly less enthusiastic. They had been among the most vociferous in objecting to the choice of far-off California in the first place.[30] Their team had suffered cutbacks for financial reasons, and with fewer victories to celebrate press coverage was more subdued. High-brow political papers like *Le Matin* covered the Games in a perfunctory way, with rather dry summaries of results, while more popular broadsheets like *L'Echo de Paris* had more plentiful and more colorful coverage. The sport-hungry British devoted considerable space to the Olympics in papers such as the *London Times* and the *Daily Mail,* but the focus was still overwhelmingly on sports results and the occasional controversy over judging or rules. Everywhere, the wired reports journalists sent home described the Olympics with a narrow focus on sport, leaving observations of other notable aspects such as advertising or tourism for the occasional memoir or popularized book published after the event.[31]

Other media got into the act as well, as movie newsreels recorded every phase of the Games for international audiences. Televised broadcasts would begin only at the 1936 Olympic Games, and even there only on an experimental basis, but Los Angeles had the next best thing: highlights of the Games were rushed from the field to laboratories in Hollywood and shown in local theaters and at the Olympic Village the same night or the next day.[32] Radio, making its Olympic debut, was the one area where organizers stumbled. Like major-league baseball and other commercial sport enterprises, Olympic organizers were slow to recognize the enormous potential of radio (and later television) to expand the popular appetite for sports. Hollywood studios saw radio as an unwelcome rival in the entertainment business and pressured the organizers to limit broadcasting. These factors, combined with a dispute with the National Broadcasting Corporation over fees, meant that in 1932 reports were limited to summaries of results and interviews with athletes rather than live broadcasts.[33]

Commercialization and the Hollywood Connection

Setting the Games in the capital of the American entertainment industry was a crucial element in their success. Hollywood studios, directors, and actors provided critical funds and celebrity backing. The Hollywood connection added glamour to the events and reinforced the idea that athletes, like movie stars, were fundamentally entertainers. At previous Olympics kings and queens had opened the ceremonies and titled aristocrats had staffed official positions. In Los Angeles, it was "the royalty of the screen" who lent the Games cachet.

Among the scores of entertainments thrown for visiting athletes, officials, and journalists, the studio parties were the most sought-after invitations. MGM head Louis Mayer threw a party at his studios, where two hundred Olympic guests from thirty nations toured the facilities and lunched with film stars. The toastmaster at the lunch greeted the guests in Spanish, French, German, Japanese, and Hindi.[34] At Fox Studios comedian Will Rogers hosted a luncheon and tour for female athletes. Pickford and Fairbanks, dubbed "the king and queen of Hollywood," held a formal dinner at their estate for Olympic dignitaries. Throughout the Games, movie stars, studio moguls, athletes, Olympic officials, and local politicians mingled in swank California nightclubs.[35] Gary Cooper, Bing Crosby, Cary Grant, and the Marx brothers were among the stars who came to see the competitions.[36] The athletes, many of them celebrities themselves, proved so star-crazy about their celluloid idols that journalists dubbed autograph hunting an unofficial Olympic sport. During one visit to the Olympic Village, Fairbanks was mobbed by Finnish athletes who asked him to autograph track pants, underwear, collars, shoes, moth-eaten envelopes, and suitcases.[37]

Further indication of sport's deepening ties to the world of entertainment was MGM's release that year of the first Tarzan film, starring former Olympic swimming champion Johnny Weissmuller. A five-time Olympic gold medalist and holder of several world records, Weissmuller was one of the earliest of what would become a steady stream of attractive and charismatic athletes who parlayed Olympic medals into stardom on the screen. Paramount Pictures was hoping to replicate MGM's success when it auditioned twenty Olympic athletes after the 1932 Games, searching for a "jungle hero" to rival Tarzan. Clarence "Buster" Crabbe's swimming gold medal in Los Angeles had piqued Paramount's interest, and the studio tapped him to star as Kaspa the lion-man, launching a long and successful film career that included roles as Flash Gordon and Buck Rogers.[38] Not every Olympic athlete succeeded in Hollywood, of course. Triple-gold-winning swimmer Helene Madison sank into obscurity after one film. Glamorous Eleanor Holm, another swimming gold-medalist in 1932, was signed by Warner Brothers after the Games but stuck to bit parts for years before making what she called "a rather bad" Tarzan film with Glenn Morris, a decathlon winner at the 1936 Games.[39]

That the Games were not just about sport but also about commerce was clear to the wide mix of business, military, and political leaders from Europe, the Americas, and Japan who came to Los Angeles to mingle

Representatives of the new celebrity culture mingling at the main stadium of the 1932 Olympic Games in Los Angeles: film actor and former Olympic swimmer Duke Kahanamoku, aviator Amelia Earhart, Finnish distance runner Paavo Nurmi, movie star Douglas Fairbanks Jr., and German sprinter Arthur Jonath. IOC Olympic Museum Collections.

business and pleasure. J. Sigfrid Edström, a wealthy Swedish industrialist, was a prominent example of the many businessmen who saw international trade and international sport as mutually profitable. Edström was president of the Swedish General Electric Corporation and vice president of the International Chamber of Commerce in Paris, and was also president of the international track-and-field federation and was a member of the IOC's powerful executive committee. Though Edström called his visit to California a vacation, he spoke about international business affairs with the *Los Angeles Times,* which carried news of his arrival on the front page. The Games also drew businessmen of a less savory type, like Chicago gangster Edward "Spike" O'Donnell, who arrived in town, he told police, "to attend the Olympic Games and go to church."[40]

Foreign businessmen used their Olympic sojourns to investigate U.S. methods in aviation, textile manufacturing, refrigeration, fish- and fruit-packing, bakeries, tire and automobile companies, banks, radio, and agricultural and oil-well machinery. Local businessmen reported making new connections in markets in Europe, Latin America, and Asia. The committee formed by the Los Angeles Chamber of Commerce to facilitate such connections and to stimulate international trade gained five hundred registrants, who found abundant social opportunities for making new business contacts. The city's haute monde postponed annual retreats to summer homes to throw dozens of breakfasts, dinners, teas, concerts, ship entertainments, dances, beach parties, and garden fetes for Olympic visitors. One group of distinguished Japanese guests was reported to be attending three or four parties a day.[41] In addition to the opening Olympic Ball thrown by Garland's organizing committee, local groups threw a Ball of All Nations at the Ambassador Hotel's famed Cocoanut Grove and an International Ball at Shrine Auditorium, which featured national pavilions staffed by interpreters and hostesses in native costume and decorated with flags and banners.[42] Local ethnic-based community groups threw parties for visiting teams and gave them enthusiastic welcomes at the docks and train stations.[43]

At a time when the military in many countries provided significant numbers of Olympic competitors, top military brass also mingled at Olympic social affairs. The party thrown by Britain's Rear Admiral Sir Reginald Drax and Lady Kathleen Drax was attended by U.S. Admirals Richard Leigh and Luke McNamee, several U.S. Army colonels, the British and French consuls, California Governor James Rolph Jr., and an assortment of

European counts and princes. The U.S. secretary of the army asked Congress for special sanction to use military funds to defray expenses for army competitors at the Olympics and called it "highly desirable that the Army of the United States should be represented in these games."[44] The French consul threw a "swanky" military ball, attended by General La Font and his staff, officers from the U.S. Army, Navy, and Marine Corps, officers from other Allied forces, and other prominent guests.[45]

Local businesses catering to the tourist trade experienced a welcome boom during the Games, as out-of-state and international visitors flooded the city by car and train. Hotels, apartment houses, theaters, and local merchants had one of their best summers in years.[46] One department store hired interpreters speaking Greek, Dutch, Italian, Swedish, French, German, Spanish, and Japanese. Another opened two gift shops for Olympic shoppers, one with Chinese crafts and one with souvenirs, costume jewelry, and dress accessories in Olympic colors and motifs.[47]

Businesses also sought to capitalize on the event by harnessing their fortunes directly to the Olympic brand. The United States was home, of course, not only to Hollywood and its globally popular cinematic fare; it was also pioneering mass advertising at the time. It is not surprising, then, that despite the Organizing Committee's avowed commitment "to keep the organization of the Games on a true Olympic basis devoid of professional activities and commercialism," commercialism made deep inroads at the Games. The organizers took in revenue from the sale of advertising-free programs and from concessions sold in the stands (including sandwiches, soft drinks, candies, tobacco, souvenirs, paper umbrellas, and seat pads) and gained a share of the profits from authorizing a group of downtown businessmen to sell "official" Olympic emblems. Most of the commercialization, however, came from the many unauthorized novelties and souvenirs that companies tied to the Olympics.[48]

Businesses from clothiers to cigarette makers had sought to capitalize on the Olympic phenomenon from its earliest years, buying advertising space in programs, printing booklets combining advertising with information about the Olympics, and selling or giving away products or novelty souvenirs. For a brief moment, at the 1924 Games in Paris, advertising had even wormed its way into the stadium, and athletes competed before Ovalmaltine, Cinzano, and Dubbonnet posters until the IOC voted to prevent further such displays within Olympic venues.[49] U.S. companies had been among the first to recognize the advertising potential of the

Games. The Eastman Kodak Company had placed an ad in the Book of Official Results at the very first Olympics in 1896, and at the 1924 Games Kodak had supplied film to professional photographers.[50] In Amsterdam in 1928 similar marketing ploys included Gillette shaving kits decorated with Olympic motifs.[51]

Such efforts expanded in 1932 as U.S. companies devised ingenious ways to "market" the Olympics, in the process pushing Olympic marketing toward a focus on products aimed at the masses rather than at the upper classes.[52] Companies such as Kelloggs' Pep Bran Flakes, Weiss Binoculars, Safeway, and Piggly Wiggly inaugurated major Olympic-themed advertising campaigns. The tourism and leisure industries were naturally keen to jump on the Olympic bandwagon. Auto supply stores, railroad lines, hotels, tire manufacturers, and gasoline companies gave out Olympic tie-ins ranging from stickers to paper-holders. Standard Oil erected a giant neon sign advertising the Games.[53] "Olympic" seat cushions, hot dogs, soft drinks, sunshades, caps, and ribbons were hawked everywhere in Los Angeles.[54] An especially enterprising bread company obtained the contract to supply the Olympic Village and secured rights to market itself as the official Olympic bread company, an honor it again won for the 1936 Games.[55] The Olympics also spawned a philatelic bonanza in stamp-crazed America, producing enough commemorative U.S. postal stamps, covers, cachets, vignettes, and postcards to fill a book (literally).[56] Like the Hollywood studios, U.S. companies wooed Olympic stars, offering hefty contracts to winners willing to give up their amateur status. Springboard diver Jane Fauntz, for example, turned down a shot at a movie career but went on to endorse Wheaties cereal and Camel cigarettes.[57]

In 1928 the Coca-Cola™ Company began what would become a long-running and profitable corporate relationship with the Olympics. Hoping to expand its presence beyond Britain into the rest of Europe, the company sent a thousand cases of the soft drink along with the U.S. Olympic team to Amsterdam, where special Coca-Cola kiosks staffed by vendors with Coca-Cola caps and coats wooed more customers than competing "health drinks."[58] This effort paled beside the huge campaign Coke launched in 1932. More than two hundred teenagers in white jackets and gloves handed out Coke to spectators at the Coliseum; an Olympic record indicator, emblazoned with Coke's logo, occupied a prominent place in the stadium; and across the United States the company distributed three million disks showing Olympic records and the company logo.[59]

Local politicians also hopped with alacrity on the Olympic bandwagon. In New York City, Mayor James Walker played to the Italian American vote, for example, by welcoming the Italian team (en route to Los Angeles via steamship and railroad) at city hall, where the athletes tendered him the fascist salute.[60] Los Angeles Mayor John Porter and California's Republican Governor James Rolph Jr. were ubiquitous fixtures at events, welcoming athletic delegations, attending social events, and watching the competitions.

At the national level, however, no leader took a cue from Mussolini, who gave the departing Italian team a rousing speech linking their performance to Italian national honor.[61] President Herbert Hoover resolutely refused to recognize the Games as a political opportunity. Olympic precedent called for the host country's head of state to open the Games, and political circles in the capital had anticipated that Hoover would return to his home state to attend the Games and then make his way north to Palo Alto to accept the nomination as the Republican party's 1932 presidential candidate. Instead, just weeks before the Games began, Hoover reneged on his promise to attend. Faced with mounting economic problems and dealing with the Bonus Army march on Washington, D.C., he cited "the pressure of national affairs" in declining the invitation. His private attitude, however, is suggested by a note he wrote to Secretary of

Advertising for the Olympics: commercialization reached new heights in Los Angeles. *Source:* IOC Olympic Museum Collections.

State Henry Stimson, complaining that he was "being greatly plagued by the Olympic Games Committee" over the issuance of invitations.[62] He limited his patronage to an official statement calling the Olympics "a positive force for international acquaintance and understanding and good will."[63]

Hoping to secure the firm backing of his predecessor in the upcoming campaign, Hoover pressed former president Calvin Coolidge to open the Games in his stead, but Coolidge curtly refused, and in the end Vice President Charles Curtis was dispatched. Franklin D. Roosevelt, then governor of New York and the Democratic presidential candidate, had greater appreciation for the Olympic's public-relations potential. He had opened the Winter Games in Lake Placid, New York, and planned to go to Los Angeles for the Summer Games in what Republican leaders sneeringly called a ploy "to step into the limelight at Mr. Hoover's expense."[64] In the end Roosevelt chose not to go, leaving Curtis a full share of the limelight, although the vice president studiously avoided stepping into it. He arrived by train the day before the opening, with no entourage except for one Secret Service officer, kept his public activities minimal, and left immediately after the opening ceremony.[65]

The Department of State under Stimson was equally oblivious of the political opportunities the Olympics represented. Although the department frequently assisted international cultural conferences, officials were tepid in their enthusiasm about the Los Angeles Games. At a time when many European foreign ministries regarded sport as an affair of state, U.S. diplomats dithered over the perfunctory task of mailing invitations to the Games and initially refused to offer minor accommodations, such as waiving the usual visa requirements and import fees on sporting equipment. One bureaucrat was prompted to write testily that "while it may be none of my business, I must confess that the Department seems to me to have been unnecessarily conservative in its attitude toward participants in these Games of international interest."[66]

The Olympics Go Global

In addition to setting new standards in organization and marking new levels of public consumption, the Los Angeles Games bequeathed major innovations to Olympic symbolism. The mark that show business made on the Games was evident in the first major tradition inaugurated at

these Games: the new victory ceremony. Previously divided into separate
flag-raising and awards components, both often conducted without the
presence of the winning athletes and well after the conclusion of the
competitions, the victory ceremony was now consolidated into one formal event, orchestrated to include national anthems and flags after every
event.[67] It was a brilliant move, simultaneously enhancing the stature of
the individual athletes and tapping audiences' nationalist sentiments in
a highly effective way.

A second key tradition established at these Games was the Olympic
Village, which quickly became the most visible symbolic representation
of the Olympic creed that, as the Los Angeles organizers put it, "nations
are, after all, only members of one great family—the human family." Proposed as a way to offset the heavy cost of transportation to the West
Coast, the Village offered inexpensive accommodations to visiting male
athletes. For two dollars a day, the men could stay in one of 550 Spanish-
style bungalows specially constructed on a large tract of land overlooking
the Pacific Ocean.[68] With lawns, five miles of streets, a hospital, bank,
post office, fire department, bus service to the nearby Olympic Park, and
an open-air amphitheater showing motion pictures of the day's events,
scenic travelogues, and two-reel comedies, it was truly a "miniature
city."[69] Far more than a cheap place to stay, it was a microcosm of the kind
of international community the Olympics claimed to foster, one where, in
the words of the organizers, "the children of the nations, unscarred by
maturity and assumed nationalism, would find in each other brothers in
the flesh, regardless of color, race or creed."[70] It was no accident that female athletes were relegated to a hotel: the Olympic community was,
above all, framed as a masculine enterprise.

The contradictory impulses embedded in the organization of the Village are illustrative of the broader tensions between nationalism and internationalism that had been a major characteristic of the modern
Olympics since their founding. Billed as a way to further amicable contact among athletes of different nations, the Village also had features designed to minimize exposure to foreign cultures. Athletes roomed with
others of the same nationality, and "neighborhoods" within the Village
were segregated according to political principles. Latin American athletes were grouped together, with the exception of the Brazilians, who
were placed with southern Europeans. Other sections were made up of
the French and their Little Entente allies; the British and their Domin-

ions; and Germans, Austrians, Hungarians, and Scandinavians. Culinary segregation also prevailed. With almost fifty separate kitchens, the Village was prepared to offer every nationality meals based on its own cuisine. Organizers went so far as to consult foreign embassies weeks in advance to stock the kitchens with necessary ingredients. American hospitality did not extend to liquor: Prohibition laws remained in effect, and distraught French athletes were reduced to drinking sugar water as a substitute for the wine that normally comprised an essential component of their training diets.[71]

The limitations of the Village notwithstanding, the Los Angeles Games moved closer to adhering to the IOC's avowed principle of universality, with larger numbers of women and nonwhite participants. Women's events, though still a small percentage of the program, achieved broader acceptance and popularity. For years many IOC members had preferred to keep women off the program entirely or to limit their participation strictly to "feminine" sports like tennis. Under pressure by a group of women who formed the Fédération sportive féminine internationale to hold a separate "Women's Olympics" in 1921, the IOC began gradually expanding the program of women's events. The 1932 Games were in many ways a coming-of-age for women's participation, fueled in part by the publicity generated by star U.S. athlete Mildred "Babe" Didrikson. A brash, self-promoting, and extraordinarily talented athlete, Didrikson excelled at many sports, including baseball, golf, and track. Her celebrated victories at the Olympics included gold in the eighty-meter hurdles and the javelin, both events in which she set new world records, and silver in the high jump. If the male reporters who covered her were uncomfortable with her tough and "unfeminine" qualities, it was nevertheless clear that women were in the Games to stay and that their achievements could not be ignored.[72]

The Los Angeles Games also marked what a Swiss Olympic official praised as "a displacement . . . in the center of gravity of Olympism."[73] More non-Western countries participated, and the frequent appearances of their athletes on the victory podium offered tangible proof of the Olympics' increasingly global sweep. China made its first official appearance in 1932, sending one delegate. The Indian field hockey team carried off a gold medal after trouncing the U.S. team by a score of 24–1. Argentine Santiago Lovell took home gold in heavyweight boxing. When his compatriot Juan Zabala won the marathon in a dramatic finish, his picture appeared on the front pages of newspapers from Buenos Aires to Paris.[74] African American athletes also received new prominence, with much-ballyhooed victories by sprinters Eddie Tolan, who set a new world record of 10.3 seconds in the one hundred-meter race, and Ralph Metcalfe.

The most stunning performances were delivered by the Japanese. Participating in its fifth Olympiad, Japan sent the single largest foreign contingent, numbering about 130 athletes.[75] The effort was part of a larger drive by the Japanese government to increase Japan's prestige through victories in international sports. Highlighting Japanese sensitivity to foreign opinion, the sixteen women on Japan's team were required to complete a two-week course in American etiquette at the YWCA in Kyoto, learning how to use knife and fork instead of chopsticks, among other social essentials.[76] Despite Japan's recent seizure of Manchuria, an act of aggression the U.S. government met with a policy of nonrecognition, the Olympic team was feted in Tokyo by U.S. Ambassador Joseph Grew before its departure, filmed in a "talkie" to introduce the athletes to the U.S. public, and given a hearty welcome on its arrival in Los Angeles. As one ocean liner with Japanese team members pulled to the dock, a band played Japan's special "Olympic Games song" and ten thousand flag-waving Japanese Americans crowded the pier to greet the team, which was then paraded by motorcar first to city hall and then to the Olympic Village.[77]

The climate of hostility between the United States and Japan was not evident on the field.[78] American public opinion was generally favorable toward the team, and the Los Angeles papers began for once to use the term "Japanese" rather than the derogatory "Jap." The *Los Angeles Times,* adopting a celebratory tone throughout the Games, claimed afterward that the treatment Californians had afforded the Japanese athletes had "done much to sweep away the one-time prejudice in [Japan] against America."[79] In fact, the Japanese team reported that they received kind and fair treatment from officials and fans, but complained that they were barred, like Mexicans, from some dance halls and first-class restaurants. They were also unimpressed by the casual manners and style of dress of Americans.[80]

Shocking most Western observers and leaving their U.S. rivals scrambling for excuses, the Japanese team won six of seven events in men's swimming, a sport usually dominated by Americans. Japan's "flying fish," as one sportswriter dubbed them, won four individual events and broke three Olympic records.[81] Although Americans raced to explain these victories on absurd racial and cultural grounds (citing "webbed feet" and leg development spurred by the absence of chairs

Informal cultural exchange: Japanese Olympians sampling the fare at a Los Angeles drive-in in 1932. Some first-class restaurants in LA refused to serve Japanese athletes. *Source: Dai jikkai Orimupikku taikai hokoku, 1932.*

in Japanese houses, for example), Japanese success was due in good part to careful emulation of U.S. techniques. Recognizing the public-relations value of sports victories, the Japanese had embarked on a high-powered training program in key sports. Their efforts to win international success had included invitations to U.S. swimming stars, including Johnny Weissmuller, whose exhibition meets in Japan in 1928 and 1931 had been filmed and carefully analyzed by Japanese trainers.[82]

Reflecting the enormous public interest in the Olympics back home, Japan also sent the largest foreign contingent of newspaper correspondents. They spared no expense in covering the Games, often paying $2.62 a word to rush their copy by wire and racking up about $40,000 in total telegraph and cable tolls. Special arrangements were made to rush photographs of the Games by ship to Japan.[83] The Japan Broadcasting Corporation (NHK), prohibited by U.S. organizers from doing live radio broadcasts, instead offered simulated live broadcasts. After an event, an announcer was driven from the stadium to a nearby NBC affiliate, where he re-created the competition for broadcast. The re-creations were cabled to San Francisco and then sent by shortwave to Tokyo, where they proved widely popular.[84] The homecoming of the Olympic team in September, when they were greeted by a crowd estimated at 100,000 and saluted as national heroes, was broadcast throughout the nation.[85]

During the Games, Los Angeles was also abuzz with other meetings and conferences that were part of a growing repertoire of international activities in the realm of sport and physical education. As was traditional, an art competition and exhibition of sport-related art was staged as part of the Olympics. Conveniently located near the Olympic Stadium, the exhibition attracted displays from thirty-one countries and nearly 400,000 visitors, with prizes awarded in painting, sculpture, architecture, the graphic arts, literature, and music.[86] On August 2, the Hostesses of the Xth Olympic Games staged an elaborate pageant called California Welcomes the World, which one journalist labeled "the West's contribution to the festival side of the superb Olympiad." The lavish enterprise of "song, dance, and enthralling pictorial impressions" was seen by a capacity audience of 30,000 in the Hollywood Bowl, including the governor and Olympic officials. They watched a cast of thousands, accompanied by special lighting effects, depict the history of California, followed by national dances like Irish jigs and a Chinese tiger dance, folk songs, Swiss yodels, a human flag made by a Czech group, and other entertainments representing the cultures of the foreign countries represented at the Games.[87]

Associated conferences included those held by nine international sport federations, which continued the tradition of holding their congresses in conjunction with the Games.[88] Other organizations interested in sports, physical education, and leisure also piggybacked on the Olympics. The First International Recreation Congress attracted one hundred delegates from twenty-five countries to exchange information on democratizing facilities and opportunities for recreation. The Congress featured an opening ceremony that drew inspiration from the Olympic ceremony, with groups from many countries in national costume demonstrating local dances and songs. Invitations for the Congress were transmitted by the U.S. State Department, a function it took on only for "unusually important conferences."[89] On a smaller scale, the International "Olympics" Conference on Physical Education featured invited lecturers from England, Germany, Japan, Finland, Poland, and France.[90]

As the Games drew to a close, observers found much to praise. The Games had had their share of controversy, most prominently three days before the Games began, when the IAAF barred Paavo Nurmi, Finland's celebrated long-distance runner, for accepting compensation above expenses during a European "barnstorming" competition.[91] Yet commentators agreed that an atmosphere of goodwill had prevailed and that the Games had been free of the kind of international "incidents" that had marred earlier Olympiads.[92] Opinion was unanimous that the weather had been close to perfect, fully justifying Southern Californians' claims to have a climate ideally suited to sport. Outsiders were rarely as ecstatic as the local press—the Los Angeles Times declared that "for perfection of setting, excellence of management and brilliance of presentation it is unlikely that the Tenth Olympiad of Los Angeles will ever be equaled"— but compliments were nearly ubiquitous.[93] Baillet-Latour, who had succeeded Coubertin as IOC president, was lavish in his praise, calling the Games "an unprecedented success," "the crowning glory" of the Olympics, and flawlessly organized.

Foreigners lauded the careful preparations that had gone into staging the events and the "grand manner" in which the organizers had carried out the festival. The London Times called the Games "a triumph." A Japanese journalist declared, "No Olympiad of the modern era comes near enough to the Games that Los Angeles has so ably and magnificently prepared." A German visitor called them "one of the greatest sport successes of all time." The German National Olympic Committee declared that the Games had handily outdone all predecessors in splendor. One German official announced that "the Olympic Games at Los Angeles will stand in our memory as an unbeatable new Olympic and world record . . . the record of records." Even the cantankerous French declared the Olympics "a stunning sporting and popular success."[94]

Olympic and world records had fallen with dizzying frequency, evidence that the Los Angeles Games had ushered in an era of elite, high-performance sport based on rigorous and systematic training. The very first event of the Games saw a new Olympic record set, and not infrequently, records were made and then remade in the same afternoon. Forty-eight records were broken—a mark that was itself a new record. Thanks to ideal weather conditions and an unusually fast track, almost every one of the twenty-three events in track and field saw performances that, as one correspondent put it, "not only eclipsed" previous marks but made them look "almost ridiculous." The leap in achievements was so great that some observers predicted that little room was left for further improvement and that these records would stand for a generation. (In most cases they would last but a few years.)[95] The home team, not surprisingly, dominated the victory stand, garnering 740.5 points to second-place Italy's 262.5 on the unofficial point scale used by the *New York Times*. Japan, too, had won the title of "sport power," winning third ranking on this scale.[96]

The Los Angeles Games were also novel in accumulating a substantial surplus, an achievement that most subsequent host cities would fail to duplicate.[97] The new standards of publicity, organization, scale, and pageantry introduced by the organizing committee in Los Angeles, however, were emulated by successors. Garland's group was the first to attempt to learn systematically from the experience of the previous Olympiad, sending representatives to the 1928 Games to study their organization and bringing the Dutch committee's general secretary to Los Angeles for several months to provide advice and assistance.[98] In similar fashion, the German Olympic Organizing Committee officials in charge of the 1936 Games made copious and careful observations in Los Angeles and diligently studied the lessons of 1932.[99]

The Los Angeles extravaganza had an enduring influence on the

Olympic Games, shaping the future of the world's biggest sporting event. Long an event with aristocratic overtones that catered to an elite audience, the Los Angeles Games were democratized and made available to the masses, both at home and abroad. Americans did to the Olympic Games what they had done to so much else: commodified them, popularized them, made them into an entertainment spectacle to be consumed like the flavor of the month. By linking the Games so closely to America's most popular export—Hollywood movies—the organizers injected glitz and glamour into an event that had been pompous and stuffy. The amazing sport performances that felled so many records marked the ascendancy of the rigorous training and specialization nurtured by Americans and now increasingly imitated successfully by their competitors, but these were only the most obvious of the American influences on the Games. Americans were world leaders not only in sport performances but also in mass consumption, and the deeper and less visible effects of 1932 were to leave the Games intertwined with commercialism and consumption in ways more profound than ever before imagined.

5

Dictatorship and International Sport: Nazi Germany

When British sports first appeared in Germany in the late nineteenth century, many Germans regarded them as an undesirable foreign import. German physical culture had long been dominated by the indigenous gymnastics system known as *Turnen*, devised in the early years of the nineteenth century. Its proponents viewed sport as a form of recreation fundamentally hostile to the principles valued in gymnastics. Even as sport grew significantly in popularity in Germany after World War I, *Turnen* remained a powerful and prominent element of physical culture. It offered the Nazis, who were opposed to internationalism and to foreign cultural forms, a possible alternative to the international culture of modern sport. The Nazi regime sought to control culture for the purposes of mass mobilization, to insulate the country from transnational cultural flows, especially the influx of U.S. commercial mass culture, and to build an autarkic cultural alternative, with varying degrees of success.[1] Yet in the realm of physical culture, instead of elevating *Turnen* as the centerpiece of a uniquely German cultural program, the Nazi regime became a full member of the international sport community.

Sport was not the only international cultural product the Nazi regime tolerated. Jazz, for example, was labeled a "bacillus" of black and Jewish origin, an alien, individualistic, improvisational (hence free) form of music that had no place in a racial-collectivist dictatorship. Yet while the regime disapproved of jazz, it never stamped it out, and indeed sometimes exploited it for its own purposes. The regime expressly promoted some forms of modern dance, and consumption of that quintessentially American soft drink, Coca-Cola, rose steadily in the 1930s.[2] Whether these elements of popular culture offered Germans a site of resistance to the regime or strengthened the regime's control has been the subject of considerable debate. As with jazz and Coke, however, the Nazi acceptance of sport demonstrates, in Hans Dieter Schäfer's formulation, that "the militaristic, racist rhetoric with which the Third Reich demonstrated its power was tempered by peaceful cosmopolitanism."[3] From the boxing star Max Schmeling's exploits in the United States to friendly soccer matches against neighboring countries, international sport offered the Nazis a way to assert national power, while also opening avenues for the infiltration of internationalist ideas and values.

Louis versus Schmeling

On June 22, 1938, Joe Louis met Max Schmeling for the world heavyweight championship in a fight that would become one of the most fabled boxing bouts of the century. In one corner was Schmeling, one of the great, colorful sports figures of the 1930s, who had held the world heavyweight title in 1930–1932 and was now embraced by the Nazi regime as a symbol of Aryan manhood. In the opposite corner was Louis, an African American boxer from Detroit who had risen to fame in a country where racism was still pervasive and where sports provided one of the few avenues to wealth and standing for blacks. A talented, hard-hitting boxer, "the Brown Bomber" (among the nicknames sportswriters had tried and discarded were the Mocha Manhandler, the Tan Tornado, the Beige Bonbon, and the Almond-Colored Annihilator) was lionized by blacks, who saw his victories over white boxers as vindication for the daily humiliations they suffered. He won acceptance from white America both because of his incontrovertible talent and because he chose not to upset the color line outside the boxing ring.[4]

America's "Bomber" and Germany's "Black Uhlan from the Rhine" had met two years earlier in one of the great upsets in boxing history, when Schmeling had inflicted the first knockout of Louis's career. For two years, fans had been waiting for a rematch, their appetites whetted not just by the sporting value of the bout but by its symbolic implications: a black American pitted against a representative of a dictatorship founded on race hatred. For Americans and Germans, the rematch was one of the most eagerly anticipated sporting events of the decade, but the fight was also a global phenomenon, broadcast in Spanish and Portuguese in South America and covered by reporters from thirty-six countries.[5]

On the afternoon of the fight tens of thousands of New Yorkers jammed the Lexington Avenue subway to 161st Street and clogged the streets leading to Yankee Stadium. Thousands more came from out of state. Among the 70,000 spectators who packed the stadium that evening were the governors of four states, New York Mayor Fiorello LaGuardia, members of Congress, President Roosevelt's son, FBI Director J. Edgar Hoover, the German ambassador, former heavyweight champion Jack Dempsey, and dozens of other notables from the sports world, as well as movie stars Clark Gable, Douglas Fairbanks, Gary Cooper, Gregory Peck, and Tallulah Bankhead. From the rich, famous, and powerful at ringside to the down-and-out in the cheap seats at the back, all races and strata of U.S. society were represented in the stadium. Five German weight lifters on a U.S. tour joined a minority of the crowd rooting for Schmeling. The chief of police assigned 1,700 officers to the stadium to maintain order. Ringside seats, listed at $30 each, were sold for $125 or more. As had happened only a handful of times in the past, a boxing match took in more than a million dollars in gate receipts.[6]

It was a lot of money to spend on two minutes of entertainment. Shortly into the first round, Louis launched a fierce barrage of punches that sent Schmeling reeling to the canvas again and again. Finally, as Schmeling lay dazed and bloodied on the canvas, his manager stormed into the ring to stop the fight. The referee ended the count at five and signaled that Louis was the victor. America's "Brown Bomber" had avenged his 1936 defeat in spectacular fashion.[7]

For weeks the American press had been filled with inflated rhetoric depicting the fight as a struggle between democracy and fascism, freedom and dictatorship, good and evil. As one sportswriter from Boston put it, "Louis represents democracy in its purest form: the Negro boy who would be permitted to become a world champion without regard for race, creed, or color. Schmeling represents a country which does not recognize this idea and ideal."[8] Expressing a decidedly minority viewpoint, the editors of the *New York Times* injected a discordant note into the public discussion, arguing that "the prizefight doesn't mean anything. It doesn't mean that the Nazi philosophy is good or bad, that the Negro race is or is not rising in the economic scale, or anything else."[9]

In the United States public sentiment toward the Nazi regime had hardened since the 1936 fight. As in 1936, Jewish groups in New York City organized a boycott of the fight, calling Schmeling a "Nazi product" whose prizewinnings enriched the Nazi coffers.[10] The boycott was little supported or noticed among non-Jewish boxing fans, but Schmeling's association with Hitler dented his popularity in the United States. When Schmeling's ship docked in New York, he was met by protesters carrying anti-Nazi placards, and the boxer was flooded with hate letters.[11] After the fight, a Southern newspaper echoed widespread sentiment when it gloated: "The Aryan idol, the unconquerable one had been beaten, the bright, shining symbol of race glory has been thumped in the dust. The noise you hear is Goebbels making for the storm cellar."[12]

Joseph Goebbels, Hitler's propaganda minister, may not have made for the storm cellar, but he was one of many Germans who stayed up until the wee hours of the morning glued to his radio. Schmeling's knockout, Goebbels confided in his diary, was "a terrible defeat." He rued that the newspapers had "bet too much on a victory [and] now the whole nation is depressed."[13] According to one report, Goebbels now had to abandon grandiose victory plans to celebrate "the innate superiority of Nordic" over other races.[14]

It was a far cry from his reaction to Schmeling's 1936 victory over Louis. Then Goebbels had spent a suspenseful evening with Schmeling's wife, the Czech-born film star Anny Ondra, keeping her spirits up as they waited impatiently for the early-morning broadcast. That victory, after twelve grueling rounds, he described in his diary as "a dramatic, exciting struggle. Schmeling fought for Germany and won. The white man over the black, and the white was a German." He went on to note: "The whole family is in ecstasy. I didn't get to bed until 5 A.M. I was really happy. Today . . . we celebrate the victory with Anny Ondra." The next day Goebbels listened to a rebroadcast of the fight, remarked again that it was a victory for all of Germany, and exulted in the "fantastic press," both at home and abroad, that Schmeling's victory was garnering.[15] When Schmeling arrived back in Germany on the Hindenburg a few days after the victory, he was greeted by 70,000 well-wishers, showered with gifts and flowers, and officially feted as a national hero. Hitler, whose favorite sport was boxing, held a dinner at the Reich Chancellery in Schmeling's honor, and Goebbels produced a documentary of the fight, entitled *Schmeling's Victory—A German Victory,* that played in packed theaters across the country.[16] One author cited Schmeling's victory, along with construction of the Autobahn, occupation of the Rhineland, and introduction of Zeppelin service to New York, as one of the ten greatest "achievements of the new Germany in 1936."[17]

Schmeling was Germany's best-known international athlete and an icon to millions of Germans. As a successful professional boxer, he had become wealthy and famous in the 1920s. First a German idol, he became an international phenomenon when he went to New York and broke into the world of U.S. boxing, where he held the world heavyweight champion title (a title bestowed by U.S. authorities) from 1930 to 1932. As one historian has suggested, Schmeling's international victories functioned for Germans as a kind of "collective psychic compensation for the national humiliation of Versailles."[18] The boxer's circle of friends in Weimar-era Berlin included Emil Jannings and Ernst Deutsch from the theater world, the opera singer Michael Bohnen, film stars Hans Albers, Willy Fritsch, and Olga Tschechowa, and the hugely popular race-car driver, Bernd Rosemeyer. George Grosz painted his portrait; Joseph Thorak, Ernesto de Fiori, and Rudolf Belling sculpted him. He starred in several films, including a 1934 film called *Knockout* with his wife as costar.[19]

Rich and famous before 1933, Schmeling found that his star rose still further in the Nazi period. Although he portrayed himself as apolitical and tried to protect some of his Jewish friends, he also worked comfortably with the Nazi regime. Certainly he was assiduously courted by Nazi officials, who heralded him as a prototype of the "master race." They gave him tax breaks, assured him favorable press coverage, facilitated his international fights, and gloried in his victories.[20] Schmeling was not a party member, but he was perceived, within Germany and without, as an ambassador of the Reich, defending the regime to the outside world and acting as an unofficial spokesperson. In 1935, for example, Nazi officials asked him to use a trip to New York to work against the U.S. movement to boycott the Berlin Olympics, and he hand-delivered to Avery Brundage a letter from the German Olympic Committee that offered assurances that black and Jewish athletes would be treated fairly in Berlin. He was one of the first athletes on whom Hitler bestowed personal invitations— dinner at the Reich Chancellery, coffee on the Tegernsee.[21] The eagerness with which high Nazi officials sought to help Schmeling regain the championship title demonstrates the extent to which the regime staked its prestige on Schmeling's career. In 1937, for example, the regime offered $350,000 in scarce hard-currency reserves as a purse to draw a championship match to Berlin, where Schmeling would take on then-titleholder James Braddock. (In the end New York interests bid higher, and it was Louis who fought Braddock for the title.)[22]

His 1938 defeat at the hands of a black man—an Aryan defeated by a representative of an inferior race—came as a shock to the Nazi regime. Goebbels's propaganda ministry immediately issued orders to downplay the loss, banning the news from the front pages of newspapers. "Schmeling," the press instructions admonished, "is not Germany." The party organ *Völkischer Beobachter* argued that "the defeat of a boxer is no national loss of prestige; it is a lost battle only for the boxer himself."[23] Goebbels's paper *Der Angriff* admitted that the defeat was "bitter" but claimed it should not be considered "a national disaster."[24] In the face of the exuberant celebrations of "a victory for Germany" just two years earlier, such disclaimers rang hollow. The Nazis had staked prestige on the bout, and their claims for the supremacy of the "Aryan race" and the power of the "new Germany" were undermined when one of the regime's heroes lay prostrate on the canvas, knocked out by a black man before a global audience.

But how was it that Schmeling appeared in the ring with a black man in the first place?[25] Interracial boxing had long been a source of profound unease in the United States, where blacks had been unofficially banned from title contention in a "save the white race" campaign after Jack Johnson upset the racial hierarchy by holding the heavyweight title from 1908 to 1915. Johnson was a flamboyant character who consorted with white women and flaunted his wealth and fame; his brazen disregard for the unwritten rules requiring blacks to keep "in their place" represented such a challenge to white America that one of his fights resulted in riots and an estimated eighteen deaths.[26] Black boxers were similarly suspect in Britain, where the prospect of a Johnson bout against the British heavyweight champion in London prompted the Home Office to ban high-profile interracial boxing matches in the 1910s and 1920s for fear that they could incite black unrest in the empire and erode the mythology of white superiority.[27] If interracial boxing was fraught with symbolic implications in Britain and the United States, surely it was in the "racial state" of Nazi Germany as well. Before the first Louis-Schmeling bout, a German sports magazine declared that simply for Schmeling to fight Louis would be "a national humiliation." For an "Aryan" to appear in a sporting event with a black man implied a degree of equality between the two opponents. Participation in a boxing match entailed an acknowledgment that contestants should be bound by universal rules, and that within those rules, either could win. As Schmeling himself put it to the American press, "In sport, the Negro and the white man are just the same. The best man wins."[28]

Why, then, did the Nazi regime condone Schmeling's fights and promote him as a representative of the German nation? Up to the assumption of power in January 1933, the Nazis had condemned international sport for, among other sins, "working politically to the advantage of the Bolshevik struggle against the white race" and for "the inconsistency and lack of instinct of the nations of the white race" that led to competitions with "black serfs" (*unfreien Schwarzen*).[29] But after 1933 the Nazi regime found the advantages of participation in international sport more compelling than the disadvantages, even when participation meant competition against "inferior" races.

Sport, German Gymnastics, and National Socialism

Hitler seized power at a moment when "English sports" and German gymnastics were poised in a delicate balance. After a decade of growth, sport clubs claimed a membership roughly equal to that of the *Turnvereine* (gymnastics societies) that had long dominated German physical culture.[30] When Hitler came to power pledging a return to traditional German values—in his first speech as Reich chancellor he declared "we want to give back to our people a truly German culture, a German art, a German architecture, a German music, which will restore our soul; we shall thus evoke reverence for the great traditions of our people"— gymnasts had good reason to hope that the Nazi program would favor their movement as the preeminent version of German physical culture.[31]

The history of *Turnen* was interwoven with the rise of German nationalism. Devised at the beginning of the nineteenth century by Friedrich Ludwig Jahn, an ardent Prussian patriot and anti-Semite, German gymnastics was intended to foster *völkisch* nationalism (a racialized nationalism based on a transcendent German "essence") in the aftermath of Napoleon's humiliating defeat of the Prussian army.[32] "Love of fatherland through gymnastics" was how Jahn described his aims. Ritual and cultic elements were deeply embedded in the movement, which drew on historical symbols and traditions, such as the German oak and ancient German dress. Gymnastics exercises were accompanied by the singing of patriotic songs and torchlight parades. When Jahn's disciples held a festival at Wartburg Castle in 1817 to celebrate the 300th anniversary of German nationalism, they burned "un-German" books and made speeches glorifying the cult of the *Volk*.[33]

After a period of decline—for a time Jahn was imprisoned and the exercises were banned in public places—*Turnen* underwent a remarkable resurgence in the 1840s. Along with choir and sharpshooting associations, *Turnvereine* were the largest and most broadly based of the private, patriotic organizations that spread throughout the German states in this period.[34] Initially imbued with the spirit of liberal nationalism, *Turnen* by the eve of World War I had become a conservative social movement, allied with right-wing nationalism and chauvinism.[35] Practitioners of a uniquely German physical culture, *Turnvereine* had no interest in multinational gatherings and their leaders condemned internationalism.[36]

The German gymnastics that became formalized in the 1840s differed from sport in eschewing the competition and individualism of games and contests in favor of collective exercises and mass drills. Gymnasts saw intrinsic value in the exercises themselves and disdained the striving for achievement in the tangible form of records and victories that underpinned sport. The Deutsche Turnerschaft, established in 1860, attacked modern sport as amoral and un-German as soon as it began to appear in Germany in the 1880s.[37] Edmund Neuendorff, leader of the Deutsche Turnerschaft before the Nazi takeover, thought sport encouraged "pride" and "egotism" and undermined "what the *Turner* have dedicated themselves to creating: a national community" (*Volksgemeinschaft*).[38] Rejecting the paraphernalia of modern sport—"concrete stadium, cinder track, tape-measure, stop-watch, manicured lawn, and track shoes"—gymnasts sought "the simple meadow, free nature." Whereas sport allegedly produced a one-sided physique, *Turnen* produced healthy, well-rounded bodies. Soccer was derisively labeled the "English disease" and was judged a barbaric game similar to kicking dogs.[39]

It was not until after World War I that sport began to rival *Turnen* in popularity. Membership in sport clubs grew, and public spending on playgrounds, swimming pools, and stadiums increased. Boxing, for example, had been banned under the Kaiserreich but became popular in the 1920s. The young Schmeling moved to the occupied Rhineland specifically because the British occupying forces had started boxing clubs there.[40] Like gymnastics, sport was seen as a covert method of military training, useful because the Versailles Treaty prohibited compulsory military service in Germany. Sport in the Weimar period appealed primarily to the middle class, while workers, youth, and women preferred the *Turnvereine*.[41] Other models of physical culture flourished as well, including separate Catholic, Jewish, and Protestant sports movements and a robust workers' sport movement that abjured the individualistic and competitive aspects of the English sport model.

The conflict between English-style sport and *Turnen* that had flared up in the 1880s was reignited in the 1920s, partly over the issue of the 1928 Olympic Games. When Germany was invited to participate in the Games for the first time since World War I, the Deutscher Reichsausschuß für Leibesübungen (DRA), the umbrella organization for sport and *Turnen* clubs, accepted the invitation. The Deutsche Turnerschaft then withdrew from the DRA to protest participation in international meets.

In a lengthy published response to the withdrawal, Carl Diem, the DRA's general secretary who would play a key role in sport administration under the Nazis, argued that sport had the same aims as *Turnen*. Bristling at the gymnasts' claims to be following a higher mission than sport, he defended the nationalist sensibilities of sportsmen. "Has anyone ever heard that members of sport clubs behaved less patriotically [*vaterlandsfreudig*] in the war? . . . Is there not in sport clubs just as in the Turnerschaft a strong leaning to 'black-white-red'?" he asked, referring to the monarchist colors used to signify conservative opposition to the republic.[42]

Diem's defense of sport clubs as a bulwark of conservatism had much to support it. The leaders of middle-class sport organizations tended to be antidemocratic and staunchly antisocialist. They subscribed to the same brand of nationalism, anti-intellectualism, and glorification of militarism as did the Nazis. As a result adherents of Nazism in the 1920s were attracted not just to *Turnvereine* but also to sport clubs; in fact, the leaders of the national soccer, rowing, swimming, and track and field associations were Nazi party members.[43] Yet despite Diem's claim that *Turnen* and sport had "99% in common," the belief in a fundamental philosophical divergence persisted, and there was considerable truth to Diem's much later observation that many Nazis viewed sport groups as "liberal," "pacifist," "foreign-loving," and run by Jews.[44]

The Nazi Party took no official position on the conflict between sport and *Turnen* before its ascension to power in 1933. The 1920 party program called for "the legal establishment of a gymnastics and sport duty," but in this it was merely echoing a common call among parties of the right to use paramilitary physical training programs to subvert the provisions of the Versailles Treaty.[45] Hitler saw physical exercise as a key element in building the strength of the German nation, but appears to have made little distinction between sport and *Turnen*. In *Mein Kampf* he declared that physical training was "a requirement for the self-preservation of the nationality" and must be made a state matter, not "an affair of the individual." In particular, it must be made a compulsory element of education in schools, so that "young bodies are treated expediently in their earliest childhood to obtain the necessary steeling for later life." Hitler deplored the "gross incongruity" of devoting most of the school day to "purely mental training" while "gymnastics gets barely two hours a week and participation in it is not even obligatory." In his view, "not a day should go by in which the young man does not receive one hour's physical training in the morning and one in the afternoon, covering every type of sport and gymnastics."[46]

Sport was mentioned infrequently in the party press before 1933 but when broached was usually condemned as a hotbed of liberalism, pacifism, Marxism, and Jewish influence.[47] International competitions came in for special scorn. The *Völkischer Beobachter* wrote in 1929 that any participation in an international sport federation should be rejected for reasons of national pride.[48] Rather than subordinating German athletes to the abstract world civilization represented by international sport, the Nazi press argued, a truly "German" physical culture must be promoted.[49] Nazi ideologist Alfred Rosenberg called international competition "raceless" and disparaged it as similar to "the idea of a union of nations."[50] Such ideas reflected the party's broader anti-internationalist stance. As Hitler said in a 1928 speech, his party aimed to free the German people from "the hopeless turmoil of internationalism" and "the pathetic belief . . . in reconciliation of peoples, world peace, a union of nations, and international solidarity."[51]

The tone of the press reports underwent a subtle shift beginning in 1928, when Germany was finally allowed to reenter Olympic competition at the Amsterdam Games. The success of the German team, which came in second after the United States in the unofficial standings, apparently helped soften attitudes. In 1929 the *Völkischer Beobachter* suggested that a nation could, under certain circumstances, be associated with a transnational sport organization. After the 1936 Games were awarded to Berlin in 1931, the paper did not call for a boycott but instead demanded that Jews and blacks be excluded.[52]

On the whole, then, indications were ambiguous as to how the Nazis, in power, would regard international sport. There was, however, enough in their general hostility toward internationalism to justify the actions of a group of Berlin students who staged a small demonstration after Hitler was named chancellor in January 1933. The students dug up the running track at the Berlin Stadium and planted small oak trees, symbols of Jahn, *Turnen,* and German tradition. The new regime, the students hoped, would bring an end to the "terror of the measuring tape" and restore the primacy of the German gymnastics tradition.[53]

Their hopes would soon be disappointed. Instead of *Turnen* the regime embraced sport, in this realm taking the side of cultural modernity.[54] Soon after taking power, the Nazi regime extended the *Gleichschaltung*—a term that literally means coordination but in practice meant Nazification—to physical culture. Out of Weimar's messy patchwork of confessional, political, and regional sport and gymnastics societies, the Nazi regime gradually created a centralized, state-controlled system. Workers' sports federations were shut down; Christian clubs had to abandon their religious orientation; Jews were excluded from all sports clubs except specifically Jewish ones. As Arnd Krüger has shown, after several months of debate the Nazis decided to model their new sport structure on the Italian version, where sport federations were no longer democratically elected but rather hierarchically structured from above and "coordinated" by the government (or the party).[55] In April 1933, Hans von Tschammer und Osten, an SA-Obergruppenführer and early follower of Hitler, was named Reichssportkommissar (a title changed some months later to Reichssportführer). In May, Interior Minister Wilhelm Frick placed control of all sport organizations into Tschammer's hands.[56] Eventually Tschammer gained a measure of control in almost every area of sports life in Germany: he was adviser for sport to the paramilitary Sturmabteilung, chairman of the German Olympic Committee, and head of the sport office of Kraft durch Freude (Strength through Joy), the recreational arm of the Nazis' ersatz trade union, among other positions.[57]

Like sport groups, the Deutsche Turnerschaft, whose leaders initially hoped for special preference because of the movement's *völkisch* tradition, was not allowed to remain independent. In 1933 Edmund Neuendorff was forced to hand control of the society to Tschammer, who dissolved the organization in 1936.[58] Gymnastics nevertheless continued to be practiced in Germany and strongly influenced physical education programs, as was vividly apparent in the regime's mass athletic demonstrations. In certain respects mass physical education was "Turnified" under the regime. In the international sphere, however, the major emphasis shifted to sport.

Organized physical activities to promote fitness and military preparedness assumed great importance as a result of the regime's drive for militarization. Physical education programs at various levels of schooling were centrally mandated, and a physical fitness test became a requirement for higher education.[59] The philosophical rationale for participation in sports and physical education programs was defined strictly in terms of service to the state. Sport was now "a duty" for all Germans. "The age of individualism in sport is over," Tschammer declared in 1933. Physical education, he said, no longer existed "to promote the welfare of the individual." Instead, the health and physical ability of the individual were important only insofar as they contributed to the total strength of the *Volk*.[60] For boys and men, sport was to serve as preparation for life as soldiers. For girls and women, sport was preparation for motherhood. In Tschammer's words, physical exercise was necessary for women so that they could "provide more healthy children for state and *Volk*."[61]

The Uses of International Sport under Nazism

The emphasis on mass sport as a way to increase the nation's military preparedness did not necessarily mean that the regime would embrace international competition at the elite level or that it would organize sport along lines consonant with international rules and standards. Before World War I, Germany had been a member in good standing in the major international sport federations, competing in the Olympic Games and in other international events. In 1912 the IOC granted Germany the right to host the Olympic Games of 1916, and preparations were already under way when war broke out. After the war, however, Germany was isolated culturally as well as diplomatically. Not until the mid-1920s did the former Entente countries resume sporting contacts with Germany, concurrent with the political reintegration of Germany signaled by the 1924 Dawes Plan, the 1925 Locarno Conference, and Germany's admission to the League of Nations in 1926. Germany's international sport relations, then, had generally reflected its position within the international political system. Hitler's antipathy to internationalism, vividly expressed by Germany's withdrawal from the League of Nations in October 1933, might have suggested that the Nazis would likewise withdraw from the international sport federations they had so often criticized.

Sport editor Bruno Malitz spelled out the party line in 1933 when he criticized the "liberal" idea that sport should be used "to tie constricting bonds among nations." In a major treatise laying out "the Nazi idea" of sport, he argued that cloaking sport competitions in the guise of international reconciliation was a sham. Flags were flown, national anthems played, clever words about international peace spoken, he said, and yet the victories of German athletes had altered nothing about the onerous, unfair Versailles *Diktat*. "Frenchmen, Belgians, Pollacks, Jew-Niggers have all raced on German tracks, played on German football fields, and swum in German swimming pools," he complained. "All kinds of foreigners have been having a marvelous time at our expense. The sporting promoters have thrown great sums of money about so that the international connections of Germany with her enemies shall be made yet closer."[62]

The cross-cultural fertilization that was an essential characteristic of modern sport came in for particular condemnation. Malitz complained that commercial interests in German sport, seeking "international sensations," copied other nations' techniques. "Thus in soccer we look at English, Hungarian, Austrian models, in tennis American and French, in diving Japanese and American, in long-distance and winter running Norwegian, but never at German models." Malitz wanted to see foreign coaches and trainers banned from Germany and German sports experts prohibited from purveying their knowledge abroad. He did not propose abstaining altogether from international competitions, considering them "necessary for international propaganda reasons," but thought participation should be sharply curtailed. "One soccer match a year will be enough, and one championship in track and field as well. But we will prohibit all contests that do not accord with national honor."[63]

Once in power, however, the Nazis did far more than their predecessors to tighten and increase the international connections Malitz had derided. Tschammer himself remarked on the turnaround in a conversation with the foreign press in early 1935. "The national tendencies represented in German sport," he said, "were frequently treated as an obstacle to the development of international relations. In practice the opposite has been the case. Never before, as long as German sport has existed, have Germany's sport relations with foreign countries been stronger and . . . more welcome than they are now."[64]

In the 1920s, Germany's international sport contacts had averaged twenty a year. Between 1933 and 1939, the number tripled, to an average of sixty. Most of these were with Germany's western democratic neighbors, the Benelux countries and France, and with its Scandinavian neighbors to the north. Only in 1939 did sport contacts with Italy assume primary importance.[65] The Deutsche Turnerschaft and the German rowing association joined international federations for the first time in 1934, after refusing in the past for nationalist reasons. Similarly, under considerable pressure from Tschammer in the summer of 1933, the German Student Society returned to international competitions, in a development that its heavily Nazi membership found surprising and disturbing. The *Völkischer Beobachter,* which had in the past almost entirely ignored sport, expanded its coverage tenfold in 1933.[66]

Nazi officials promoted international sport because they saw it as a valuable instrument of foreign policy, particularly as a way to influence public opinion abroad.[67] Whereas governments in the democracies, especially Britain and the United States, were slow to see international sport as an agent of diplomacy, both fascist Italy and Nazi Germany actively exploited sport for state purposes. As the U.S. consul in Berlin reported at the end of 1933, the new regime was putting "great stress" on success in international competitions. The same attitude, he pointed out, prevailed in fascist Italy, where "the country has been scoured for athletes who could be used in international competition; and Premier Mussolini has himself decorated successful athletes and lauded them as national heroes." Fascist doctrine, now embraced by the Nazis, held that "much of a Nation's honor and glory is dependent on its success in the field of sport. In fact international athletic activities are considered a part, and not an insignificant part, of foreign policy. The Government must, therefore, do everything within its power to increase the athletic strength of the nation."[68]

In July 1933, Tschammer complained that the Foreign Ministry was not always providing enough support for German athletes abroad, even though they were acting to promote Germany's foreign relations. "All German sportsmen in foreign competitions," he noted, must in all cases "represent the nation in an impeccable way." To ensure this goal, greater oversight from foreign missions was needed. The Foreign Ministry responded by directing its missions to appoint an official to aid and supervise German athletes in major sport competitions and to act as an official representative to the public and the press.[69] In early 1935, the Foreign Ministry instructed that the Nazi flag be flown and the national anthem played at every foreign competition.[70] This was not just a matter of national pride but was also intended to accustom public audiences abroad to the symbols and spirit of the Nazi regime.[71]

Some of the foreign missions followed the instructions too evenhandedly, prompting the Foreign Ministry to offer a clarification in March 1935. "We have nothing against the participation in foreign competitions of Jewish athletes who belong to Jewish sport clubs in Germany," the circular stated, but Jewish athletes should not participate under the same conditions as German national teams. The German flag should not be flown and the national anthem should not be played. In addition, diplomatic officials should take a hands-off attitude toward such competitions, refraining from attending and from providing any advice or assistance beyond the most basic consular services such as passport control.[72] Such qualms would become moot as German Jews became subject to increasingly tight restrictions.

Those athletes sponsored by the regime were urged to act while abroad as "warriors for Germany," "ambassadors of the Third Reich," and "representatives of the German race."[73] A 1936 article in the *Frankfurter Zeitung* on the foreign policy tasks of sport explained that the Nazi regime had brought new meaning to international sport. After World War I, it noted, Germans "correctly saw in international sport contacts a wide bridge to mutual rapprochement and understanding," but the Weimar government had failed to exploit sport's full potential. Even though athletes understood one another "faster than the delegates nations sent to political conferences," German teams traveling abroad before 1933 saw such trips mainly as a personal opportunity and did not feel entrusted with a special government mission. Under the Nazi regime, however, sport's political meaning was fully understood, and German teams in foreign competitions were treated as "auxiliary troops of German foreign policy." "The successes that German teams abroad bring," the article's author asserted, "are not successes for one sport or another; they are entirely German successes." Sport, the author concluded, was "called to stand in the front lines of foreign policy."[74]

Unlike promoters of sport in democracies such as England and the United States, who often justified international sport competitions on the basis of their supposed role in promoting peace and mutual understanding, Nazi officials viewed international sport predominantly as a way to assert German power. German superiority, they felt, ought to be reflected in all spheres of life, including sport. The expression of one sport official was typical: "Germany must secure a place that its significance as a great power requires."[75] The idea was that sport victories would not just impress foreign political leaders but could also play an important role in winning support from foreign publics that could indirectly lead to government policy changes more favorable to Germany.

The 1935 soccer match between Germany and England, as well as a similar match against France in 1935 and a return match against England in 1938, demonstrate how these considerations influenced the German deployment of international sport contacts. The 1935 match in Britain was proposed by British soccer authorities who wished to promote British contacts with continental soccer. Anti-Nazi groups in Britain quickly coalesced to oppose the match, disquieting the British Foreign Office, which preferred not to antagonize German opinion.[76] The calls for a boycott prompted Hitler to consider withdrawing from the match, but he decided the advantages outweighed the disadvantages, which would have included forfeiting the financial proceeds, damaging German sport pride, and giving an indirect boost to the movement to boycott the 1936 Berlin Olympic Games.[77] In the end the match itself was a success, providing prime opportunities for German officials to cultivate friendly relations. The German team arrived by plane accompanied by Tschammer and other high-ranking officials, who were treated to lavish dinners hosted by British public figures eager to improve Anglo-German relations. At a welcoming reception for the players, German spokesmen emphasized British-German links, including the fact that British soccer stars were household names in Germany. Ten thousand German fans arrived to cheer on their team, which lost gracefully 3–0, and, despite the presence of protesters, the game passed without incident. The match's successful staging and the impression made by the visitors had notable effects on British opinion, in the assessment of some observers. In May 1936, a German official in London reported that cultural ties, and sport in particular, had played an important role in turning British public opinion in favor of Germany.[78]

The "New Order" in International Sport

Nazi participation in international sport may have been successful in some respects, but it entailed compliance with international norms that many Nazis found distasteful. By the late 1930s their dissatisfaction led to efforts to create an international sport system under Nazi control. After the grand success of the 1936 Berlin Olympics (see Chapter 6), the regime embarked on a concerted dual-track campaign, intended first to seize a major share of power in the Olympic movement and second to create an international sport system in its own image and under its own control. On the second track, German sport officials sought to reorganize international federations or to create new ones subject to German control.[79]

The Germans achieved a surprising level of success on the first track. The regime succeeded both in appropriating Olympic symbolism domestically to enhance its own legitimacy and in gaining more control over IOC operations. Immediately after the Games, Tschammer forced the resignation of the long-time German IOC member Theodor Lewald, filling Lewald's spot with his own man, Walter von Reichenau, a leading Nazi military commander.[80] The Ministry of the Interior financed the founding of an International Olympic Institute in Berlin, under the authority of the Reichssportführer.[81] The IOC's official bulletin was incorporated into the German-published *Olympische Rundschau*.[82] The IOC awarded its Olympic Cup to Kraft durch Freude, the Nazi's popular leisure association, and presented the Olympic Diploma to Leni Riefenstahl for her film *Olympia*. Finally, Werner Klingeberg became IOC secretary-general.[83]

Even after the German annexation of Bohemia and Moravia and the Kristallnacht pogrom in 1938, IOC President Baillet-Latour made no moves to downgrade his organization's close association with the Nazis. In early 1939 the IOC withdrew the Winter Games of 1940 from St. Moritz, which had stepped in after Norway was forced to relinquish them, and awarded them instead to Garmisch-Partenkirchen, which had hosted the Winter Games of 1936. Baillet-Latour did not bring up the issue of nondiscrimination against Jews, as he had in 1936.

Later that year it became clear that neither the Winter nor the Summer Olympics could be held, but Germany continued to increase its influence over the IOC. In July 1940 Diem visited Baillet-Latour in occupied Brussels, under instructions from Tschammer to transfer the top positions in the IOC to German hands.[84] The Germans were willing to see Baillet-Latour continue as president, but they wanted to "rejuvenate" the committee—in other words, to pack it with their own men. According to Tschammer, Baillet-Latour agreed that "the wishes of the authoritarian States should be respected; firstly, a radical rejuvenation of the Committee, and secondly, recognition of the principle that, in the authoritarian States, the representatives proposed by them should be appointed members."[85] The latter point was in contradiction with IOC principles according to which members were chosen by the committee and acted as the committee's representatives in their respective countries, not as national representatives to the IOC. Baillet-Latour, however, refused to convene an IOC session that would have been necessary to enact any substantive changes to the Olympic statutes. By settling the IOC into inactivity rather than submitting to German influence during the war, he effectively derailed a German takeover.[86]

After igniting the war the regime stepped up its efforts on the second track—the creation of a "new order" in international sport in occupied and neutral countries. Responding to a newspaper report in November 1940 that the "new order" meant that Germany and its Italian ally would withdraw from international sport federations, Tschammer asserted that the regime intended to work "constructively" within existing structures.[87] Efforts to Nazify the federations, however, were of limited success. Most federations preferred to adopt a wait-and-see approach during the war, while others more readily submitted to Nazi blandishments. Although FIFA President Jules Rimet, along with the French presidents of the international swimming and ice-hockey federations, opposed Nazi sports policy, such resistance was ineffectual.[88] After 1940 FIFA was run almost single-handedly by its German secretary in Zurich, who served Nazi interests.[89] The head of the IAAF, J. Sigfrid Edström, had profascist leanings but nevertheless sought to maintain the IAAF's autonomy. He chose not to admit new member countries under Nazi control (like Slovakia and Croatia) and newly Nazified federations (as in Norway), displeasing the Germans. Edström, however, did appoint the Nazi functionary Karl Ritter von Halt as chair of the European commission of the IAAF, with Diem as his secretary.[90] But as the demands of war became ever more pressing, the goal of a Nazi international sport system receded.

The Nazi use of international sport represented the most focused and coordinated drive of any country during the interwar years to direct international competitions toward specific foreign-policy goals. Both mass and elite sport were subject to state control, and sporting contacts were carefully chosen and stage-managed to serve state interests. Nazi success in using sport to serve regime aims was facilitated by top officials in international sport federations and the IOC (such as Brundage, Baillet-Latour, and Edström), conservatives who were often sympathetic to Hitler's regime. As a result, they sought fewer compromises from the Nazis than they could have and were often willing to flout their own principles for the sake of cooperation with the Nazi regime.

But the Nazis' relationship with the international sport system was not entirely one-sided. The regime's success in developing an elite athletic system and the favorable impressions abroad and at home won by international sport victories should be considered alongside the defeats of German sportsmen by Joe Louis and Jesse Owens, whose achievements upset the Nazis' carefully calibrated racial theories. By its nature, competition in sport produced uncertain outcomes, which did not always redound to the advantage of the regime. More generally, transnational cultural flows in sport, as elsewhere, posed challenges to state sovereignty.[91] Participation in the international sport system entailed acceptance of a transnational cultural form, leaving the indigenous German strain of physical culture—*Turnen*—in a peripheral position. The internationalist principles associated with modern sport had been anathema to the Nazi Party before it came to power and continued to produce discomfort throughout the 1930s. At a meeting of a local physical education section in 1938, to cite one example, officials suggested that "sport competition according to international rules and norms" should be rejected because it failed to instill "race-appropriate" feelings.[92] Like other elements of mass culture, sport conveyed messages that subverted as well as supported Nazi ideology. Participation in international sport allowed the Nazi regime to demonstrate national power on an international stage, but the universalist international sport system also imposed constraints on the expression of racist ideology. The mixed legacy was evident in the one sporting event to which the Nazis accorded utmost importance: the 1936 Berlin Olympics.

6

Between Nazism and Olympism:
Berlin, 1936

In August 1936 Berlin played host to the most grandly staged Olympic Games held to date, a monumental spectacle and an astounding organizational feat that was greeted with awe and acclaim around the world. Building on the successes and innovations of the Los Angeles Olympics, introducing significant new features, and operating on a massive scale, the Berlin Games set a new benchmark for the Olympic ritual. Many of the elements introduced in Los Angeles were visible in Berlin, providing an element of continuity often overlooked in accounts of the 1936 Games. Commercialism, tourism, the commoditization of sport as an element of mass culture, and the cult of celebrity were as prevalent in Prussia as they had been in California. Indeed, much of what the German organizers achieved was an elaboration of what had been undertaken in 1932, and part of what made the 1936 Olympics so successful was that Los Angeles had already transformed the Games into a different kind of festival.

The 1936 Olympics, however, were novel in one very important respect. Politics has always influenced international sport, but the "Nazi Olympics" saw an unprecedented politicization of the Games. They were politicized on the German side because, under Hitler's dictatorship, the Games were a government-run enterprise. Hitler himself approved the hosting of the Games, oversaw the preparations, and spent many hours gleefully cheering on the Reich's representatives. For the first time a state provided resources on a massive scale to carry out the Games. Almost every branch of local and national government played a role, and propaganda extended to reach virtually every German citizen—and millions around the world. In the polarized international climate of the mid-1930s, the Nazi connection to the Games inevitably provoked reactions from other governments. The Soviet Union, not yet a participant in the Games, strongly condemned them, and boycott movements sprang up in many countries, most worrisomely (from the German perspective) in the United States. Communists and socialists planned a huge counter-Olympics in Barcelona, though the festival had to be aborted when Spain was engulfed by civil war.

In retrospect the Berlin Games have come to be seen as an embarrassing stain on the Olympic record, a form of appeasement akin to the infamous Munich agreement of 1938 and a capitulation that served to strengthen the Nazi regime. There is much truth to this view. The IOC and other sport organizations were often quiescent—even willing—partners to their manipulation by Nazi propagandists who used the Games to present a whitewashed version of the "new Germany" to the world public. But there is another side to the story. The 1936 Olympics was an international festival run in large part in accordance with international norms,

Hitler at the opening ceremony at the 1936 Olympic Games, flanked by IOC President Henri de Baillet-Latour. The Führer was an avid spectator at the events. *Source:* IOC Olympic Museum Collections.

Nazified at the margins but not at the core. Pressed (though not hard enough) by the international sport community and by the force of world opinion, the Nazis briefly mitigated some of the most repugnant aspects of their repressive dictatorship. The "Olympic pause" instituted by the Nazis was short-lived and left no lasting imprint on the Reich's murderous racism, but if the Nazis used the Games, it was at the price of an accommodation, however fleeting, with ideas and ideals antithetical to Nazi ideology.

Prelude: The Politics of Participation

In 1931, when the IOC awarded the 1936 Olympic Games to the capital of the Weimar Republic, the move was intended as a gesture of reconciliation and a symbol of Germany's reintegration into the Olympic community.[1] The unanticipated Nazi seizure of power, coming just eighteen months after the awarding of the Games, posed an acute dilemma for the growing Olympic movement. In addition to the well-known Nazi distaste for internationalism in general, the Nazi press disparaged the Olympics as "Jewish international enterprises."[2] Already in the summer of 1932, even before the Nazi Party won nearly a third of the votes in the November Reichstag elections, IOC President Baillet-Latour worried about how a possible Nazi government would view the Games. At the Los Angeles Games Theodor Lewald, an IOC member and head of the German Organizing Committee, told Baillet-Latour that Hitler would be "absolutely opposed" to holding the Games in Berlin.[3] The *Völkischer Beobachter* demanded that if the Games were held in Berlin, blacks must be excluded. Hitler as yet took no public position, although when Karl Ritter von Halt, one of three German members of the IOC and a Nazi with close business ties to the party, sounded him out in 1932 he agreed not to interfere with the Games.[4]

Once Hitler came to power, the IOC, as historian Allen Guttmann has put it, braced "in anticipation for Hitler's announcement that he wanted another authentic *Turnfest* in 1936—not some international celebration of human solidarity."[5] Instead, Hitler quickly came to the conclusion that staging the international festival presented an ideal propaganda opportunity. Shortly after becoming chancellor, Hitler met with Lewald's organizing committee, which itself had been formed just weeks earlier, and pledged to support the Games.[6] His motives, it seems, were twofold.

Hitler saw in the Olympics a way to promote sport among German youth and thus build national strength. Staging an event of such global significance also offered international legitimacy and an unrivalled platform from which to garner the world's attention. In October 1933, even as Hitler was pulling out of the Lausanne Disarmament Conference and the League of Nations, he explained his support of the Olympics to Goebbels in the following terms: "Germany is in a very bad and difficult situation internationally. It should therefore try to impress world public opinion by cultural means. In this context it is fortunate that the Olympic Games will be held in Germany in 1936, at which all countries of the world take part. If one invites the world to such a festival one has to show the world what the new Germany can do culturally."[7]

To his intense frustration on several occasions, however, Hitler found that he could not dictate the terms on which the Games would be held. The first hurdle he encountered was in putting his own men in charge of organizing the festival. He was able to appoint Tschammer as head of the German Olympic Committee and to remove Lewald, whose father was a Jewish convert to Protestantism, from the presidency of the main sport organization, the Deutscher Reichsausschuß für Leibesübungen, since both of these were national bodies. The organizing committee, however, was bound by the Olympic charter, which required that it remain free from political interference. While the organizing committee did work in tight connection with the regime—indeed most of the preparations for the Olympics were handled directly by state agencies, and in important respects the organizing committee was subordinate to the Reichssport-führer—Hitler was not able to pack it with his own men. Thanks to international pressure, Lewald and Carl Diem, leaders appointed in the Weimar era, remained in place.[8]

The regime also came under pressure in regard to discrimination against Jews. In general, international sport organizations dismissed Nazi repression against Jews (and others) in political, social, and economic life as "internal affairs." But the elimination of Jews from German sports was harder to ignore. Jews were excluded from German sport clubs, prohibited from using public swimming pools, and forbidden even to engage in horseback riding because German horses were not supposed to be in physical contact with Jews. Jewish athletes were confined to allegedly "separate but equal" Jewish sport organizations until 1938, when the Kristallnacht pogrom brought an end to Jewish sport in Germany.[9]

Concerned that such blatant, wholesale discrimination by the host country would discredit Olympic ideals, Baillet-Latour sent the German IOC members a sharply worded ultimatum in May 1933, demanding that the government produce a written guarantee that it would observe Olympic rules, among them that "the Games are conferred to a city and not to a country . . . and that they should have no political, racial, national, or confessional character." If "differences of opinion" over Olympic principles continued to surface, Baillet-Latour threatened, Berlin's right to host the Games might be revoked.[10] U.S. IOC member Charles Sherrill pressed for more. Instead of agreeing to abide by vague rules, the Germans, he insisted, must reverse their stated intention to exclude Jews from the German Olympic team.[11]

The IOC demands produced the desired response. At the IOC's annual meeting in June, its German members delivered a document guaranteeing that "all the laws regulating the Olympic Games shall be observed" and that "as a principle, German Jews shall not be excluded from German teams at the Olympiad."[12] Opinion in the United States, where cries for a boycott were already being heard, was mollified. As the *New York Times* noted, in the eyes of some observers the German agreement showed that "a real blow had been struck in the cause of racial freedom at least in sports." The paper assurances were also enough to placate Baillet-Latour, who was, as he once confided to a colleague, "not personally fond of Jews and of the Jewish influence."[13] The German declarations, he eagerly concluded, "have in my opinion settled [the] Jewish question quite satisfactorily."[14] Privately he admitted that "everything is perfect" only on the surface, because German national sport federations were continuing to exclude Jews. But in his opinion it was not the IOC's job to monitor the makeup of the German team; rather it was the national Olympic associations preparing their Olympic teams that should take up the issue. With appropriate pressure, the Germans would give in "out of fright," he said, because they were counting on making the Games a great success.[15]

Having secured the minimal guarantees from the Nazis necessary to soothe public opinion, Baillet-Latour hoped to avoid further public controversy. In 1934, for example, Baillet-Latour privately expressed agreement with the views that the absence of Jews from top-level training in Germany was a reflection of their poor athletic qualities and that anti-Jewish policies in Germany were "minor unimportant details."[16] The controversy subsided until international outrage was reawakened in 1935 by the passage of the Nuremberg laws, which deprived German Jews of their citizenship, banned marriages between Jews and "Aryans," and stripped Jews of political rights.

As a boycott movement gathered steam in the United States, Sherrill prodded the regime to honor its commitments. Sherrill, a former ambassador who was a staunch anticommunist and an admirer of Hitler and Mussolini, sharply disapproved of the boycott movement, and his determination to see "at least one Jew on the German Olympic team" was in part designed to weaken the rationale for a boycott. Acting on his own initiative—Baillet-Latour was annoyed at Sherrill for "mixing politics and sport"—he gained a personal meeting with Hitler in August 1935 at which he pressed for guarantees that Jews would be included on the German team.[17] Contradicting the text of the 1933 guarantee, Hitler argued that the agreement with the IOC meant only that *foreign* teams would be allowed to have Jewish members; the German team need not. If the IOC insisted that Jews be permitted to represent Germany, he threatened, Germany would stage its own purely German Olympics. When Sherrill dined with him again shortly thereafter, however, Hitler had changed his tune, pledging to honor the original commitment.[18] Sherrill declared himself satisfied. "As for obstacles placed in the way of Jewish athletes or any other in trying to reach Olympic ability," he told a reporter, "I would have no more business discussing that in Germany than if the Germans attempted to discuss the Negro situation in the American South or the treatment of the Japanese in California." He grimly warned that a wave of anti-Semitism would sweep the United States if a boycott succeeded.[19]

Baillet-Latour, too, was naturally opposed to boycott efforts and took strong action against one IOC member who supported the boycott. Ernest Lee Jahncke, another American on the IOC and a former assistant secretary of the navy, adamantly opposed holding the Games in Berlin on the basis that the Nazis were violating the principles of Olympism and exploiting the Games purely for financial and political gain. Incensed at Jahncke's highly public airing of opinions that ran contrary to IOC decisions, Baillet-Latour expelled him from the committee in an unprecedented move shortly before the Olympics began, replacing him with Avery Brundage.[20]

Jahncke's opinion was shared by vocal minorities in many countries.

Only in the United States was national participation seriously at risk, but the prospect of a boycott was debated across Europe. The stakes were high, according to a November 1935 report by U.S. diplomat George Messersmith:

> The youth of Germany believe that National Socialist ideology is being rapidly accepted in other countries . . . To the Party and to the youth of Germany, the holding of the Olympic Games in Berlin in 1936 has become the symbol of the conquest of the world by National Socialist doctrine. Should the Games not be held in Berlin, it would be one of the most serious blows which National Socialist prestige could suffer within an awakening Germany . . .
>
> There are many wise and well informed observers in Europe who believe that the holding or the non-holding of the Olympic Games in Berlin in 1936 will play an important part in determining political developments in Europe. I believe that this view of the importance of the Olympic Games being held in Berlin in 1936 is not exaggerated.[21]

In the end, however, no country refused to participate on political grounds, although a handful of athletes engaged in individual boycotts.[22]

The campaign against the Nazis was hamstrung by one critical fact. Nazi repression, as of 1935, was unusually severe, but racial and religious equality was an ideal many countries could be accused of violating. In the United States, for example, many athletic clubs excluded Jews, blacks, and women. In the American South the Jim Crow system relegated African Americans to second-class status, depriving them of constitutionally guaranteed rights; lynching remained a common occurrence through the 1930s. Blacks hoping to make the 1936 Olympic team were subject to discrimination. During a regional trial for the U.S. Olympic team in Maryland, for example, the white director barred four African Americans from competing. When they complained, national officials qualified the men for the semifinals in Massachusetts but did nothing to sanction the Maryland official. Despite such incidents, 1936 saw the highest number to date of blacks on the U.S. team: 18 out of 357.[23]

It was, however, the United States, and its vocal Jewish and Catholic organizations, in particular, that took the lead in protesting the Nazis' extraordinary racial and religious persecution. When the boycott movement seemed on the verge of winning, the Nazis, aware that a U.S. withdrawal would significantly diminish the value of the Games, agreed to a significant concession. In late 1935, in response to American pressure,

Tschammer invited Helene Mayer to join the German Olympic team. Considered a "half-Jew" under the Nuremberg laws, Mayer had won gold in fencing for Germany at the 1928 Games. Now living in California, she accepted Tschammer's invitation (and on the victory stand in Berlin, after winning the silver medal, she would offer the Nazi salute). Tschammer promptly forwarded copies of his correspondence with her to the IOC and to German embassies around the world to use in countering adverse publicity. Top hockey player Rudi Ball, who had emigrated to Italy and was also considered a "half-Jew" under the Nuremberg laws, was likewise invited to play on the German team at the Winter Games. Open discrimination, however, kept other Jews off the German team. Of the twenty-one Jews allowed to try out for the team, none was accepted. The most glaring omission was Gretel Bergmann, a top high jumper. Despite a performance in June 1936 that equaled the German record, she was excluded from the team, and instead the third spot in the women's high jump squad was left vacant.[24]

By inviting two non-Aryans to join the German team—significantly, both "half-Jews" who were living abroad—the regime placated international opinion and averted a U.S. boycott. The regime was also forced to keep the Games free of overt racial or religious discrimination against foreign visitors and its own citizens. With international opinion in mind, the viciously anti-Semitic face of the Reich was temporarily masked. After Baillet-Latour objected to anti-Jewish signs near the Winter Games in Garmisch-Partenkirchen (held in February), the Minister of the Interior ordered all such signs removed, along with exhibits of the viciously anti-Semitic SS newspaper, *Der Stürmer*. When the prevalence of military uniforms in Garmisch garnered unfavorable attention in the foreign press, orders were given to use civilian dress in Berlin.[25] For the Summer Games in Berlin the worst anti-Semitic slanders disappeared from the papers, *Der Stürmer* vanished from newsstands, many (but not all) of the ubiquitous signs warning Jews not to enter—"Jews and animals not allowed"—came down, and Germans were instructed to treat all foreign guests, even Jews, with equal courtesy. Despite some anti-Semitic incidents in bars and restaurants, for the most part they did so. One Nazi "race researcher" lamented having been forced to exercise so much "consideration for our foreign guests" that he was unable to use the Games for research purposes. As Victor Klemperer observed, "Jew-baiting, bellicose sentiments, everything offensive" disappeared from the newspapers for the duration of the Games.[26]

Advertising for the Third Reich

In its main aim—the staging of an extraordinarily well-run and impressively choreographed festival that could claim the title of "best Olympic
Games ever"—the Nazi regime rightfully claimed success. As American
sportswriter John Kieran put it, "everything that was done at Los Angeles
[was] outdone at Berlin."[27] By the end of the Games, one correspondent
remarked, newspaper readers abroad had probably tired of "the constant
iteration that [these Olympics were] the biggest athletic games ever held,
the most largely attended, the best organized, the most picturesque and
the most productive of new and startling records."[28]

The first step in the years of preparation was to learn from the Games in
Los Angeles. The officials accompanying the German team in the 1932
Games conducted "a complete survey of the American method" of staging
the events.[29] Diem, the chief organizer of the Berlin Games, spent several
weeks in California gathering information behind the scenes. He collected
a huge quantity of printed material, copied information from the designers
of the telephone systems, took photos of garages and workshops, copied
blueprints of the stadium, the swimming pool, and the playing fields, and
took measurements of the Olympic Village cottages. Later he, Lewald, and
German architects traveled far and wide to study athletic facilities in other
countries.[30]

After 1933, Hitler put a high priority on the Olympics, intent on ensuring that they successfully showcased the regime's ability to stage a major
international festival. To that end he spared no expense in making the
Berlin Olympics bigger and better than any before. Organizers, architects,
and builders were granted unprecedented access to resources, financial
and otherwise, deemed necessary for success. Preparations involved tens
of thousands of people and, according to one estimate, expenses exceeded
100 million Reichsmarks.[31]

To impress the world with the Reich's achievements, Hitler put in motion
an enormous construction campaign for new and revamped facilities for
the Games. The budget for the main stadium and its associated buildings
in the Reich Sport Field would eventually reach 40 million Reichsmarks.
Touring the stadium built for the failed 1916 Games, Hitler promptly
deemed it inadequate, ordering it expanded to accommodate 100,000
spectators with room for 250,000 in the staging area outside. The 325-acre
Reich Sport Field would also include a swimming stadium, a riding field,

an open-air theater, an enlarged gymnasium, a large administration building, and a 243-foot bell tower holding a specially designed Olympic Bell.[32] A half-million truckloads of dirt were brought in to elevate the sport complex above the surrounding area.[33] New underground stations were built linking the grounds to the center of the city five miles to the east, and roads were widened to create a Via Triumphalis along which Hitler's motorcades could drive from the Reich Chancellery to the stadium. Direction of the huge construction project, which employed more than 500 companies and up to 2,600 workers a day for more than two years, was placed under the Ministry of the Interior.[34] In 1934 Hitler vetoed architect Werner March's plans to make the stadium a modern structure of concrete and glass, instead calling in his chief architect Albert Speer to redraw the plans and cover the concrete with natural rock for a more classical look.[35]

The final result was an impressive, state-of-the-art complex with one of the biggest and best-equipped stadia in the world. Touring the new stadium after its completion, an enraptured British delegation gushed over its amenities:

> It is equipped with every sort of facility and convenience, from an elegant apartment for the Führer to large batteries of floodlighters and loudspeakers, accommodation for the wireless service and the great news agencies, apparatus for word and picture telegraphy, refreshment rooms, two large "departmental stores," a police post, a fire brigade station, first-aid rooms, post offices, sanitary conveniences, cloakrooms and 52 changing-rooms for athletes.[36]

Replicating one of the Los Angeles organizers' most successful innovations, the Nazis constructed an Olympic Village for male athletes. Built by the German Army (and converted to army barracks after the Games), the village was located in an idyllic setting near forest and lakes outside Berlin. Like the Los Angeles village, the 1936 village had all the attributes of a small community, including a hundred buildings, an artificial lake, a hairdressing salon, playing fields, gymnasia and exercise tracks, and thirty-eight dining halls catering to the particular tastes of different national cuisines.[37] There was no apparent order to the placement of national teams: Danes were put next to South Africans, Americans next to Chinese and Swedes, Greeks next to Brazilians. The athletes were entertained by films, variety shows, and daily open-air concerts by the German Army music corps, as well as by visits from Max Schmeling, Charles Lindbergh, and other celebrities.[38] Like the Los Angeles Olympic Village, the German version gained virtually unanimous accolades for its comforts and the spirit of harmony and goodwill that prevailed among the athletes. As had been the case in Los Angeles, female competitors were housed separately. In Berlin the women, who numbered only 360, compared to more than 4,400 men, were placed in an old dormitory, where conditions were far less comfortable than those provided for the men.[39]

Diem also added his own innovation to Olympic symbolism, one that, like the Olympic Village, would become a treasured part of the Olympic ritual. His Olympic torch relay, in which a flame was carried from the home of the ancient Greek Olympics to the host city, was an ingenious way to dramatize the fictional links between the ancient and modern Olympics and between ancient Greece and modern Germany. Eleven days before the Games began, a group of Greek maidens lit a torch on Mount Olympus whose flame was then carried by a series of runners—in three thousand torches specially made by Krupp, Germany's largest arms producer—via Saloniki, Sofia, Belgrade, Budapest, Vienna, Prague, and Dresden to Berlin, where the final torch was then used to light a cauldron in the stadium during the opening ceremonies.[40]

Exceeding the first-class public-relations and media services the Americans had set up four years earlier, the Nazis created communications and publicity systems that were a marvel of complexity and engineering. Miles of phone lines, dozens of switchboards, and nearly a thousand connections were installed to field the thousands of requests for information and tickets that came in every day, to connect the various groups involved in organizing the Games, to communicate within the sports facilities while the events were taking place, and to transmit radio broadcasts. Mimicking the Dow-Jones electric writing machines that had proved so successful in Los Angeles, the Germans disseminated results instantaneously through an extensive system of Siemens teletypewriters, run from a central office staffed by the Luftwaffe's information service. Using these teletypewriters, newspapers and news agencies could have results in print within a few minutes after an event concluded.[41]

The organizing committee accorded pre-Olympic publicity an especially high priority, recognizing that "a thorough, well-considered press campaign" was critical to the festival's success. Functioning as part of the organizing committee but directed and generously financed by the Propaganda Ministry, this campaign had two faces, one directed internally toward the German population and the other directed internationally.[42] The internal campaign was intended to impress the Germans with the importance of the Olympics and to educate them as to their role as hosts. The international campaign attempted to develop as much interest as possible among people "in every country of the world" to ensure the widest participation in the Olympics. In 1933 the committee established a monthly Olympic Games News Service that sent information and high-quality photographs to sports organizations and press outlets. First printed in runs of 7,000 copies in five languages, the numbers were eventually increased to 24,000 copies in fourteen European languages, with a distribution that included 615 German newspapers and magazines and 3,075 foreign periodicals. Information from the bulletins was published throughout Europe, in India and Asia, and in the Americas. As the Games drew nearer and more rapid communication became essential, this news service was supplemented by the official German News Agency, along with the German Broadcasting Company and the German Railway Publicity Department, which sent out immediate press releases. Large numbers of foreign journalists visited Berlin to inspect the construction of the new stadium and the Olympic Village.[43] Tschammer, Lewald, and Diem toured Europe to build interest in the Games, visiting London, Paris, Stockholm, Oslo, Copenhagen, Budapest, Helsinki, Lausanne, Istanbul, Athens, Belgrade, Zagreb, and Zurich, holding news conferences and meeting both with foreign sports officials and politicians.[44]

These efforts were supplemented with a staggering array of additional publicity materials and activities, including Olympic rings, slide shows, postcards, special seals, publicity badges, radio lectures, exhibition and display-window material, invitations to foreign travel experts, receptions hosted by German embassies or legations, lecture tours by prominent German sports officials, advertisements in newspapers and magazines in seventeen countries, and guidebooks with German history rewritten to conform to the Nazi script. In Chicago the Germans hired a stunt flyer to give a demonstration in a plane decorated in Olympic motifs. At the Oxford-Cambridge boat race forty men carried large Olympic placards along the river and through crowded London streets. Subway stations in Buenos Aires sported Olympic placards. About 200,000 official Olympic posters were printed in nineteen languages, including a thousand in Japanese, and distributed to thirty-five countries (including Japanese-occupied Manchuria). The German Railway Publicity Bureau printed more than four million pamphlets for use in dozens of countries and arranged for poster displays in shop windows and hotel showcases from Buenos Aires to London. A lavishly illustrated magazine, *Olympic Games 1936,* printed on high-quality enameled paper and intended as a permanent keepsake of the Games, was given a print run of more than 60,000 copies. A lecture text accompanied by sixty-five slides was sent to thirty-three countries.[45]

The interest generated by the campaign was reflected in the unprecedented press coverage in many countries both before and during the Olympics—partly because of the intense political controversies the Games had fueled, but also because the event promised to be, as the organizers put it, "the only genuine world festival of our age."[46] In Argentina, to cite just one example of pre-Olympic promotion, radio reports on Olympic preparations were broadcast twice a week in the first months of 1935 and daily beginning in April 1935.[47] Once the Games began a flood of journalists arrived in Berlin to cover the events. It was, the *New York Times* remarked, the biggest gathering of newspaper writers since the Geneva disarmament conference of 1932–1933 (which had failed in the face of Hitler's determination to rearm Germany).[48]

Media interest exceeded even what the organizers had expected. Although they had equipped the main stadium with an unusually large press section holding more than 1,100 seats, demand far outstripped supply. About eight hundred newspapers and magazines from Germany alone applied to report on the events, and the large Berlin publishing companies sent as many as fifty journalists each on important days. More than seven hundred journalists from fifty-eight countries, from Afghanistan to Venezuela, were officially registered with the authorities, and perhaps a thousand more were in the city without official press badges. At the conclusion of the Games, the organizing committee estimated the number of journalists in attendance at more than 2,800.[49] Few of them took seriously Goebbels's promise, made at a dinner party thrown for a thousand visitors, that he had no intention of using the Olympics for propaganda purposes, but many came away with favorable impressions of life under the new regime.[50]

Radio coverage of the Games reached an estimated 300 million listeners worldwide, making the Berlin festival, as Arnd Krüger notes, "by far the largest media event of the world to that time."[51] Live radio broadcasts were used for the first time in Olympic history. In keeping with Goebbels's vision of radio as the chief instrument of propaganda in modern society, the Nazis devoted enormous technical resources to creating a state-of-the-art broadcasting system for the Games, one that a U.S. correspondent called "one of the most remarkable engineering feats created since the war."[52] The centrally run German Broadcasting Company and German shortwave stations serving German émigrés abroad gave the Olympics saturation coverage, and the 105 foreign broadcasters who covered events were given superb facilities and assistance. Directed from a central control station under the Führer's loge at the main stadium—"a nerve center for the whole globe," as the *New York Times* put it—radio operators at a gigantic switchboard directed three thousand transmissions in dozens of foreign languages to forty countries, from Argentina to South Africa.[53] In the United

Cameramen snapping shots of the winners in a swimming event at the 1936 Olympics. The nearly three thousand journalists who covered the Olympics in Berlin made it the biggest media event to date. *Source:* IOC Olympic Museum Collections.

States alone more than one hundred stations in the Columbia Broadcasting Company and National Broadcasting Company networks covered the Games regularly.[54]

The 1936 Olympics were the first sporting event to be televised. Closed-circuit television cameras used 15 kilometers of specially laid television cable to transmit 138 hours of coverage to 25 public viewing rooms in the Berlin area, where 160,000 people watched part of the Games. The grand experiment turned out to be the one aspect of the Nazi media offensive that netted less than satisfactory results, as the signal was weak and the images transmitted were fuzzy.[55]

The Los Angeles Games had set a record by attracting more than a million spectators; Berlin attracted more than 3 million, with ticket sales totaling 9 million Reichsmarks, and an additional 600,000 complimentary tickets given to the media, competitors, and guests of honor.[56] Tourism thrived under the Nazi dictatorship, which encouraged it as a way to bring in much-needed foreign currency, and the Olympic Games were naturally a prime opportunity to attract visitors to the Reich, though the numbers fell considerably short of predictions. As in other areas of organization, the Nazis directed enormous amounts of attention, energy, and money to bring in visitors and keep them happy and entertained while in Germany. In addition to the massive publicity campaign already described, the organizing committee set up information kiosks, interpreter centers, guide centers for motorists, and a special hotel bureau to oversee lodging requests. Organizers estimated the total influx of visitors to Berlin in late July and early August at half a million, including more than 75,000 foreign visitors, 15,000 of them from the United States.[57] Foreign guests included ambassadors, foreign ministers, royalty, and other high officials, many from countries allied with or being wooed by Germany, such as King Boris of Bulgaria and Crown Prince Umberto of Italy.[58] As in Los Angeles, icons of popular culture, including Schmeling and Lindbergh, attended the Games, though the celebrities who drew the most attention were Hitler and his top cronies, who were frequent spectators at the events.[59]

Commercialism, too, was present in Berlin. German companies like Lufthansa and German subsidiaries of foreign companies like Coca-Cola™ marketed the Olympic connection. Since the late 1920s the Coca-Cola™ Company had been making a concerted campaign to break into the German market, and by the end of the 1930s there were forty-three bottling plants in Germany and more than six hundred distributors. Company president Robert Woodruff came to the Olympics with a large entourage. He was annoyed that the Nazi health ministry had decreed that summer that a warning about Coke's caffeine content be placed on every bottle, but was pleased to see Coke prominently on sale in Olympic venues. Although a Berlin brewery had been granted an exclusive concession at the stadium and Ovomaltine had secured the status of official Olympic drink, Nazi authorities authorized Coca-Cola to market its "ice-cold refreshment" at sidewalk stands outside Olympic venues, where they found a ready audience. Sales were reported as "middling," but many Germans were introduced to Coke at the Games. As it had in Los Angeles, the company mass-produced Olympic tie-ins, in this case promotional brochures with information on Olympic records and event schedules. After the Games, Woodruff interceded with economics czar Hermann Göring, who had just cut imports as part of the new four-year plan, to permit the continued importation of Coca-Cola's secret concentrate. The company continued to promote its ties to sports, appearing at bicycle races and soccer matches, and even obtained a promotional photograph of Göring sipping from a bottle, all of which helped sales surge to 4.5 million cases by decade's end.[60]

Race and the Question of Success

In the months before the Games, Hitler denounced the Locarno Pact, reoccupied the demilitarized Rhineland, and began sending arms to support Franco in the Spanish Civil War, but what visitors and the press saw when the Games opened on August 1 was a spirit of friendly celebration. Returning for the Games after the Bayreuth festival, Goebbels noted approvingly that Berlin had "Olympic fever."[61] France's *Le Jour* said "it is no longer Berlin; it is a film set."[62] The entire city was adorned with festive decorations. White Olympic flags jostled next to black-bannered swastikas.[63] The city was scrubbed and cleaned, unsightly buildings were covered with greenery, "disturbing and unattractive advertising" was removed, outlying sections of the city were landscaped, and wet laundry was banned from balconies. On the Via Triumphalis alone the city government had spent 710,000 Reichmarks on decorations. Military tunes and political programs on the radio were reduced to a minimum. Public transportation had been expanded, additional police officers brought in from other cities, and new post offices opened to handle the influx of mail. Schmeling recalled that "Berlin regained its uniquely cosmopolitan atmosphere": books by Thomas Mann, Hermann Hesse, and Stefan Zweig, banned since 1933, reappeared in bookstores, and Berliners lined up to see Teddy Stauffer, "the King of Swing," play music the regime normally forced underground. Local women were allowed to wear their hemlines five centimeters higher than previously allowed, gay bars were reopened, and the Gestapo was ordered to turn a blind eye to offenses committed by foreign homosexuals. As Victor Klemperer observed, "It's constantly being drummed into the country and into foreigners that here one is witnessing the revival, the flowering, the new spirit, the unity, steadfastness and magnificence, pacific too, of course, spirit of the Third Reich, which lovingly embraces the whole world." The clean-up efforts also had a nasty underside. Known criminals were preemptively locked up, prostitutes were removed from the city center, and hundreds of Roma (gypsies) were interned to remove them from the eyes of tourists. In 1943 they were shipped to Auschwitz and killed.[64]

In the weeks and months leading up to the Games, Nazi leaders had exhorted the German people to behave as gracious and friendly hosts. In Berlin the Labor Front decreed "a week of laughter" in July, "eight days . . . of jollity and cheerfulness" to help Berliners greet their guests with "merry heart and friendly expression."[65] The editor of *Der Angriff* declared that "we must be more charming than the Parisians, more easy-going than the Viennese, more vivacious than the Romans, more cosmopolitan than London and more practical than New York."[66] Goebbels urged every German to consider himself a representative of the National Socialist state with a significant political mission: to reestablish Germany's world position by winning over tourists. "The future of the Reich," he claimed, "will depend upon the impression that is left upon our guests."[67]

On opening day, 100,000 spectators filled the stadium to capacity for what would prove to be an opening ceremony far more grandiose and spectacular than any before. As the crowd waited for the festivities to begin, the great zeppelin *Hindenburg* cruised overhead, trailing a huge Olympic flag and symbolically demonstrating, as the organizing committee put it, "German inventive genius and workmanship" and revived German ambitions in aviation. Loudspeakers blared reports on the progress of the Führer's motorcade as it left the chancellery and sped to the stadium down streets crowded with cheering Germans. Hitler, along with Lewald, Baillet-Latour, and their entourages, entered the stadium to the

Spectators at the main stadium in Berlin. Tens of thousands of foreign visitors flooded Berlin for the 1936 Olympics, but not all of them imitated the Nazi salute. *Source:* U.S. National Archives, Hoffman Collection.

accompaniment of Wagner's "March of Homage," proceeding down the stairs from the two Marathon Towers and along the track to the tribune of honor. As Richard Strauss directed an orchestra in the playing of *Deutschland über alles* and the *Horst Wessellied,* the flags of participating nations were hoisted slowly to the tops of masts surrounding the stadium.[68]

In the centerpiece of the ceremony, the four thousand participating athletes from forty-nine countries entered the stadium in the Parade of Nations.[69] The French received roars of applause when they appeared to offer the fascist salute while passing the tribune where Hitler and dozens of foreign dignitaries stood. In fact they were offering the Olympic salute, which coincidentally resembled the Nazi version.[70] When Hitler, as head of the host government, at last announced the Games open, a huge Olympic flag was raised, trumpets sounded, guns saluted, and twenty thousand doves were released to flutter over the stadium. Strauss conducted the new Olympic hymn he had written for the occasion. Finally, a single runner entered the stadium, carrying the flame that had been lit at Olympia.[71]

For the next two weeks normal life in Berlin came to a halt, and the city was filled with congresses, rallies, receptions, parties, and exhibitions. Hitler gave a dinner at the Reich Chancellery for two hundred guests, including Baillet-Latour and diplomats such as Sir Robert Vansittart from the British Foreign Office and Poland's State Secretary for Foreign Affairs, Count Jan Szembek. At roving diplomat Joachim von Ribbentrop's estate in Dahlem, "champagne flowed like water" for six hundred guests, including leading Germans and British aristocrats, admirals, and press lords. Göring invited guests to the opera and threw a lavish garden party for which he had constructed an entire eighteenth-century village in miniature, complete with an inn, post office, bakery, craft shops, and a merry-go-round. U.S. ambassador William Dodd called the performances of the evening, which included stunt airplane flights and an ensemble with actors and actresses in eighteenth-century costume, "the greatest display I have ever seen." Not to be outdone, Goebbels threw an even more elaborate party for 2,600 guests on Pfaueninsel, near Potsdam, with a pontoon bridge wide enough for two rows of automobiles specially built to connect it to the mainland and a bevy of girls dressed as Renaissance pages to lead the guests to their places. The cost of the party—32,000 Reichmarks—was equivalent to the yearly salaries of 160 factory workers.[72]

It is not surprising that with the purse-strings left open, the Games did not match the economic success of the Los Angeles festival. The Californians managed to turn a profit, but the Nazis spent far too lavishly to recoup expenses. The numbers of foreign visitors fell below expectations, netting fewer hard currency reserves for the regime than the organizers had anticipated. Moreover, although the hard currency derived from foreign visitors to the Games was funneled directly into the coffers of the arms manufacturer Krupp, the regime spent more on food imports intended to showcase German prosperity than tourists brought in to the country, resulting in a net loss. Nor did the Nazis use the Olympics, as California businessmen had, as an opportunity to promote business interests. Aside from inviting prominent foreign businessmen to a lavish evening at the opera, the regime and business leaders failed to see the Olympic Games as a means to promote German industry abroad.[73]

In purely sporting terms, however, the Games marked a tremendous success for Germany. Although U.S. athletes, and African Americans in particular, dominated the popular track and field events, German athletes won more victories than ever before, ending for the first time with the top ranking. Exulting over the medal count, *Der Angriff* declared it "truly difficult to endure so much joy."[74] Observers agreed that the German team had been propelled to new heights by rigorous and systematic training and the psychological boost of competing before the Führer and enormous home crowds rooting for any German victory. In a preview of the state sponsorship that the East Germans would perfect after the war, and in a clear violation of amateur rules, many German athletes had been paid to train full time for months before the Games.[75]

Japan continued its success in men's swimming, winning six gold medals in those events. Korean Kee-Chung Sohn (Kitei Son), forced to compete on the Japanese team because Korea was then under Japanese control, won a spectacular victory in what was heralded as the Olympics' most authentic event, the marathon. He set a new world record, and his friend and rival from Korea, Song-Yong Nam (Shoryu Nan), came in third.[76]

Americans, though disappointed to come in second in the overall standings, scored many successes. The eighteen African Americans on the national team won six gold medals and accounted for 83 of the team's 167 total points.[77] The hero of the Games was the African American track and field star Jesse Owens, billed by U.S. journalists as "the world's fastest human." He won four gold medals—in the one hundred-meter dash, the two hundred-meter dash, the long jump, and the four hundred-meter relay—and his graceful athletic style and friendly demeanor won him accolades from the world press. Hitler, who attended almost every day of the track meets, dourly saluted with outstretched arm as the U.S. anthem was played again and again.[78]

Owens was celebrated as well in the German press and became the darling of the German crowds. Leni Riefenstahl's famous propaganda film about the Games, *Olympia,* paid special homage to Owens.[79] Even Hitler's alleged snubbing of Owens, which remains an entrenched part of American folklore, is a myth. After personally congratulating the first medal winners (two Germans and a Finn), Hitler decided not to congratulate further winners—not to avoid shaking Owens's hand, but rather because Baillet-Latour had pointedly reminded him that, as the Olympic host, he ought to bestow his accolades impartially, either to all or to none.[80]

The victories by inferior races irked Nazi leaders. According to Albert Speer, Hitler was "highly annoyed" by Owen's victories but shrugged

Jesse Owens signing autographs at the 1936 Olympic Games. The African American track star won four gold medals and was the darling of the press and the hero of the Games for many fans, including Germans. *Source:* U.S. National Archives, Hoffman Collection.

them off by explaining that "people whose antecedents came from the jungle were primitive" and represented unfair competition. They must be excluded from future Games, Hitler said.[81] Goebbels privately noted that the medals won by African Americans were "a disgrace. The white race ought to be ashamed"—though what else could one expect from "a country without *Kultur*."[82] But in the instructions given at the daily press conferences his ministry held to telling the German press what and how to report, firm guidelines were laid down prohibiting criticism based on race. When *Der Angriff*, a leading Nazi organ, deviated by calling Owens and his African American compatriots "black American auxiliaries," it was swiftly cautioned. Overall the Nazi press acknowledged the victories of African Americans and published a large number of profiles of international sport stars.[83]

Despite the problem of race, as Nazi leaders reflected on the outcome after the Games had ended, they had good reason to be satisfied with their achievements. Having followed the events with great excitement, Hitler was pleased at the results, in sporting and in propaganda terms; he convinced himself that international animosity toward the Third Reich had vanished.[84] Goebbels's diary entries for the two weeks of the Games convey a pleased, self-congratulatory tone. He was especially gratified by the favorable foreign press. On August 3, he noted: "This Olympiad is a really big breakthrough. Fantastic press here and abroad. On Sunday alone [Germany] won 3 gold medals. The result of reawakened national ambition. I'm so pleased about it. It's possible to be proud of Germany again . . . The foreign press is quite wild with enthusiasm."[85] Toward the end of the Games, when Germany's standing as the top medal-winner was confirmed, he exulted that the country was "the best sport nation in the world!"[86]

In judging the organization of the Games, assessments from abroad were nearly unanimous in their praise. The *New York Times* called the Olympics "a very great success" for the Germans. "However much one may deplore or detest some of the excesses of the Hitler regime, the Games make clear beyond question the amazing new energy and determination that have come to the German people."[87] Reporting back to the State Department, Dodd agreed that "from the German point of view the Games were an almost unqualified success" and that "the tremendous advance that German sport performance has made under Nazi regulation cannot be gainsaid." The regime, he noted, had also generated much favorable opinion abroad. The "effusions of the 'Olympic Spirit'" that had crowded out "the usual provender of vilification" in Berlin for two weeks had had a powerful effect on American visitors to the Games. The conditions in Germany—"as they perceived them to be"—did not match what these visitors had been led to expect from negative portrayals in the U.S. press. They were impressed by "the orderliness and apparent prosperity of a country which they had believed was on the verge of collapse, and the popularity of Hitler who had been represented to them as a tyrant."[88] Visiting athletes and tourists did little to peer below the Olympic façade. When anonymous letters of protest or critical leaflets reached foreign visitors despite the Gestapo's postal censorship, visitors sometimes passed the materials on to the police, and some foreign guests who heard critical statements also reported them to the police.[89]

But the propaganda value of the Games should not be exaggerated. Krüger's study of worldwide reactions to the Berlin extravaganza concludes that the Games helped to consolidate Hitler's popularity at home but had little effect abroad. The success of the Games, Krüger writes, "led Germans to believe that their new regime was universally admired." Yet while foreigners were impressed with the organizational capabilities the regime put on display in staging the Games, in political terms the Games tended to reinforce opinions already held.[90]

At a formal ceremony on opening day, Baillet-Latour formally thanked Hitler for his support of the Games. "The excellent organization of the Festival," he declaimed, "will constitute a permanent monument to the contribution that [Germany] has made to human culture in general."[91] Looking back after the war, most observers would argue precisely the opposite. Historians have tended to agree that the Games represented an unqualified propaganda coup for the Nazis. Many have argued that the Olympics were Nazified, its ideals politicized and made to serve as base propaganda for an evil regime.[92] And certainly, it was a betrayal of grand proportion to allow a festival that claimed to stand for peace and the transcendence of racial and religious differences to be staged in the capital city of a regime based on race-hatred.

Christiane Eisenberg, however, has suggested that the view of the Olympics as a Nazi performance is too colored by the ex post facto Nazification of the Games that Riefenstahl effected in the highly influential *Olympia*, released to widespread acclaim in 1938. As Eisenberg points out, much about the Olympics was relatively unpoliticized. For once Nazi party uniforms were pushed to the background. The SS, the SA, and even the Hitler Youth were relegated to the sidelines and kept away from the main arenas. The well-mannered, multilingual officials who checked in the foreign teams were dressed in civilian uniforms. Despite military-style parades on the Via Triumphalis on opening day, one United Press reporter said there was "nothing military about the atmosphere" at the Games.[93]

For two weeks in August 1936, the regime's vicious racism and anti-Semitism temporarily went underground.[94] Blacks and Jews raced on German tracks, swam in German pools, played on German courts. When they beat Germans, Germans applauded them, shook their hands, and asked for their autographs. Foreign opinion was favorably impressed by the Olympics only because they were remarkably free of the Nazis' extremist views. The concessions offered by the regime as part of the staging of the event were temporary and had no long-term effects on racial policies or attitudes, and the Games were very much part of a broader Nazi campaign to deceive the world about the regime's nature and intentions. If there is any truth to one American reporter's assessment that "this contact with many nations and races has made the Germans more human again after four long years" of Nazism, it is nonetheless clear that the Games did nothing to alter the character of the Third Reich. But the Third Reich did little to alter the character of the Olympics.[95] The Nazification of the Games was significantly constrained. The Olympics was a festival staged as much on the world's terms as on the Nazis'. As the U.S. Olympic runner Marty Glickman later wrote, "I have always thought of the 1936 Olympics as the Jesse Owens Games rather than the Nazi Olympics."[96] The Nazis succeeded in conveying to the world an impressive display of organizational efficiency, but it was at the price of allowing other messages—about the virtues of internationalism and the achievements of other races—a prominent place in the narrative of the Berlin Games.

7

The Soviet Union and the Triumph of Soccer

Hitler avidly seized on international sport as a tool of propaganda. Did Joseph Stalin, too, recognize the new medium's value? Unlike Hitler, Stalin showed little personal interest in sports, and physical fitness was accorded relatively low priority in the Soviet Union, where the regime focused on more urgent needs, especially building an industrial base. But here, too, physical fitness was recognized as a matter of national power. In the 1920s the Soviet regime promoted its own "proletarian" brand of *fizicheskaia kultura* (physical culture) as part of broader programs of health, hygiene, and premilitary training. But by the 1930s even the USSR, under the dictatorship of a xenophobe deeply distrustful of the West and of Western culture, was pulled to a significant extent into the orbit of the emerging global sport culture, developing a professionalized spectator sport culture with transnational connections. In the end, proletarian *fizkultura* lost to capitalist soccer.

The Revolution of 1917 and its aftermath had left the Soviet Union isolated from the West. The severing of diplomatic relations and border closings were followed by the upheavals of civil war, collectivization, and rapid industrialization. In the relatively liberal atmosphere of the 1920s the Soviet Union had continued to share in an international culture, and Western films, books, and other elements of "low-brow" culture were popular.[1] Even into the 1930s, jazz was popular and even officially patronized; the Soviet trade establishment copied Western commercial techniques and enthused over customer service at Macy's department stores; French fashion magazines were sold; and Soviet youth embraced the foxtrot and Western fads in fashion. Despite restrictions on foreign film imports, Soviet filmmakers sought to emulate Western techniques and ideas, producing what one historian calls a "Stalinization of Hollywood style."[2] Such foreign cultural influences, however, declined dramatically when Stalin assumed dictatorial power in the late 1920s, as the regime sought tight control of culture for the purposes of mass mobilization. Like Mussolini's Italy and Hitler's Germany, Stalin's regime attempted to build an autarkic alternative to internationalized forms of mass culture.[3] Contacts with foreigners, travel abroad, and the importation of foreign products, literature, and films were strictly circumscribed in the effort to build a new, internally controlled culture. The result was an extraordinary degree of isolation.

The Anglo-American brand of sport, as a form of culture steeped in an ethos of individualism, competition, and achievement that reflected its origins as an offshoot of capitalism, was particularly suspect. In the 1920s the Soviet Union largely opted out of the Western system of international sport, condemning it as inherently capitalist and exploitative. Instead the Soviet Union attempted to build an alternative international system based on a distinctly "proletarian" brand of sport and physical culture that eschewed individualism and record-seeking. Like other efforts to develop a unique national version of mass sport, however, the Soviet attempt to develop a domestic and international system of physical culture that was class-based, collectivist, and mass-oriented was ultimately overtaken by the expanding powers of the capitalist, consumer-oriented, and elite-centered transnational sport culture.[4] As a result, in the early 1930s the Soviet regime dropped its opposition to "bourgeois" sport and moved toward integration into the international sport system it had previously denounced.[5] This integration went furthest in the case of soccer, a sport whose accessibility and spectator appeal were making it the world's most popular team sport.

The Soviet move toward engagement with Western international sport was partly a product of a new orientation in Soviet foreign policy. The introduction of the Popular Front and Soviet entrance into the League of Nations in 1934 signaled a new willingness to work with the "bourgeoisie" to combat the fascist threat. Internally, the shift toward a competitive, high-achievement sport system modeled on Western lines was consonant with the regime's "Great Retreat" from radical toward more conservative social and cultural policies, and with its effort to overtake capitalist achievements in other spheres, such as industry and agriculture.[6] But in a deeper sense it was also a reflection of the ways the Soviet Union was caught up in broader modernizing processes that affected all of Europe in this period and that reached the USSR despite its relative isolation. State regulation and supervision of populations expanded under the new Soviet regime, as elsewhere, including the introduction of sport and physical education programs.[7] International sport's apparently objective capacity to measure national success in harnessing population resources was a political lure that proved irresistible even to a Stalinist mentality deeply hostile to capitalist forms of internationalism.

The Soviet rapprochement with international sport remained tentative and incomplete. The forces drawing the regime into engagement were offset by suspicion of the West and by fears of weakness and ideological contamination. Yet the significance of the shift should not be underestimated. To an extent that would have been unthinkable in the 1920s, the Soviet regime accepted the authority of "bourgeois" organizations based in liberal democratic countries in determining much of the form and content of the sports played in the Soviet Union. It accepted a vision of global sport, defined not by political or ideological parameters but by ostensibly universal membership, inclusive of all countries and all classes. Although modern Western sport was modified in the process of adaptation to the Soviet context—it was, in other words, Sovietized—it retained a core set of values resistant to Soviet ideological transformation. Nationalist aspirations propelled the Soviet Union into participation in the Western sport world, but at the price of opening Soviet culture to internationalist currents that sometimes ran counter to broader regime goals.

The Failure of "Proletarian" Physical Culture

The brand of modern sport pioneered in Britain first began to appear in Russia, as in the rest of Europe, in the last decades of the nineteenth century. The fin de siècle fads for body-building, professional wrestling, and bicycling that swept Europe came to Russia as well, and in the years before World War I, private groups in Russia formed hundreds of sport clubs. When new international sport competitions were established, tsarist Russia was an early participant. In 1894 Russians were among the founding members of the IOC; in 1908 a handful of Russian athletes competed in the Olympic Games in London; in 1912 the All-Russian Football Union joined the international football federation; and Russian soccer players competed in more than a dozen international soccer matches. Recognizing the value of sport and physical education for international prestige and for the health and fitness of the population, the tsarist government provided a generous subsidy for the 1912 Olympic team and opened an office to promote physical fitness.[8] The level of state interest and of working-class involvement in sport were lower than elsewhere in Europe, but Russia was nonetheless part of the nascent international sport community.

The Bolshevik Revolution and the ensuing civil war created a rupture in Russia's cultural relations with the West, in sport as in other realms. By disbanding tsarist-era sports organizations and replacing them with new Soviet organs, the Bolsheviks severed the relationships that had been established between Russian and Western organizations. Although the All-Russian Football Union, for example, continued a shadowy existence until the mid-1920s and the international soccer federation continued to list it as an official member until 1932, Soviet authorities showed no interest in using tsarist-era bodies as conduits to Western organizations or in establishing relations through new ones. Instead, the Bolsheviks set out to create their own separate and distinctive structure for "proletarian sport."

Bolshevik policy toward Western sport reflected a principled rejection of "bourgeois" culture. In the 1920s Soviet theorists sought to dismantle the remnants of "decadent" capitalist culture and to create new cultural forms appropriate for the new proletarian state. In physical culture, as in art, music, cinema, theater, and literature, the search for proletarian cultural forms generated controversy. The new Soviet physical culture, all sides agreed, ought to increase labor productivity, ready workers for defense, and inculcate habits of collectivism, good hygiene, and discipline. To achieve these goals, physical educators created widely divergent systems combining labor, gymnastics, corrective exercises, games, pageants, and excursions. Some theorists rejected competitive sport altogether as inherently capitalist and corrupt, whereas others believed that certain sports could be used in moderation to draw the masses into a regimen of hygiene and exercise. All agreed, however, that individualism, record-seeking, and competitive habits were vices to be discouraged.[9] A. A. Zikmund, the head of the Physical Culture Institute in Moscow, for example, strongly disapproved of records and individual distinctions. "It is completely unnecessary and unimportant," he wrote, "that anyone set a new world or Russian record."[10]

In accordance with such ideas, the government implemented a variety of antisport policies, targeting soccer and boxing as the most harmful sports. In some cities, for example, teenagers were forbidden to play soccer, and in 1926 schools were forbidden from organizing soccer competitions.[11] Commissar of Education Anatolii Lunacharskii defended boxing as a socially useful sport, but he criticized the "fetishization of sport" in capitalist countries, with their endless quest for records, unhealthy competition, and professionalization.[12]

Internationally as well as domestically, the Soviet Union sought to build an alternative to the capitalist sport system. The Red Sport International (or Sportintern), formed in 1921 as an adjunct to the Comintern, oversaw an international "proletarian sport" culture that posed as an alternative both to the workers' sport system run by the larger and better organized Socialist Workers' Sport International, founded in 1920, and to the still larger and more popular capitalist sport model advanced by the IOC and international sport federations. By sponsoring parades, demonstrations, and meetings, as well as athletic competitions between Soviet athletes and European workers, the Sportintern tried to advance revolutionary goals through political education directed at members of communist (and socialist) sport clubs. At various times during its sixteen-year existence, the Sportintern claimed member sections in Europe, Latin America, and North America, but its total membership never exceeded several hundred thousand workers outside the Soviet Union— a small fraction of the working class interested in sport. Even at its peak it remained a marginal organization, poorly funded, poorly organized, and often ignored by the Comintern. In its main task—bringing the socialist workers' sport movement under communist control—it was spectacularly unsuccessful.[13]

Despite occasional denunciations of the Olympic Games and other international competitions as militaristic and exploitative, the Sportintern devoted little attention to "bourgeois" sport. Although most European workers who participated in sport belonged to nonpolitical sport organizations (in Soviet parlance, bourgeois organizations), Sportintern policy largely ignored them.[14] The main government body for sport, the Supreme Council for Physical Culture and its successors, showed more interest in Western sport.[15] Technically the Sportintern's Soviet section, the council often pursued its own line in international sport relations and frequently clashed with the Sportintern. Although there were fac-

tions within both the Sportintern and the council, as a rule council officials were less concerned with the international workers' sport movement than with raising the level of Soviet sport. They therefore tended to
look more favorably on Soviet relations with non-workers' clubs in Europe. Whereas the Comintern and the Sportintern opposed meetings
with non-workers' clubs except in countries where no proletarian organizations existed, the council argued in the mid-1920s that Soviet athletes could benefit from competition with the stronger "bourgeois" clubs
and that victories in such competitions would confer more prestige.[16]
Stalin, then in the process of maneuvering toward dictatorial power, is
reported to have remarked on the issue: "We compete with the bourgeoisie economically, politically, and not without success. We compete
everywhere possible. Why not compete in sport?"[17] But despite Stalin's
endorsement, for most of the 1920s competitions with non-workers' organizations were discouraged, and only a handful were permitted under
exceptional circumstances.[18]

Conflicts over the role of sport in the system of physical culture, over
the proper balance between collectivism and competition, and over the
relationship with "bourgeois" sport were never definitively settled, and
contradictory tendencies coexisted throughout the 1920s. From the beginning one of the aims of Soviet participation in international meets was
to showcase the achievements of the Soviet physical culture movement, a
goal that fostered elements of competitiveness.[19] The popularity of competitive sports like soccer grew by leaps and bounds despite official dis-
couragement, and manifestations of professionalism emerged. Even in
the mid-1920s soccer was drawing enough spectators that forms of semiprofessionalism had arisen. The better soccer teams drew crowds of up to
ten thousand, and foreign matches drew tremendous interest. Illustrating
soccer's prosperous conditions, players in 1926 asked the Physical Culture Council for better traveling conditions, including a doubling in their
daily allowance, accommodations in single rooms in hotels instead of in
dormitories, and beer, cigarettes, and other privileges.[20]

The main thrust of Soviet international engagement in the 1920s,
however, centered on mass sport and revolutionary agitation in European workers' clubs, not on athletic achievement. The emphasis remained on promoting collectivism and discouraging individualism and
record-seeking, and on creating a separate international system for proletarian sport rather than measuring Soviet achievements against "bour-

geois" standards.[21] With international competitions limited to friendly meets within the socialist sphere, dedicated fans found little satisfaction in the level of competition. Long-standing soccer official George Diuperron concluded that "nothing good can be said" about the kinds of matches that were permitted in the 1920s: "True, our teams have visited . . . Germany, Austria, France, Latvia, Turkey; they won everything, even ties were rare, but it's impossible to hide one circumstance: our opponents were always of a low class, and these victories did not bring us much honor. What's more, it's difficult to imagine that they even were very useful to us, since we can learn only from the strongest teams, which are capable of beating us."[22] *Krasnyi sport* expressed similar frustration at the end of the 1927 season, complaining that the level of Soviet soccer had actually deteriorated because "we are stewing in our juice. We have no one to study from, and no one teaches us the newest tactics and techniques. There are no games with the strongest of opponents who can enliven our play."[23]

The consensus among experts was that Soviet soccer at the end of the 1920s had still not regained its prerevolutionary levels, while soccer in other European countries was advancing rapidly. Soviet soccer players traveling abroad to play workers' teams in the 1920s were amazed whenever they had the opportunity to watch a professional match. "All our players who have been abroad and have seen first-class teams," Diuperron remarked in 1929, "know that to play well means to play completely differently than we do."[24] The frustration engendered by isolation from the international sports mainstream would soon lead to a reassessment of the relationship between Soviet and "bourgeois" sport.

The Soviet Embrace of Western Sport

The emphasis on disengagement from mainstream Western sport underwent a dramatic transformation beginning in 1930, as the main aim of Soviet international sport contacts shifted from revolutionary agitation within an independent sport system to results-oriented competition within the Western sport system.[25] Frustrated by the weakness of the communist sport movement and impressed with the growing power of mainstream sport, the regime came to see Western international sport as a useful way to reach large numbers of foreign workers, impress foreign governments with Soviet strength, and bolster its legitimacy at home.

The Sportintern, cut off from contacts with socialist clubs as a result of a disastrous policy of confrontation, moved to increase its influence in Europe by devoting more attention to the large numbers of workers in non-workers' organizations.[26] By 1933 the Physical Culture Council was debating whether to offer general sanction to competitions between Soviet athletes and athletes from non-workers' clubs.[27]

Official hostility toward the Western model of competitive, achievement-oriented sport was reversed. The idea of surpassing capitalist sport first appeared in the Soviet press in late 1933, and the slogan "catch up to and overtake bourgeois records in sport" was officially launched in 1934. Typical of the regime's rhetoric, the goals set for Soviet sport had little correspondence to reality. The aim was "to bring worldwide glory to Soviet sport" and "to win first place in the world for Soviet sport. We want victories, records, success."[28] Initially the calls were to surpass half of all world records within two to three years, but even as the impossibility of achieving that goal became apparent, the mantra became "*all* world sport records should belong to the USSR."[29] Paralleling the introduction of social hierarchies in other areas, as in the creation of a privileged class of high-achieving "Stakhanovite" workers, in 1934 the regime introduced a new category of elite athlete, the "distinguished master of sport."

New channels of information flow and direct contacts with European and U.S. sport established connections that drew the USSR into the world of transnational sport. The Physical Culture Council set up a foreign department that carefully monitored Western sport, acquiring and translating training manuals, rulebooks, physical-education journals, films, and newspapers. It began publishing informational bulletins summarizing developments, achievements, and methods in foreign sport.[30] Working with the All-Union Society for Cultural Relations Abroad (VOKS), Intourist, and—with somewhat less success—the Commissariat of Foreign Affairs, the council hosted foreign sports delegations, hired foreign trainers (such as French tennis star André Cochet) to come to the Soviet Union as teachers, and organized tours of Europe for its own trainers and coaches to study the latest techniques.[31] The Soviet press began to devote more space and more favorable coverage to international competitions and to sports achievements and events in foreign countries.

The council also tried to disseminate information about Soviet sport achievements abroad. It was involved, for example, in designing a sport and physical culture section for the Soviet pavilion at the 1937 Paris Exhibition. In the same year Intourist began organizing special sport tours for foreign tourists, which included visits to skating rinks, stadiums, institutes of physical culture and other sport organizations, as well as visits to soccer games and other competitions.[32]

As in other areas, the regime's grand goals in sport were hamstrung by limited resources. While Germany had hundreds of periodicals that covered sports and physical education, the Soviet Union produced only about a dozen, and these appeared in insufficient numbers to meet demand. The main sport newspaper, *Krasnyi sport,* had a circulation of only 50,000 in 1935, and its coverage of events was often dry and formulaic.[33] Foreign tourists often found it impossible to secure tickets to sports events. Although foreign interest in sport in the USSR was high, the regime's isolation ensured that access to information and coverage of Soviet sport remained minimal in other countries.[34]

As the council acknowledged, direct contact in the form of face-to-face meetings with bourgeois opponents was the critical element necessary for the new policy of engagement to succeed. Soviet athletes would reach the highest levels, authorities agreed, only by competing against the strongest opponents—those formerly denounced as bourgeois. Thus, in the most visible aspect of the new program, the regime arranged high-profile competitions between Soviet athletes and top-level Western athletes (often professionals or record-holders) in select sports. As one sport official put it, "raising our sporting class and accomplishing the goal of 'catching up to and overtaking world records' depend to a large degree on the existence of systematic meetings between Soviet athletes and the best representatives of foreign sport," in which Soviet athletes could both test their skills and learn firsthand the latest tactics and techniques.[35]

What officials called Soviet sport's "entry into the world arena" was fixed for the year 1934.[36] "Never before," council chairman Nikolai Antipov said, "has there been such a sharp turn in our international work."[37] Marking the Soviet debut on the world stage was a trip to Czechoslovakia by a delegation of Soviet boxers, runners, and soccer players, sent to compete against Czech professionals in October. The visit—the first major exchange with "bourgeois" clubs—was part of an effort to consolidate improved relations after Czechoslovakia extended official recognition to the USSR in June. The highlight was a soccer match played between Spartak Moscow and Zidenice Brno, a highly ranked Czech professional team, which drew extraordinary public interest both at home and in Czechoslovakia. It was the first time a Soviet team had met a top-flight European professional team: the Czechs were among the top soccer powers in Europe and just a few months earlier had barely lost to Italy in the second World Cup final.[38]

For Soviet soccer players and their fans, the transition to competition against top athletes produced high levels of both excitement and anxiety. Soviet fans greeted the Czech match with tremendous enthusiasm precisely because it represented a new, higher level of competition. As the team's captain observed, "No foreign trip of Soviet sportsmen has generated as much interest in sporting circles as the trip to Czechoslovakia . . . We still know little about foreign soccer, and therefore all kinds of legends about professional teams were often created . . . Just the word 'professionals' inspired in some people a kind of admiration that had absolutely no basis."[39] Both players and officials hoped for success but feared that European professionals would outclass them. Nikolai Starostin, the team coach and head of the Spartak sport society, recalled that the players were so nervous that no one slept before the match. The onus of their mission—"to defend the honor of Soviet sport"—weighed heavily.[40]

For the Soviet soccer world, the Soviet victory in a close match against the Czech "capitalists" offered the ultimate validation of the strength of Soviet soccer. From the Czech point of view, Soviet success was modest. As the head of the Czech soccer federation put it, "the Russians behaved like correct and capable sportsmen, without at all having shown any extraordinary qualities."[41] For the Soviets, however, the intoxicating victory led to overstated assessments. Players and officials quickly claimed that the match proved Soviet soccer ranked among Europe's best. In Starostin's view, "we had firmly secured our right to be considered first-class soccer players in international estimation."[42] The delegation's leaders were similarly enthusiastic. "To the general surprise of all circles of Czech society," they gushed, "in soccer our team showed that Soviet soccer players, who had never been seen before in a serious international match, had an international class of game that set them at the same level as the best clubs of Europe."[43]

The successful debut of Soviet sport led to more matches against top European athletes, resulting in an exchange of information and experience that proved highly influential in shaping Soviet sport. The following year marked the high point of Soviet international exchanges, as more than 150 Soviet swimmers, wrestlers, skaters, weight lifters, cyclists, tennis players, fencers, boxers, and runners sallied forth to Scandinavia, Turkey, France, and Belgium. French tennis stars and Norwegian skaters and skiers competed in the USSR, and a Prague professional soccer team toured Moscow, Leningrad, and Kiev, winning or drawing a tie in all matches. Helping to cement friendly relations with France after the conclusion of the Franco-Soviet mutual-assistance pact in May 1935, a Ukrainian soccer team played Red Star, the twelfth-ranked team in the French league, in Paris; the Ukrainians won handily. In women's basketball, a Soviet team played the French national team. In a major event in January 1936, a Moscow soccer team lost a close match to Racing Club, the team that had just won the French championship, in front of sixty thousand spectators at the Parc des Princes stadium in Paris.[44]

Although Soviet athletes continued to compete occasionally against workers' clubs, such meets were of marginal importance in the new scheme favoring Western over workers' sport. While Soviet sport offi-

The Soviet soccer team playing Racing Club at the Parc des Princes in Paris in 1936, one of the key moments of a Soviet opening to the West in sports. *Source: Sto let Rossiiskomu futbolu.*

cials turned unrelenting criticism of Western sport into modulated admiration, the Sportintern—with its revolutionary, anticapitalist stance and focus on workers' sport—slipped into irrelevance. As the Physical Culture Council assumed primary control of international sport contacts in the mid-1930s, the Sportintern was relegated to insignificance, and in 1937 the Comintern officially dissolved it.[45] Rather than focusing their attention on workers' organizations, communists were now instructed to work with (and within) "bourgeois" organizations.

Soviet rhetoric toward international competitions like the Olympic Games underwent a reversal that paralleled the broader goals and tactics of the Popular Front. Instead of condemning sports events like the Olympics as imperialist and militarist spectacles, Soviet sports authorities celebrated the ideals and traditions of modern sport. The communist campaign to boycott the 1936 "Nazi Olympics" in Berlin accepted as genuine the Olympic ideals of pacifism and racial equality and denounced the Nazis for violating these principles.[46] Drawing on Olympic rhetoric, one Sportintern appeal described international sport as associated with "culture, humanity, health, physical and mental purity, progress, peace and friendship of the peoples, freedom and self-determination of all peoples and races."[47] A Comintern commission on the sport question recommended that communist parties use "the strong Olympic traditions which exist in the sporting world" to strengthen "peace and friendship among peoples" and to secure "the progressive and cultured development of sport." Where possible, communists were to reinforce national Olympic committees with democratic and progressive members.[48]

Despite these substantial moves toward rapprochement with Western sport, the relationship remained unconsummated in one key respect. The USSR did not become a participant in the Olympic Games or a member of the international sport federations that exerted increasingly tight control over international competition. Part of the problem lay in the attitude of these organizations toward the Soviet Union. The IOC claimed to be a universalist organization that ignored politics, but it was disinclined to extend membership to the Soviet Union. The hosts of the 1924 and 1932 Olympics had considered inviting the Soviet Union but were rebuffed by the IOC.[49] In 1934 the now-retired Coubertin privately protested that the failure to invite the Soviet Union to the 1936 Olympic Games violated the Olympic spirit of universalism. The Soviets, he said, "had long abandoned the idea" of holding separate international events and now "would be favorable to participation" in the Olympics. IOC President Baillet-Latour, however, refused to consider Soviet participation. "I am absolutely opposed," he wrote to an associate, "not wanting at any price to facilitate the corruption of the youth of the entire world by putting them in contact with these reds, who would take advantage [of participation] to make wild propaganda. Let's not lapse into the errors of the League of Nations."[50] Soviet officials, their main priorities elsewhere, most likely did not give serious consideration to the expenditure of energy and resources an Olympic entry would have entailed.

Several of the international federations governing international sports were more welcoming of Soviet membership than was the IOC. The federations typically prohibited their members from engaging in matches against nonmembers. But when national associations, often for their own political reasons, began to clamor for contacts with the Soviets in the early 1930s, several federations made exceptions to allow competitions with Soviet athletes. In October 1934, for example, FIFA granted permission to the Czech national football association for a match against a Soviet team. The result was the Spartak-Zidenice match described earlier in this chapter. In their deliberations, FIFA's leaders noted that contact with the Soviets was "a delicate question" because Soviet sport organizations maintained relations with workers' sport organizations that were antagonistic toward FIFA's national associations. Nevertheless, genuinely desirous of securing Soviet membership, FIFA officials decided to grant "provisional" authorization for meets in the interest of "studying the possibility of a rapprochement" with Soviet soccer.[51] The policy of granting "exceptional" permission for Soviet matches was extended until April 1936, when the Soviets appeared to renege on a promise to join FIFA during negotiations to bring a Scottish team to the USSR. FIFA's leadership then decided that further matches would not be permitted until the Soviets joined, and no further matches between Soviet teams and FIFA members took place until 1940.[52] The IAAF similarly voted to allow meets with Soviet teams beginning in 1934 and then discontinued the practice in 1937.[53] The result was that the outpouring of Soviet-Western contacts in 1935–1936 slowed to a trickle by 1937.

The "blockade," as Soviet officials saw it, quickly took a toll on the Soviet Union's efforts to achieve first-class sport results. In 1938 the Physical Culture Council expressed frustration that despite the imperative to increase the number of international meets, efforts to do so "in recent years have run into a very serious obstacle": the exclusivity of international federations. As an official wrote:

> In view of the fact that the Soviet Union is not a member of a single one of these associations, it has found itself in recent years in a position of isolation, with extremely rare opportunities to invite individual, technically strong sportsmen (out of the small number who have the right to compete without special permission from international associations), and without any opportunities to invite in systematic order the strongest national teams.[54]

To ensure continued progress in elite sport, the council considered joining a number of federations, including those for soccer, tennis, weight lifting, swimming, track and field, and skating—all sports in which Soviet athletes could claim respectable, if not top-level, results. In the second half of the 1930s the council initiated exchanges of information, acquired statutes and rulebooks, and opened informal or indirect negotiations on membership. When council chairman Ivan Kharchenko was in Paris for the match against Racing Club, for example, he met informally with FIFA head Jules Rimet.[55] Within the council, the view seems to have been that membership was both necessary and inevitable, and the council began to adopt many federation rules to bring Soviet practices in line with international standards. At a 1937 Comintern meeting, Kharchenko declared that "we evidently are going to participate in international organizations."[56]

The Soviet tango with FIFA illuminates both the suspicion and the ignorance of the West that plagued the Soviet rapprochement with Western sport. Because soccer was the country's most popular sport and one of the USSR's strongest, Soviet officials were most eager to join FIFA, but they hesitated because they viewed FIFA's leadership as hostile. FIFA, according to the council, was "led by fascist elements" who had "a clearly unfriendly attitude toward the USSR"—a reference to FIFA secretary Ivo Schricker, a German with close ties to the Nazi sport establishment.[57] Although FIFA's internal correspondence indicates that it was genuinely interested in Soviet membership, the Soviets likely feared that a request to join would be publicly rejected or that onerous conditions would be attached. In an effort to bridge the impasse, in mid-1938 Soviet sports authorities held talks with Rudolf Pelikan, a member of FIFA's executive committee and the president of the Czech soccer association whose contacts with Soviet sport dated back to 1934.[58] Pelikan proposed a technical agreement, evidently short of full membership, that would allow the Soviet Union to compete against FIFA members of its own choosing. The council then sought permission from the Council of People's Commissars (Sovnarkom) to join FIFA under the terms of the technical agreement, as well as the federations for track and field, skating, weight lifting, and swimming. In its application the council noted that the initiative for Soviet entry came from FIFA, which had virtually guaranteed admission, and that Klement Gottwald, head of the Czech Communist Party, supported the agreement.[59]

In the end the Sovnarkom and the Politburo, the ultimate authority in determining international sport contacts, chose not to grant permission, possibly fearing that subordination to international bodies would entail too great a loss of control over Soviet sport.[60] The timing was also inopportune, as international tensions mounted and the internal purges of the Soviet leadership reached their peak. Another obstacle was the restrictions that membership in federations would have imposed on competitions with workers' sport organizations. Although such meetings had diminished in importance by 1938, renouncing them altogether would have been politically difficult. Soviet authorities likely hesitated, too, because of doubts about the strength of Soviet sport. Where Soviet achievements were indisputably at world-class level, the regime was willing to join "bourgeois" international structures. In aviation, a field akin to sport but one accorded higher priority by the regime, the Soviet Union joined the international federation in 1936 immediately after famed pilot Valerii Chkalov's world distance record was refused official standing in the record books because Chkalov did not belong to a federation member country. From then on, Soviet authorities followed federation requirements for certifying records and soon held a commanding lead in aviation world records.[61] In sport, however, where direct contacts with foreigners were required and where federations imposed more stringent requirements for participation, submission to international authorities entailed greater sacrifice.

Domestic Repercussions

The Soviet regime, then, did not become a full member of the Western sport club, but its efforts to emulate Western sport had significant internal consequences. In soccer, for example, the high-profile loss to Racing in 1936 led to a substantial organizational restructuring that mirrored developments elsewhere in Europe. Across the European continent, soccer was rising to new heights of popularity in the interwar years; previously limited to middle classes in major cities, it now became a mass phenomenon. One reason for the increase in popularity was the creation of leagues in most European countries. Before the systematization of competition within leagues, it was impossible to document the relative progress of teams, and fan enthusiasm was consequently short-lived.[62] Leagues brought fixed schedules and regular championships. Results and rankings were published regularly in the new sport sections of newspapers and in new sport dailies, and fans increasingly identified with "their" teams. With spectators willing to pay to see matches, clubs became profitable, and the pressures for players to devote more time to the game increased as well, resulting in the professionalization of the game. Between 1924 and 1934, professional leagues formed in Hungary, Austria, Czechoslovakia, Spain, France, and Switzerland.[63]

As in Europe before the advent of leagues, Soviet soccer lacked a framework for regular, organized competition before 1936. City and national championships were sometimes held, but there was no fixed structure for such competitions.[64] The 1936 loss in Paris prompted Nikolai Starostin, head of the Spartak sport society and a leading figure in Soviet soccer, to propose a radical restructuring around an openly professional league, quite deliberately modeled on those in Europe. "In the last two or three years," Starostin wrote in a February 1936 memo to the council and the Komsomol, "Soviet soccer has shown that it stands at the level of the best European teams . . . At the same time, a better acquaintance with working conditions for foreign professional soccer players—and all the best teams in Europe consist of professionals—showed us that professional soccer has a number of advantages over amateur." Professionals, he explained, practiced daily, had "absolute discipline," and gained "colossal experience" from frequent international matches. He proposed establishing eight professional club teams in six cities around the country, with two championship seasons per year. This system, he argued, would simply "legalize the professionalism that already exists in our soccer." Setting up a league comparable to what existed in the West, Starostin felt, would inevitably lead to a higher class of Soviet soccer.[65] The memo—striking in its uncritical admiration of Western, commercialized sport, the absence of any effort to distance Soviet sport ideologically from the Western version, and the assumption that the best way to advance Soviet sport was to implant Western practices and structures—represented a dramatic departure from the discourse of earlier years.

The council accepted most of Starostin's proposals, remodeling soccer along Western lines. Replacing the haphazard organization of previous years, the council created a league similar to those in Europe, consisting of "demonstration teams of masters" sponsored by individual sport societies and factories.[66] Although they were never officially acknowledged as professional teams, players and coaches received wages, a fact that was openly discussed in the press.[67] In accordance with Starostin's recommendation, two annual championships were held, as well as a USSR Cup, open to any team and organized according to the Olympic system—very much like the national cup competitions that had become common in the West. As in the rest of Europe, the league system helped expand soccer's popularity, and by 1939 the USSR Cup matches attracted 10 million spectators.[68] Similar leagues were also established in basketball, wrestling, shooting, ice hockey, and boxing.[69]

The new league system did not work perfectly, and over the next few years officials constantly tinkered with its structure and schedule.[70] Nevertheless, the league structure did enhance soccer's popularity, both among ordinary workers and the party elite. Stadiums had government loges, and in the late 1930s Spartak regularly gave out a thousand tickets per game, many of these to members of the Central Committee. High-ranking party officials sought to dictate team lineups and to appoint and dismiss coaches.[71]

Soviet sport came to resemble the European variety in other important ways. The council adapted rules in various sports to conform to Western standards, and it studied and emulated European and U.S. tactics and training techniques. In soccer, for example, the matches in Czechoslovakia and France prompted Spartak to adopt the "W" formation, a defensive tactical innovation practiced by some English and other European clubs. It soon became standard among Soviet teams.[72] Competing within the Western sport system, moreover, placed limits on Soviet sport. In 1938, for example, Lavrentii Beria, a serious soccer fan who was then the secretary of the Georgian party but would soon head the secret police, pushed for several changes to Sovietize the organization of soccer, including redesigning the league around one team per Soviet republic. The council rebuffed his efforts on the grounds that the requirements of international competition would not allow them.[73] The Westernization of Soviet sport also had broader social consequences, including competition among clubs for the best athletes that led to buying and selling of athletes, violence and corruption, and the creation of a class of privileged, professional athletes who often failed to demonstrate proper "Soviet" behavior both on and off the field.[74]

The effort to remodel Soviet sport along Western lines and to compete on Western terms produced tensions and conflicts. One symptom of discontent was the conflict that erupted in 1937 and 1938 between the council and the Komsomol (along with Spartak, the Komsomol-supported sport society). Driven by the dynamics of the ongoing purges, the conflict was also shaped as a reaction to the effort to create an elite sport system capable of competing with the West. When a visiting professional soccer team from the Basque region of Spain, on an international tour to raise funds for the Republican cause, handily beat the best Soviet soccer teams in six of seven games in July 1937, the party and the Komsomol attacked the council for failings in sport policy. *Pravda* sharply criticized the council for failing to produce "the best sportsmen in the world," but—indicative of the contradictions within Soviet sport—ascribed blame to the council's neglect of mass work and its overemphasis on elite sport.[75]

In defense, the council's leadership instituted sundry organizational changes; it also initiated an investigation of Spartak. Nikolai Starostin, Spartak's head, and his brothers were accused of buying and selling players, doing insufficient political-educational work, squandering state funds, placing too little emphasis on militarized sports, bringing back foreign goods from trips abroad, using Spartak funds to pay for apartments, and—most important—"of introducing bourgeois methods of work in sport."[76] Spartak track stars, the brothers Serafim and Georgii Znamenskii, wrote denunciations accusing the Starostin brothers of corruption. They also criticized Starostin's management style, which they regarded as too close to what they had seen in capitalist sport. As Georgii Znamenskii wrote, "Starostin's leadership and his education of sportsmen are directed to the exact opposite of a social-cultural organization . . . [His] method is similar to an entrepreneurial, private sport club."[77] Serafim Znamenskii echoed this sentiment: "Nikolai Starostin's manner is not like that of a leader of a Soviet sport society, but is like that of the owner of a private sport club, like the owner of the Palais de Sport in Paris." In visits abroad, Znamenskii suggested, Starostin felt all too at ease with capitalist sportsmen.[78]

Reflecting the unresolved tension between elite and mass sport, criticism of Spartak often centered on its deficiencies in promoting mass-participation and defense-related sport. Yet the press was also full of calls to eradicate "self-seeking frames of mind," "parasitic attitudes," and "bourgeois customs," and to root out "enemies of the people" who were "contaminating" the spirit of Soviet sportsmen by paying stipends and promoting "bourgeois professionalism," all of which suggest a deeper unease with the effects of cultural transfer resulting from the engagement with Western sport.[79] It was, after all, precisely Starostin's "bourgeois methods of work" that had made Spartak one of the two most successful sport societies in the country (along with Dinamo, the sport society run by the secret police). Starostin paid players well, gave them contracts, lured good players from other teams with promises of higher salaries, and provided coveted privileges, including apartments, dachas, and hard currency to buy foreign goods during trips abroad. These practices were employed by other sport societies, but they were used most effectively by Spartak, and the society's very success made it a target for Soviet officials uncomfortable with the necessary by-products of the quest for records. Despite complaints that "the planting of elements of bourgeois professionalism in Soviet sport" was hindering "the battle for world records,"[80] Soviet sport would not have achieved the results it did without the introduction of elitism, salaries, and privileges.

Official discomfort with the unintended effects of cultural transfer eventually intersected with the onset of the purges to temporarily suspend the program to tighten Soviet-Western sport contacts. In 1938 and 1939 the Soviets did not participate in any major international matches.[81] In 1938 the only Soviet athletes to travel abroad were sent to France: ten runners, two swimmers, and the Torpedo soccer team.[82] The council continued to propose exchanges, but the Sovnarkom refused to permit them.[83] In late 1939, after the Nazi-Soviet Pact, the council drew up an ambitious proposal for sport exchanges in 1940, primarily with Germany and the Baltic republics, but again the Sovnarkom refused to approve the plan.[84]

Even so, the regime continued occasionally to use international sports events as diplomatic tools. Soccer matches with Bulgaria in the autumn of 1940, for example, were used as a lever in the German-Soviet struggle for influence in the Balkans. (FIFA officials apparently chose to ignore the Bulgarian violation of the blockade; even this late they hoped the USSR would join.) As one participant recalled, the visit had "special political significance." Georgii Dimitrov, the Bulgarian who headed the Comintern, had proposed the visit, but pro-German elements in the Bulgarian government had tried to derail the plans.[85] Indicating the importance of the trip, a special commission—including Aleksandr Shcherbakov, first secretary of the Moscow *oblast* party committee and a Central Committee member; Lev Z. Mekhlis, head of the Main Political Administration of the Red Army; and Vice Premier Andrei Vyshinskii—was formed to oversee preparations. The three personally visited the team to check on its preparations before departure.[86] There seems to have been considerable debate as to which team to send. Tblisi Dinamo was recommended on the basis that the Georgian climate was closer to Bulgaria's. In the end, Moscow Spartak was sent but with the addition of players from other teams, including Central House of the Red Army and Dinamo. No expense was spared: players flew in two large planes instead of taking the train, and the total cost of the expedition was estimated at 361,000 rubles.[87]

When the team landed in Sofia, they were greeted by perhaps a hundred thousand well-wishers.[88] The applause that greeted them in the stadium on the day of the first match (August 11) was, as the delegation's head noted, something of "a political demonstration." Tightly sequestered during their stay, the players were kept away from the press, prohibited from making public statements, and confined to a hotel inaccessible except to Bulgarian government representatives. The Soviets won both matches handily, and upon their return to Moscow, five players were immediately awarded the prestigious title master of sport.[89]

In September 1940 the Bulgarian team Slaviia returned the visit, flying to Moscow. Again, preparations were intense. The Physical Culture Committee, VOKS, and Intourist representatives greeted the delegation at the airport, and VOKS arranged a series of cultural events, including an evening welcoming party with a jazz orchestra, and later a tour of the city and evenings at the cinema and the Bolshoi Theater. For the first match against Spartak at Dinamo stadium, the Moscow police prepared a detailed security plan that called for more than two thousand police and other troops. The Bulgarian Embassy in Moscow was given a loge; tickets were sold at ten, eight, five, and three rubles; and the match was broadcast over the radio. Banners reading "Welcome" and "Hello to the Sportsmen of Bulgaria" were displayed (an earlier suggestion to write "Hello to the sportsmen of *friendly* Bulgaria" had been countermanded).[90] On the eve of war, the Soviet regime, like many others in the last decade, turned to sport contacts in a desperate search for diplomatic leverage.

The USSR-Bulgaria soccer matches are a hallmark of the importance sport had attained in Stalin's Soviet Union by the end of the 1930s, both in terms of its domestic popularity and its foreign-policy significance. These developments formed the basis for the surge in Soviet sport after World War II. Emerging from the war with its international standing greatly enhanced, the regime now placed a much higher priority on the use of sport to project and enhance its superpower status. The new tack was apparent in 1945 when the Moscow Dinamo soccer team took a highly publicized tour of Britain. In short order the Soviet Union began to join the organizations it had flirted with in the 1930s. It chose first to enter the federations governing those sports at which it was most confident of international success: soccer and weight lifting (both in 1946). Track and field, basketball, wrestling, swimming, volleyball, skating, skiing, boxing, and gymnastics quickly followed.[91] The regime now felt confident enough not simply to petition for membership in federations but to negotiate concessions. The policy adopted in 1947 was to request that a Soviet official be given a position in the federation's governing body (typically a vice presidency or membership in the executive committee), that Russian be made an official language, and that fascist Spain be excluded. Federations generally acceded to the first request, but the Soviets had less success with the latter two. Soviet officials also tried to include Ukraine and Belorussia as separate members and to create European groupings within federations to counter U.S. influence.[92]

By devoting new resources and attention to elite sport, the regime quickly registered impressive gains. Although the Soviets declined to participate in the 1948 London Olympics, a delegation sent to observe the Games concluded that the Soviet Union would have been second only to the United States. In the late 1940s, however, the regime made it a priority to engage in international competitions mainly in sports with wide popular followings, where the effects on public opinion would be greatest, and to participate only when Soviet athletes were guaranteed success—a policy that (not surprisingly) led to relatively few matches.[93]

Although the foundations of what became "the big red sports machine" can be traced to the 1930s, the Soviet Union could not then have claimed status as a major sport power. Its achievements in particular sports— notably soccer, where the best Soviet teams were roughly equivalent to high-ranking professional teams in the West, and weight lifting, where Soviet athletes had set marks exceeding twenty-two of the thirty-five world records then in place—were impressive, but in most sports Soviet athletes lagged far behind world levels. During the 1930s the regime de- voted greater attention to sport, particularly as a form of paramilitary training, but it was not yet the state priority it became during the Cold War. Funding, except for a few elite sport societies, was low. Facilities and equipment tended to be of poor quality and in short supply, and low stan- dards of living and poor nutrition affected athletic performance.[94]

In the interwar years, the global hegemony of modern Western sport and its international institutional structures, achieved with astonishing rapidity in the postwar years, was not a foregone conclusion. Alternative visions of modern body cultures, including an international workers' sport movement, remained viable. That the Soviet Union abandoned the quest for an independent system of physical culture in favor of adapting to the Western international sport system is related to other shifts noted earlier, including Stalin's move away from proletarian internationalism toward a more statist and security-oriented approach to both domestic and foreign policy. It can, however, also be explained in part by the growing appeal of internationalized forms of mass culture. The spread of modern Western sport was propelled in part by its demonstrated popu- larity among the masses. By the 1930s, governments had also come to see it as a preeminent means of rationalizing the body—of producing better workers and, especially, better soldiers. It was, however, in elite sport that modern states came to see the greatest political benefits to par- ticipation in international culture. International proletarian sport, by the 1930s, simply did not offer the same kind of benefits that participation in the "bourgeois" system offered.

Soviet authorities consistently portrayed Soviet sport as intrinsically different from capitalist sport, and there were indeed differences, both real and rhetorical. "Physical culture," notably in the form of mass gymnastics demonstrations highlighted in the annual "day of physical culture" parades on Red Square, continued to exist alongside competitive sport. Within sport, authorities continued to inculcate a collectivist ethos. Individual stars, though they were celebrated and received privileges, never attained the level of fame or idolatry (or riches) that became common elsewhere in Europe and in the United States. Popular media stressed the message that the achievements of Soviet athletes were the product of, and a tribute to, the Soviet system, downplaying the Western notion that achievements primarily reflected individual effort and will. State funding and control of sport within a planned economy, moreover, gave Soviet sport a distinctly different character than its highly commercialized Western counterpart.

Yet the Sovietization of competitive sport should not obscure a reciprocal Westernization of Soviet physical culture. By setting as its goal the overtaking of Western sport, the Soviet sport establishment opened the door to widespread imitation of Western practices. Competing on Western terms involved changes not just in rules, tactics, training methods, and the organization of a competitive system of leagues and championships, but also in the promotion of management styles and patterns of thought that clashed with communist ideology—and hence were condemned as bourgeois even as they produced success. Many of the growing pains experienced in Soviet sport—player misbehavior, player transfers, salary disputes, fighting on the field, and poor officiating—mirrored those that were occurring in the rest of Europe.[95] Even the exhortations to create new Soviet styles, different from foreign canons, echoed similar calls across Europe to nationalize and domesticate international sport.[96] Participation in international sport hardly constituted a Westernization of Soviet society, but it did connect an important element of Soviet culture to an increasingly global cultural form. Modern Western sport involved the Soviet public in new consumption patterns and cultural habits that were shaped by distinctly Soviet mentalities and practices, but that also implicitly situated the Soviet Union within an international and avowedly universalist culture.

Conclusion

Looking back over the interwar years, Avery Brundage observed that "the world-wide development in competitive athletic sport and in physical training was no less than phenomenal. All over the world, in nearly every country in Europe, in South America, and in the Orient, stadia, playing fields, swimming pools and arenas were built by the hundreds . . . . Country after country recognized the importance of physical training and sport and tried to make themselves nations of athletes."[1] As countries became "nations of athletes," they increasingly sought to demonstrate their achievements to international audiences. Building national strength through physical training was not enough; an essential part of the endeavor meant testing and demonstrating national achievements in international venues.

As a result, international sports competitions, too, experienced phenomenal growth in the 1930s, growing from festivals of marginal significance into global mega-events that drew millions of fans, miles of column inches in newspapers, prime coverage in the emerging medium of radio—and the avid attention of politicians and diplomats. The bigger sport competitions became, the greater was the imperative for every country to participate. As the growth of international competitions helped spread sport to every corner of the globe, nations were increasingly bound together in a common cultural pursuit. Like other elements of the new mass culture, sport became internationalized, part of a network of cultural flows increasingly unconstrained by national borders. The spread of modern competitive sport—not just particular sports like soccer but a general philosophy of physical recreation—provided the world with what exponents celebrated as "a universal language."[2]

The extent and rapidity of modern sport's spread during the twentieth century is remarkable. Sport occupies center stage in today's conceptions of "physical culture" to such an extent that we now find it difficult to grasp just how historically conditioned and narrowly framed it is.[3] The spectrum of options in the realm of physical recreation was far greater in the first half of the twentieth century than it was in the second half. Before World War II sport had powerful rivals: in Europe, workers' sport and gymnastics; in the rest of the world, traditional games and contests.

In the interwar years sport was subject to a sustained critique from the Left. Socialist theorists saw "capitalist sport" as a tool for the subjugation of workers, a senseless diversion invented by the ruling class to distract workers from their true interests. Sport, in this view, was not a genuine form of leisure but a replication of the conditions of work, a disciplinary regime that inculcated bourgeois norms of achievement-oriented action, respect for authority, and the specialized routines of factory work. Instead of "capitalist sport," the Left offered a different brand of physical culture: "workers' sport." Rejecting competition, the iconization of elite athletes, male dominance, and nationalist rivalries, workers' sport promoted instead collectivism, mass participation, gender equality, and international solidarity. Though strongest in Germany, workers' sport organizations existed in almost every country in Europe. The Socialist Workers' Sport International counted more than 2 million members at its high point and staged international festivals—in Vienna in 1931 and Antwerp in 1937—that drew not just a few thousand elite athletes but tens of thousands of participants and hundreds of thousands of spectators.[4]

When the Nazis came to power in Germany, they disbanded workers' sport organizations, just as they attempted to destroy the Left in general. In the rest of Europe, Nazi occupation or the rigors of war pushed workers' sport to the margins. Although there were postwar efforts to revive a workers' sport movement in Europe, its fortunes declined into insignificance. But even in the USSR, where the Soviet state generated its own brand of proletarian sport as part of its efforts to create a new socialist culture, workers' sport did not last. In the early 1930s the Soviet regime shifted its priorities away from the Red Sport International, a Comintern affiliate that promoted contacts between Soviet athletes and workers' sport groups in Europe, and toward an engagement with "bourgeois sport." Partly the turn was an acknowledgment that proletarian *fizicheskaia kultura*, with its mass displays and pageants, its message of service to state, and its disdain for individualism and record-seeking, never achieved popular appeal. Partly it was prompted by recognition that international competitions were now such an important venue for seeking internal and external legitimacy that they could not be ignored, especially when the regime was desperately trying to build an antifascist coalition to counter the German threat. In the Soviet Union, soccer triumphed over *fizkultura*. Mass physical culture displays of the kind showcased in the famed Red Square parades continued, but the resources of the state and the attention of the sport-minded public were directed primarily to a brand of sport that had only recently been condemned as an exploitative tool of capitalists. Soviet weakness would keep the country from full membership in the international "bourgeois sport" community until after the war, but the fundamental ideological rapprochement came in the mid-1930s.

The Nazis, who like the Soviets were deeply suspicious of international culture, also had an alternative to modern sport. Like the Czech Sokol and the Ling system in Sweden, German gymnastics sprang from a quite different philosophy of the body than did modern sport, and it was a specifically German, not a transnational, variety of patriotic physical exercise. *Turnen* showcased process rather than quantifiable results, posture rather than objectively measured achievements. A snapshot of the physical cultural landscape of the European continent around 1930 would reveal that sport and gymnastics, in their various national iterations, were equally powerful. But in the 1930s sport quickly co-opted gymnastics, turning it from a rival system into just another sport. Like the Soviets, the Nazis used mass gymnastics displays to great effect and continued to promote *Turnen* to inculcate collectivist ideals. But as was the case in the USSR, despite an ingrained hostility to cultural internationalism, Nazi Germany turned its focus to modern, competitive, international sport.

Why did the version of competitive sport enshrined in the Olympics and the World Cup win such a dramatic victory over its rivals in the interwar years? Certainly modern sport's popular appeal—the pull from below—explains much of its success. The competitive nature of sport and its inherent drama seem to make sport uniquely well suited as a means of entertainment in the modern age. But sport was not merely entertainment. It was also seized on as a way to express nationalism on an international stage. Governments and private groups in countries across the world used international sport as a medium for mediating between national identity and an emerging international society.

The international organizations that provided sport with its uniquely powerful institutional apparatus did much, especially in the interwar years, to establish sport as an international "regime," a form of "governance without government" in which actors recognize the legitimacy of and abide by widely accepted rules and norms.[5] Instead of establishing regional groupings or bringing together clubs or individuals athletes, the IOC, FIFA, and other international federations claimed global jurisdiction and argued for the universal relevance of sport. They claimed that sport transcended class, race, and religion (though not gender), but they enshrined national representation as the organizing principle for international competition and for representation in their own bodies. They established the rules that gave sports a degree of autonomy from local contexts, allowing them to be played the same way everywhere. They constructed the rites and symbols of the global sport community, and in their increasingly popular festivals they provided a physical locus for an "imagined world."

The Olympic Games of 1932 and 1936 provided the central referents for this imagined global community. In 1932 Los Angeles boosters transformed the Olympics from a stodgy European festival into an entertainment extravaganza with global appeal by harnessing the powers of advertising, public relations, and Hollywood's celebrity appeal. As with sport more broadly, Los Angeles Americanized the Olympics in much the same way that mass culture and consumerism were being Americanized in this period.

In organizational scale, the 1936 Berlin Olympics went much further. The Nazi state spent lavishly, with a largesse that the Los Angeles organizers, even with the financial backing of city and state governments, never came close to achieving. In California the Games were locally run; in Germany the Games were an affair of state, accorded national importance and overseen by dozens of national and local agencies. From the hiring of interpreters to the expansion of postal services, German organizational efficiency was everywhere in evidence during the Berlin Games. But aside from enlarging the scale of the Games and adding the highly significant torch relay from Olympia to the host city, the 1936 Olympics largely repeated what had made the 1932 Games a new kind of Olympics.

Although the world's participation in Berlin—with the exception of boycotts by a few individual athletes—despite the Nazi regime's viciously discriminatory policies was itself an odious example of appeasement, the stark contradiction between Olympic ideals and Nazi repression did lead to an unprecedented intervention in the affairs of the host nation. No one on the IOC would have dreamed of demanding that the United States ensure that African Americans qualify for the U.S. team in 1932—at a time when blacks, especially in the South, suffered from severe legal and extralegal oppression. But under pressure from outside groups, the IOC did demand, despite the anti-Semitic and profascist leanings of many of its top leaders, that the Nazis include Jews on the German Olympic team.[6]

With all the zeal of a dictatorship intent on presenting a false face to the world, the Nazis arguably proved to be better hosts than their U.S. predecessors. In 1932 first-class restaurants in Los Angeles turned away Japanese Olympians with the sign "No Mexicans Allowed"; Louise Stokes and Tidye Pickett, African American Olympians traveling with white teammates to Los Angeles, were refused service at a Denver hotel. In Berlin, blacks and foreign Jews were generally treated with courtesy, and the Nazis turned a blind eye to the homosexual behavior of foreign guests that would otherwise have been subject to criminal prosecution.[7] The Nazi hierarchy also found that it could not stage the Games on its own terms in many less obvious ways. Everything from the watches used in the races to the protocol of the opening ceremony to the length of the track was determined by international bodies. Hitler could bedeck Berlin in swastikas, but the form and content of the sports events were determined from outside. Blacks and Jews won races on "Aryan"—now Olympian—fields. Hitler's determination in the years after the Games to build his own international sport order, one where he could determine the size of the track and the race of the competitors, is in part a testament to the constraints that the international sport system succeeded in imposing on the Nazi regime.[8]

Had Germany won the war, Hitler would have created an "Aryanized," exclusionary sport system subordinated to German interests, and the international sport system would have looked far different than it did in the 1930s. It is apparent, then, that the sport internationalism that existed in the interwar years, run primarily by men in Western democracies, was dependent on a system of international politics undergirded by a liberal capitalist world order.[9] And indeed the international sport system in many ways mirrored the international political system and the emergent world polity. The sport community of the interwar years had much in common with the League of Nations and drew on many of the same currents of thought that had given rise to the League. Dedicated to safeguarding international order, the League was an association of independent states that was considered to represent more than the sum of its members, namely, the human community.[10] Both the world of sport and the League, however, fell short of encompassing all of humanity. The League, for example, was neither universal nor democratic. Its initial membership of forty-two states conspicuously excluded colonies, the defeated Central Powers, the Soviet Union, and Mexico. The United States, the country that provided the main inspiration for its founding, refused to join. The League's structure gave power to a council dominated by the Great Powers; smaller countries in the assembly had a voice without real authority. So, too, were international sport organizations dominated by wealthy white European men and run according to Western principles. Yet just as the principle of national self-determination would help to undermine European empires, so, too, would the idea that sport offered a universal platform for representation provide opportunities for peoples in other parts of the world to claim international power and legitimacy.

The appeal of international sport proved greater than the appeal of world community in other forms. Germany and Japan withdrew from the League, the United States never joined, and the Soviet Union came only late, but all were eager to be members of the new global athletic club. The symbols and events of the international sport world were arguably more recognizable to and resonated more deeply with much of the world's population than the League's. And the international sport community had greater capacity in its own sphere to breach the rigid walls of national sovereignty with its dictates.

Like the League, the globalizing sport culture of the 1930s did not prevent nations from engaging in a bloody and immensely destructive global conflict. On the one hand, sport in this period was deeply intertwined with military training, and governments often promoted sport as a way to increase national strength, whether for offensive or defensive purposes. As the approach of war became ever more apparent, international sport competitions took on a distinctly militarist flavor, and athletes became increasingly indistinguishable from soldiers. For many governments the men who tossed javelins and sprinted down cinder tracks were in effect soldiers in a different kind of uniform.[11] The jockeying for points on the green "battlefields" of stadiums was partly a tool for accruing forms of power (stronger alliances, friendlier neighbors) that might translate into victories on real battlefields. In this sense the spread of sport fed into the currents leading toward war.

On the other hand, by furthering contacts among sporting publics and accustoming government officials and civic leaders to working within the constraints of common international norms, sport arguably represented a countercurrent to the decade's rising levels of conflict and aggression.[12] It was a countercurrent that had no significant impact on the trajectory of political events in the interwar years, but in the long term its influences on the global community have been profound. The system fashioned in the 1930s laid the foundation for the extraordinary flowering of international sport after World War II, when membership in the international sport community became a *sina qua non* of nationhood, more so than membership in any other type of international organization except the United Nations. Nor were the immediate effects of the international sport system in the 1930s insignificant, despite being swamped by nationalist excesses at the end of the decade. By displacing workers' sport and traditional gymnastics, modern sport became the predominant form of physical recreation in Europe, where its preeminence in turn helped further its rise in popularity in Latin America, Asia, and elsewhere.

The internationalization of sport shows elements of both commonality and difference with the broader explosion of transnational mass culture in the years after World War I. The new mass culture, in its commercial and consumerist guise, was produced primarily in the United States and was closely identified with Americanism and its dual valences: epitomizing modernity and progress and, at the same time, embodying the empty-minded conformity many critics saw as the essence of "lowbrow" culture. Sport, however, was not controlled or produced in a single country. Modern sport as a general mode of physical recreation and training (as well as many specific sports) originated in Britain, and when it initially spread beyond Britain's borders it was often disdained as an alien import. Though marked by its British roots, sport became transnationalized with relative speed, in part because Europeans seized the initiative from an indifferent British in forming international organizations to promote and oversee the global expansion of sport. The result was that most sports came to be identified not so much as products of a foreign culture but as transnational forms adapted to national circumstances and invested with individual meaning in each country. As a result of this nationalization of international culture, each nation could claim that its participation in any international contest, though outwardly conforming to the same rules and conditions as every other nation's, was nevertheless fundamentally an expression of intrinsically national characteristics.[13]

Though dissociated relatively quickly from the taint of foreign cultural origin, sport nevertheless posed challenges to sovereignty similar to those represented by U.S. mass culture. In some respects sport could be indigenized more readily than Hollywood films, but it was not infinitely malleable. Like U.S. mass culture, sport could be subversive of state efforts to shape culture in conformity with tradition or political ideology. The transnational influences on elite sport were particularly powerful, affecting even countries as isolationist as the Soviet Union, as major stars developed cross-national reputations and followings, top players were traded across borders, expertise and innovations diffused freely, and the best teams and athletes ranked their achievements by international standards. Sport had very different meanings depending on its cultural and political surroundings, but oversight of international sport by a network of international organizations that exercised increasingly tight control over rules, eligibility, certification of records, and world championships placed limits on the extent to which sport could be molded to support nationalist ends. As a form of culture steeped in an ethos of individualism, competition, and achievement, sport also promoted new consumption patterns and cultural habits not always consonant with broader state goals. Everywhere, sport publics had increasingly international horizons. Manipulation of the international sport system for nationalist ends came at the price of opening national cultures to internationalist values and influences.

The case of sport highlights the reciprocal relationship between nationalism and internationalism, particularism and globalism: these are two sides of the same coin, not contradictory processes.[14] Nations joined the global sport system in part as a way to promote nationalist objectives, such as supporting foreign policy goals and demonstrating national strength. Thus, the existence of a competitive international sport system furthered expressions of nationalism. Yet if internationalism drove nationalism, nationalism reciprocally promoted internationalism. International competition served nationalist goals most effectively if the international system was truly so uniform and universalist that it appeared to offer a uniquely objective and quantifiable means of measuring national strength. A powerful and rigid system thus paradoxically furthered the aim of using international competition to facilitate comparisons among nations. Even as they engaged in the same forms of competition, then, Americans, Germans, and Soviets could claim sport as representative of unique national characteristics, and even as they used sport to "prove" national superiority, they were drawn into a web of transnational connections and influences.

The expansion of international sport in the 1930s suggests the importance of international sources and structures in the construction and maintenance of nation-states and national identity. Theorists of nationalism situate the process by which nations came to be "imagined" in a world of multiple nationalisms that influenced each other, in particular by using others as models or antagonists.[15] And they acknowledge that national consciousness, at least in Europe, arose in the context of an international society.[16] But theorists have looked at nationalism primarily as a phenomenon created from the inside. As some social scientists have noted, however, the external environment—the international community in general and global institutions in particular—also shapes nationalism. The transnational cultural environment has influenced many features of nation-states, shaping structures and policies and leading to an accommodation with values and beliefs that have become institutionalized in the world community.[17] The importing of modern sports, their cultivation and promotion, participation in international sports competitions, and membership in global bodies that dictate the conditions of that participation: all are part of a process whereby international structures and activities had dramatic effects on the shape and content of national identities.

International sport also shaped the broader outlines of internationalism in the twentieth century. As Benedict Anderson has argued, the modern conception of time as homogeneous and empty provided the basis for the birth of the imagined community of the nation. The creation of a sense of community among disparate individuals was made possible by a sense of the simultaneous existence of others within the community.[18] In similar fashion the spread of modern sport has disseminated a sense of homogeneous, empty time around the globe, and participation in international sports contests has linked people all over the world to a uniform clock and calendar. Every four years the world participates in the Olympics. The results of every contest, measured and quantified, are available instantaneously not just as the patrimony of the contestants but as part of the record of human achievement. The Olympic flag, the victory ceremony, and the passing of the World Cup trophy from one country to another are all symbols of an international community, global analogs to national flags, anthems, parades, and rituals. Rulebooks, referees, and training regimens provide a common language for the world of sport; records and the feats of international stars provide a common history, even if that history is told differently in different places. Race, class, religion, and nation are today no less salient markers of identity than in the past—they still motivate people to kill each other—but these identities coexist, to varying degrees, with a sense of global citizenship that has been shaped to a large degree by international sport.

Abbreviations Used in the Notes

1894–1994	*1894–1994, The International Olympic Committee: One Hundred Years. The Idea, the Presidents, the Achievements,* 3 vols. (Lausanne: International Olympic Committee, 1994)
ABC	Avery Brundage Collection, Archives of the University of Illinois, Champaign-Urbana
FIFA	Archives of the Fédération internationale de football association, Zurich, Switzerland
GARF	Gosudarstvennyi arkhiv Rossiisskoi Federatsii, Moscow, Russia
HAA-WB	Harvard Athletic Association, Records of William J. Bingham, Director of Athletics, Harvard University Archives, Cambridge, Massachusetts
IJHS	*International Journal of the History of Sport*
IOC	Archives of the International Olympic Committee, Lausanne, Switzerland
LAT	*Los Angeles Times*
NYT	*New York Times*
OR 1932	Xth Olympiade Committee of the Games of Los Angeles, *The Games of the Xth Olympiad, Los Angeles, 1932: Official Report* (Los Angeles: Xth Olympiade Committee, 1933)
OR 1936	Organisationskomitee für die XI. Olympiade Berlin 1936 e. V., *The XIth Olympic Games, Berlin, 1936: Official Report* (Berlin: Wilhem Limpert, 1937)
PAdAA	Politisches Archiv des Aswärtigen Amts, Berlin, Germany

RGASPI   Rossiiskii gosudarstvennyi arkhiv sotsial'no-politicheskoi istorii, Moscow, Russia

SDDF   State Department Decimal Files, U.S. National Archives, College Park, Maryland

USOC   U.S. Olympic Committee Archives, Colorado Springs, Colorado

Notes

Introduction

The quotation in the epigraph is from Ali Mazrui, *A World Federation of Cultures: An African Perspective* (New York: Free Press, 1976), 411.

1. "An International Sovereignty Created" [1936], ABC, Box 233, Clarence Bush folder.

2. To use Anthony Giddens's terms, stadia became spaces separated from places, modern "locales" whose nature was determined by "distanciated relations." Anthony Giddens, *The Consequences of Modernity* (Stanford, Calif.: Stanford University Press, 1990), 19. John Bale has also argued that "the globally enforced rules of sport," particularly with regard to standardized spatial and environmental forms, "encourage sameness, homogenisation and placelessness to an extent not so commonly found in such global common denominators as tourism, leisure or work." He argues that sports can "eliminate regional differences as a result of their rule-bound, ordered, enclosed and predictably segmented forms of landscape." Bale, *Landscapes of Modern Sport* (Leicester, England: Leicester University Press, 1994), 8, 2.

3. Benedict Anderson, *Imagined Communities* (London: Verso, 1983). Arjun Appadurai has suggested that the landscapes of global cultural flows can be seen as "imagined worlds." "Disjuncture and Difference in the Global Cultural Economy," *Theory, Culture and Society* 7 (1990): 296–297.

4. On modern perceptions of time and space see Giddens, *Consequences of Modernity*, 21, 64, and the discussion of Giddens in John Tomlinson, *Globalization and Culture* (Chicago: University of Chicago Press, 1999), 47–58.

5. Some scholars object to the term "global culture" as an oxymoron. For an argument about the value of distinguishing between culture—necessarily unique, local, and parochial (and thus never global)—and ideology (the actual vehicle of global cultural transformation), see Frank Ninkovich,

"Culture, Power, and Civilization: The Place of Culture in the Study of International Relations," in *On Cultural Ground: Essays in International History,* ed. Robert David Johnson (Chicago: Imprint, 1994), 11–15.

6. Michael Geyer, "The Militarization of Europe, 1914–1945," in *The Militarization of the Western World,* ed. John R. Gillis (New Brunswick, N.J.: Rutgers University Press, 1989), 77.

7. In the influential book *Homo ludens* (1938; repr., London: Routledge, 1949), the Dutch cultural historian Johan Huizinga argued that play is the essential experimental and creative force in human development. For a philosophic inquiry into the nature of play and the definition of sport (inspired in part by Huizinga), see Roger Callois, *Man, Play and Games* (New York: Free Press, 1961).

8. Henning Eichberg's works presented the earliest comprehensive argument for sport as a unique adaptation of modern society, first in *Der Weg des Sports in die industrielle Zivilisation* (Baden-Baden: Nomos, 1973) and more fully in *Leistung, Spannung, Geschwindigkeit: Sport und Tanz im gesellschaftlichen Wandel des 18./19. Jahrhunderts* (Stuttgart: Klett-Cotta, 1978). For summaries of his major ideas, see Henning Eichberg, "Stronger, Funnier, Deadlier: Track and Field in the Way to the Ritual of the Record," in *Ritual and Record: Sports Records and Quantification in Pre-Modern Societies,* ed. John Marshall Carter and Arnd Krüger (New York: Greenwood Press, 1990), 129–131, and Eichberg's essays, especially "Olympic Sport: Neo-Colonialism and Alternatives" and "The Societal Construction of Time and Space as Sociology's Way Home to Philosophy: Sport as Paradigm," in Eichberg, *Body Cultures: Essays on Sport, Space and Identity,* ed. John Bale and Chris Philo (London: Routledge, 1998). The latter collection includes a useful overview of his ideas and influence by Susan Brownell: "Thinking Dangerously: The Person and His Ideas," 22–44. See also Allen Guttmann's influential survey of modern sport, *From Ritual to Record: The Nature of Modern Sports* (New York: Columbia University Press, 1978), and Norbert Elias and Eric Dunning, *Quest for Excitement: Sport and Leisure in the Civilizing Process* (New York: Basil Blackwell, 1986). On the standardization of sport space, see Bale, *Landscapes,* especially 100–119.

9. For example, rule-making bodies made efforts to control for variation in weather by disallowing records set under certain wind conditions. Bale, *Landscapes,* 45.

10. The rationalization process is perhaps best illustrated by the evolution of high-jump techniques, with each innovation producing better performances: the scissors (1876), the modified scissors (1880), Sweeney's Eastern style (1895), the Eastern cut-off and the Western roll (1912), the straddle (1936), and the Fosbury flop (1968). Eichberg, "Stronger, Fun-

nier, Deadlier," 130. On the history of the scientization of athletic training, see John M. Hoberman, *Mortal Engines: The Science of Performance
and the Dehumanization of Sport* (New York: Free Press/Macmillan, 1992).

11. On "sportization" (the transformation of traditional games and contests
into modern sports) in non-Western societies, see G. Cameron Hurst III,
Armed Martial Arts of Japan: Swordsmanship and Archery (New Haven,
Conn.: Yale University Press, 1998), 147–176, which emphasizes the substantial contact with Western athletic ideas that prompted the transformation. Susan Brownell offers an insightful personal and anthropological
perspective on sport in China in *Training the Body for China: Sports in the
Moral Order of the People's Republic* (Chicago: University of Chicago Press,
1995). A pioneering sociological study of soccer in Brazil is Janet Lever's
Soccer Madness (Chicago: University of Chicago Press, 1983). C. L. R.
James's memoir about cricket in the West Indies, *Beyond a Boundary* (1963;
repr., New York: Pantheon, 1983), is a classic study of sport diffusion.

12. International Olympic Committee, "The Games of the Olympiad: Facts
and Figures," at www.olympic.org/uk/news/media_centre/press_release
_uk.asp?id=1363; and "Highlights of the Week, 11 October 2004,"
at www.olympic.org/uk/news/olympic_news/week_uk.asp?weekDate=10/
11/2004 (accessed July 2005).

13. See Barrie Houlihan, *Sport and International Politics* (New York: Harvester
Wheatsheaf, 1994).

14. See Pico Iyer, *The Global Soul: Jet Lag, Shopping Malls, and the Search for
Home* (New York: Knopf, 2000), 173–231; David Rowe, *Sport, Culture and
the Media: The Unruly Trinity* (Buckingham, England: Open University
Press, 1999); and Walter LaFeber, *Michael Jordan and the New Global Capitalism* (New York: W. W. Norton, 1999).

15. Lever, *Soccer Madness,* 1–5; Eugen Weber, "Pierre de Coubertin and the
Introduction of Organised Sport in France," *Journal of Contemporary History* 5, no. 2 (1970): 6.

16. For one recent example see Terry Eagleton, *The Idea of Culture* (Oxford,
England: Blackwell, 2000), 70.

17. Arjun Appadurai, *Modernity at Large: Cultural Dimensions of Globalization*
(Minneapolis: University of Minnesota Press, 1996), 90. Appadurai is referring only to cricket but suggests that all rule-governed sport has some
of this hard quality.

18. Mark Johnson, *The Body in the Mind: The Bodily Basis of Meaning, Imagination, and Reason* (Chicago: University of Chicago Press, 1987), xix. For an
overview of the body as a carrier of social values, see Mike Featherstone,
Mike Hepworth, and Bryan S. Turner, eds., *The Body: Social Process and Cultural Theory* (London: Sage, 1991), and Catherine Gallagher and Thomas

Laqueur, eds., *The Making of the Modern Body: Sexuality and Society in the Nineteenth Century* (Berkeley: University of California Press, 1987), vii.

19. Jacques Ellul, *The Technological Society,* trans. John Wilkinson (New York: Knopf, 1965), 383–384.

20. John Tomlinson provides useful overviews of these debates in *Cultural Imperialism: A Critical Introduction* (London: Pinter, 1991) and *Globalization and Culture.* (He ultimately stresses adaptation more than transformation.) Also useful in exploring the cultural side of globalization are Appadurai, *Modernity at Large;* Jonathan Friedman, *Cultural Identity and Global Process* (London: Sage, 1994); and Roland Robertson, *Globalization: Social Theory and Global Culture* (Newbury Park, Calif.: Sage, 1992). A critique of the concept of cultural imperialism is provided in Jessica C. E. Gienow-Hecht, "Shame on US? Academics, Cultural Transfer, and the Cold War—A Critical Review," *Diplomatic History* 24, no. 3 (Summer 2000): 465–494. Notable works on U.S. cultural influence abroad include Reinhold Wagnleitner, *Coca-Colonization and the Cold War: The Cultural Mission of the United States in Austria after the Second World War,* trans. Diana Wolf (Chapel Hill: University of North Carolina Press, 1994), and Richard Kuisel, *Seducing the French: The Dilemmas of Americanization* (Berkeley: University of California Press, 1993).

21. For one such argument, see Richard Pells, *How Europeans Have Loved, Hated, and Transformed American Culture Since World War II* (New York: Basic Books, 1997), especially xiv–xv.

22. On the international diffusion of sport, a general overview is provided in Allen Guttmann, *Games and Empires: Modern Sports and Cultural Imperialism* (New York: Columbia University Press, 1994). Joseph Maguire provides a more contemporary, sociological analysis in *Global Sport: Identities, Societies, Civilizations* (Cambridge: Polity Press, 1999). Important perspectives on the Olympics are provided in John Hoberman, "Toward a Theory of Olympic Internationalism," *Journal of Sport History* 22, no. 1 (Spring 1995): 1–37, and Eichberg, "Olympic Sport."

23. In recent years many historians have called for new approaches that move beyond the nation-state as the locus of inquiry. History as a professional discipline developed concurrently with the rise of the nation-state in the nineteenth century, and since then history has used the nation-state as its central organizing narrative. The assumption of the centrality of the nation-state, however, has come under question in a globalizing age. See David Thelen, "The Nation and Beyond: Transnational Perspectives on United States History," *Journal of American History* 86, no. 3 (December 1999): 965–975; Akira Iriye, "The Internationalization of History," *American Historical Re-*

view 94, no. 1 (February 1989): 1–20; Michael Geyer and Charles Bright, "World History in a Global Age," *American Historical Review* 100, no. 4 (October 1995): 1034–1060; Ian Tyrrell, "American Exceptionalism in an Age of International History," *American Historical Review* 96, no. 4 (October 1991): 1031–1072; and Eric Foner, "American Freedom in a Global Age," *American Historical Review* 106, no. 1 (February 2001): 1–16. In his study of transatlantic social-reform networks, Daniel Rodgers notes that the boundaries of the nation-state can become an analytical cage, producing histories "lopped off at precisely those junctures where the nation-state's permeability might be brought into view." *Atlantic Crossings: Social Politics in a Progressive Age* (Cambridge, Mass.: Harvard University Press, 1998), 2.

24. To cite just a handful of examples on these topics, see Kristin Hoganson, *Fighting for American Manhood: How Gender Politics Provoked the Spanish-American and Philippine-American Wars* (New Haven, Conn.: Yale University Press, 1998); Michael Hunt, *Ideology and U.S. Foreign Policy* (New Haven, Conn.: Yale University Press, 1987); Chris Endy, *Cold War Holidays: American Tourism in France* (Chapel Hill: University of North Carolina Press, 2004); and Jane Hunter, *Gospel of Gentility: American Women Missionaries in Turn-of-the Century China* (New Haven, Conn.: Yale University Press, 1984).

25. Exceptions that examine the use of sport as a tool of diplomacy include Peter Beck, *Scoring for Britain: International Football and International Politics, 1900–1939* (London: Frank Cass, 1999); Pierre Arnaud and James Riordan, eds., *Sport and International Politics: The Impact of Fascism and Communism on Sport* (London: Routledge, 1998); Pierre Arnaud and Alfred Wahl, eds., *Sports et relations internationals* (Metz: Centre de Recherche "Histoire et Civilisation de l'Europe Occidentale," 1994); and Hans Joachim Teichler, *Internationale Sportpolitik im Dritten Reich* (Schorndorf: Karl Hofmann, 1991). A useful overview from a political-science perspective of the various uses of sport in foreign policy is provided in Houlihan, *Sport and International Politics*.

26. On the role of international nongovernmental organizations in international affairs, see Akira Iriye, *Global Community: The Role of International Organizations in the Making of the Contemporary World* (Berkeley: University of California Press, 2002), and John Boli and George M. Thomas, *Constructing World Culture: International Nongovernmental Organizations since 1875* (Stanford, Calif.: Stanford University Press, 1999).

27. Japan relinquished the 1940 Games in July 1938 as the militarist government focused on war.

28. The history of the American YMCA's involvement in physical education is covered in the celebratory work by Elmer L. Johnson, *The History of YMCA Physical Education* (Chicago: Follett Publishing/Association Press, 1979).

29. On gender and sport, see, for example, Michael A. Messner and Donald F. Sabo, eds., *Sport, Men, and the Gender Order* (Champaign, Ill.: Human Kinetics, 1990), and Susan Birrell and Cheryl L. Cole, eds., *Women, Sport, and Culture* (Champaign, Ill.: Human Kinetics, 1994). On the tight strictures surrounding female athleticism in fascist Italy, see Victoria de Grazia, *How Fascism Ruled Women: Italy, 1922–1945* (Berkeley: University of California Press, 1992), 218–221; on France, see Mary Lynn Stewart, *For Health and Beauty: Physical Culture for Frenchwomen, 1880s–1930s* (Baltimore, Md.: Johns Hopkins University Press, 2001).

1. Sport, the State, and International Politics

1. British Board of Education, 1936 circular decree on "Health and Physical Education in English Schools," no. 1445, quoted in Hajo Bernett, "National Socialist Physical Education as Reflected in British Appeasement Policy," *IJHS* 5, no. 2 (September 1988): 171.

2. John J. MacAloon, "The Turn of Two Centuries: Sport and the Politics of Intercultural Relations," in *Sport . . . The Third Millennium: Proceedings of the International Symposium,* ed. Fernand Landry, Marc Landry, and Magdaleine Yerles (Sainte-Foy: Les Presses de l'Université Laval, 1991), 42.

3. Recounted in Pierre de Coubertin, *Olympic Memoirs* (Lausanne: International Olympic Committee, 1989), 11; emphasis in the original.

4. 1894 speech in Pierre de Coubertin, *The Olympic Idea: Discourses and Essays,* ed. Carl-Diem-Institut an der Deutschen Sporthochschule Köln, trans. John Dixon (Schorndorf bei Stuttgart: Karl Hofmann, 1967), 8.

5. Michael Budd, *The Sculpture Machine: Physical Culture and Body Culture in the Age of Empire* (London: Macmillan, 1997), 42–44; David L. Chapman, *Sandow the Magnificent: Eugen Sandow and the Beginnings of Bodybuilding* (Urbana: University of Illinois Press, 1994).

6. On fears of degeneration in France, see Robert A. Nye, "Degeneration, Neurasthenia and the Culture of Sport in *Belle Epoque* France," *Journal of Contemporary History* 17 (1982): 51–68. For similar views in the United States, see Hoganson, *Fighting for American Manhood,* 34–36, 138–148. On health and public hygiene in the nineteenth century, see Deborah Lupton, *The Imperative of Health: Public Health and the Regulated Body* (London: Sage, 1995).

7. Bruce Haley, *The Healthy Body and Victorian Culture* (Cambridge, Mass.: Harvard University Press, 1978), 124, 133, 140.

8. Quoted in Harvey Green, *Fit for America: Health, Fitness, Sport, and American Society* (New York: Pantheon, 1986), 183.

9. Speech by Coubertin at the Paris Congress, 1894, in Coubertin, *Olympic Idea*, 6–7. As John MacAloon notes, this idea is "a rebellion from the main lines of Western cultural tradition," which insisted on a fundamental separation of mind and body. MacAloon, *This Great Symbol: Pierre de Coubertin and the Origins of the Modern Olympic Games* (Chicago: University of Chicago Press, 1981), 175.

10. See J. A. Mangan, *Athleticism in the Victorian and Edwardian Public School: The Emergence and Consolidation of an Educational Ideology* (Cambridge: Cambridge University Press, 1981), 16–18. The book, first printed in a French edition in 1875, was an important influence on Coubertin. For a thorough explication of the influence of the Rugby model on Coubertin, see MacAloon, *This Great Symbol*, 43–82.

11. Quoted in Richard Holt, *Sport and the British: A Modern History* (Oxford: Oxford University Press, 1989), 76. The famous remark that "the battle of Waterloo was won on the playing-fields of Eton" was attributed to the Duke of Wellington as early as 1856. Though apocryphal, it was widely accepted as true. Haley, *Healthy Body*, 170.

12. Quoted in Peter Gay, *The Bourgeois Experience from Victoria to Freud*, vol. 3, *The Cultivation of Hatred* (New York: W. W. Norton, 1993), 430.

13. Holt, *Sport and the British*, 98–117. Haley notes that although sport can encourage a meritocracy based on strength, agility, and tenacity, it was also considered a possession or attainment and therefore proof of social position. It thus played "a considerable role in maintaining social distinctions." Haley, *Healthy Body*, 208–210.

14. Mark Dyreson, "Regulating the Body and the Body Politic: American Sport, Bourgeois Culture, and the Language of Progress, 1880–1920," in *The New American Sport History: Recent Approaches and Perspectives*, ed. S. W. Pope (Urbana: University of Illinois Press, 1997), 122–123; Mark Dyreson, *Making the American Team: Sport, Culture, and the Olympic Experience* (Urbana: University of Illinois Press, 1998). According to Dyreson, this ideology was reshaped in the 1920s by a new ethic of consumption and entertainment; Mark Dyreson, "The Emergence of Consumer Culture and the Transformation of Physical Culture: American Sport in the 1920s," *Journal of Sport History* 16, no. 3 (Winter 1989): 261. On U.S. sport in the Progressive Era see also Stephen W. Pope, *Patriotic Pastimes: Sporting Traditions in the American Imagination, 1876–1926* (New York: Oxford University Press, 1997); Kathryn Grover, ed., *Fitness in American Culture: Images of Health, Sport, and the Body, 1830–1940* (Amherst: University of Massachusetts Press, 1989); and Dominick Cavallo, *Muscles and*

Morals: Organized Playgrounds and Urban Reform, 1880–1920 (Philadelphia: University of Pennsylvania Press, 1981).

15. Nye, "Degeneration," 51. For more on German gymnastics, see Chapter 4.

16. Robert Mechikoff and Steven Estes, *A History and Philosophy of Sport and Physical Education: From the Ancient Greeks to the Present* (Madison, Wisc.: Brown & Benchmark, 1993), 155.

17. Nye, "Degeneration," 51.

18. Ibid., 52–61; and Robert A. Nye, *Crime, Madness, and Politics in Modern France: The Medical Concept of National Decline* (Princeton, N.J.: Princeton University Press, 1984), 324–328; Eugen Weber, "Gymnastics and Sport in *Fin-de-Siècle* France: Opium of the Classes?" *American Historical Review* 76, no. 1 (February 1971): 70–98.

19. Jean-Michel Faure, "Forging a French Fighting Spirit: The Nation, Sport, Violence and War," in *Tribal Identities: Nationalism, Europe, Sport,* ed. J. A. Mangan (London: Frank Cass, 1996), 79.

20. Quotations in Haley, *Healthy Body,* 171, 221.

21. See Christiane Eisenberg, ed., *Fußball, soccer, calcio: Ein englischer Sport auf seinem Weg um die Welt* (Munich: Deutscher Taschenbuch, 1997); Guttmann, *Games and Empires;* Weber, "Gymnastics and Sport," 84–85.

22. Elliot J. Gorn and Warren Goldstein, *A Brief History of American Sports* (New York: Hill & Wang, 1993), 179; Guy Lewis, "World War I and the Emergence of Sport for the Masses," *Maryland Historian* 4 (Fall 1973): 109–122.

23. For the Italian case see David Horn, *Social Bodies: Science, Reproduction, and Italian Modernity* (Princeton, N.J.: Princeton University Press, 1994).

24. Pierre Arnaud, "French Sport and Authoritarian Regimes, 1919–1939," in Arnaud and Riordan, *Sport and International Politics,* 117.

25. Eric Hobsbawm, "Mass-Producing Traditions: Europe, 1870–1914," in *The Invention of Tradition,* ed. Eric Hobsbawm and Terence Ranger (Cambridge: Cambridge University Press, 1983), 288–291, 298–302, 306.

26. The literature on sport and nationalism is substantial. One useful overview for soccer is provided in Vic Duke and Liz Crolley, *Football, Nationality, and the State* (Harlow: Addison Wesley Longman, 1996).

27. Quoted in Cyrus Schayegh, "Sport, Health, and the Iranian Middle Class in the 1920s and 1930s," *Iranian Studies* 35, no. 4 (Fall 2002): 359.

28. Quoted in Andrew Morris, *Marrow of the Nation: A History of Sport and Physical Culture in Republican China* (Berkeley: University of California Press, 2004), 167.

29. Schayegh, "Sport, Health, and the Iranian Middle Class," 344–347, 362; H. E. Chelabi, "The Juggernaut of Globalization: Sport and Modernization in Iran," in *Sport in Asian Society, Past and Present,* ed. J. A. Mangan and Fan Hong (London: Frank Cass, 2003), 279, 287.

30. Donald Roden, "Baseball and the Quest for National Dignity in Meiji Japan," *American Historical Review* 85, no. 3 (June 1980): 511–534.

31. Avery Brundage, "For Honor of Country and Glory of Sport," *Olympic News,* August 1934, 3f, ABC, Box 42.

32. Sandra S. Collins, "Orienting the Olympics: Japan and the Games of 1940" (Ph.D. diss., University of Chicago, 2003), 25–27; Tosheo Saeki, "Sport in Japan," in *Sport in Asia and Africa: A Comparative Handbook,* ed. Eric A. Wagner (New York: Greenwood Press, 1989), 54–55.

33. Morris, *Marrow of the Nation,* 3–15, 99, 140; quotations on 9, 15, 171. In the 1930s a debate erupted between traditionalists and Westernizers. Those in the first camp urged that traditional Chinese martial arts should be the basis of a national revival. As one writer argued, "We should not just copy Western sport. Modern sport is just entertainment." Defenders of Western sport countered that "there are no national boundaries in culture, let alone in physical education." In the end a combination of modernized martial arts and modern sport became the dominant model. Fan Hong and Tan Hua, "Sport in China: Conflict between Tradition and Modernity, 1840s to 1930s," in Mangan and Hong, *Sport in Asian Society,* 203–207.

34. George Godia, "Sport in Kenya," in Wagner, *Sport in Asia and Africa,* 269.

35. Pierre Arnaud, "Sport and International Relations before 1918," in Arnaud and Riordan, *Sport and International Politics,* 21; *1894–1994,* 1:27; Jules Rimet/Encyclopédie des Sports Modernes, eds., *Le Football* (Monaco: Union Européenne d'Éditions, 1954), 2:82; MacAloon, *This Great Symbol,* 161.

36. MacAloon, *This Great Symbol,* 120–122.

37. *1894–1994,* 1:49, 57; MacAloon, *This Great Symbol,* 161.

38. Arnaud, "Sport and International Relations," 22–23. Within Great Britain, "national" teams representing Scotland, England, Wales, and Ireland were fielded against one another beginning in the nineteenth century.

39. Budd, *Sculpture Machine,* x. Budd also suggests that "the physical body's commodification as an object of social reform was significantly linked to the depiction of the globe as an understandable totality . . . More elaborate international communication linkages allowed nations to be defined and compared as if they were physical bodies . . . In a sense, bodily metaphors helped make the unification of the globe possible at an ideological and conceptual level." Ibid., 121.

40. Coubertin, *Olympic Idea,* 10.

41. Quoted in MacAloon, *This Great Symbol,* 125. On Coubertin's English inspiration see also ibid., 51, 80–81, and Weber, "Gymnastics and Sports," 73. On Coubertin's life and thought see also Thomas Alkemeyer, *Körper,*

Kult und Politik: Von der "Muskelreligion" Pierre de Coubertins zur Insze-nierung von Macht in den Olympischen Spiele von 1936 (Frankfurt: Campus, 1996).

42. MacAloon, *This Great Symbol,* 108–109.
43. Thomas Alkemeyer suggests that Coubertin preferred sport to gymnastics because he saw the former as structurally homologous with modernity. Coubertin associated gymnastics with the old order, with compulsion and stasis, whereas sport developed initiative, dynamism, self-reliance, and mobility. Alkemeyer, "Sport, die Sorge um den Körper und die Suche nach Erlebnissen im Kontext gesellschaftlicher Modernisierung," in *Modernisierung und Sport,* ed. Jochen Hinsching and Frederik Borkenhagen (Sankt Augustin: Academia, 1995), 37–38.
44. Pierre de Coubertin, *Textes choisis,* ed. Norbert Müller (Zurich: Weidmann, 1986), 2:115.
45. MacAloon, *This Great Symbol,* 125.
46. Ibid., 127–128; *1894–1994,* 1:80–82, 97; Coubertin, *Olympic Memoirs,* 9–10.
47. Coubertin visited one such festival at Wenlock in Shropshire in 1889. MacAloon, *This Great Symbol,* 147; *1894–1994,* 1:36–40.
48. Pierre de Coubertin, *Olympism: Selected Writings,* ed. Norbert Müller (Lausanne: International Olympic Committee, 2000), 350.
49. MacAloon, *This Great Symbol,* 128–145, 160.
50. Coubertin, *Textes choisis,* 2:115–116. See also MacAloon, *This Great Symbol,* 163.
51. Coubertin, *Olympic Memoirs,* 8, 11; 1894 Circular, reproduced in Norbert Müller, *One Hundred Years of Olympic Congresses, 1894–1994: History, Objectives, Achievements,* trans. Ingrid Sonnleitner-Hauber (Lausanne: International Olympic Committee, 1994), 27.
52. Coubertin, *Olympic Idea,* 2–3.
53. Müller, *One Hundred Years,* 29. There were in addition fifty honorary members—kings, ministers, ambassadors, and other notables, most of whom were not directly involved in the congress.
54. Coubertin, *Olympic Memoirs,* 39.
55. Coubertin, *Olympic Idea,* 27.
56. In 1931, for example, Coubertin defended himself against accusations that the Olympic Games favored sport over gymnastics. Ibid., 119–122.
57. Ibid., 129.
58. In his 1931 memoirs Coubertin wrote: "Today I can admit it; the question [of amateurism] never really bothered me . . . Realising the importance attached to it in sports circles, I always showed the necessary enthusiasm, but it was an enthusiasm without real conviction. My own conception of sport has always been . . . [that] sport was a religion . . . and it seemed to

me as childish to make all this depend on whether an athlete had received a five franc coin as automatically to consider the parish verger an unbeliever because he receives a salary for looking after the church." Certain definitions of amateurism were, he said, "a relic of the class system." Coubertin, *Olympic Memoirs*, 65–66.

59. Müller, *One Hundred Years*, 34–35; MacAloon, *This Great Symbol*, 172.
60. Müller, *One Hundred Years*, 96n5; *1894–1994*, 1:105.
61. Wolf Lyberg, *Fabulous 100 Years of the IOC: Facts, Figures, and Much Much More* (Lausanne: International Olympic Committee, 1996), 359–372, 31–32. For Coubertin's attitude, see, for example, Coubertin, *Olympic Idea*, 129.
62. Coubertin, *Olympic Idea*, 49.
63. Coubertin, *Olympic Memoirs*, 13–14. In an 1894 speech he said, "Modern athletics . . . shows two trends . . . It is becoming firstly democratic and secondly international. The social revolution already accomplished among men and perhaps shortly to be accomplished among things also, is the explanation of the first trend; fast transport and easy communication are the explanation of the second." Coubertin, *Olympic Idea*, 9.
64. Coubertin, *Olympic Memoirs*, 13–14.
65. MacAloon, *This Great Symbol*, 137.
66. 1894 address at Athens, in Coubertin, *Olympic Idea*, 9.
67. Dietrich R. Quanz, "Formatting Power of the IOC: Founding the Birth of a New Peace Movement," *Citius, Altius, Fortius* 3 (Winter 1995): 6–16; Dietrich R. Quanz, "Die Gründung des IOC im Horizont von bürgerlichen Pazifismus und Internationalismus," in *Die Aktualität der Sportphilosophie*, ed. Gunter Gebauer (St. Augustin: Academia, 1993), 191–216; and Dietrich R. Quanz, "Civic Pacifism and Sports-Based Internationalism: Framework for the Founding of the International Olympic Committee," *Olympika: The International Journal of Olympic Studies* 2 (1993): 1–23.
68. Coubertin, *Olympism*, 360.
69. MacAloon, *This Great Symbol*, 262–267.
70. Beck, *Scoring for Britain*, 164.
71. *Amateur Athlete* (November 1935): 7; *Malayan Sports Pictorial*, 2 (1932): 19, quoted in Janice N. Brownfoot, " 'Healthy Bodies, Healthy Minds': Sport and Society in Colonial Malaya," in Mangan and Hong, *Sport in Asian Society*, 135.
72. Circular letter, January 15, 1894, reprinted in Müller, *One Hundred Years*, 27.
73. MacAloon, *This Great Symbol*, 188–189, 258–261.
74. Charles Maurras, "Le Voyage d'Athènes," *La Gazette de France*, April 19, 1896, 1–2. See also MacAloon, *This Great Symbol*, 111–112, 258, and Arnaud, "Sport and International Relations," 28–29.

75. John Lowerson, *Sport and the English Middle Classes, 1870–1914* (New York: Manchester University Press, 1993), 265. The German government had offered a small subsidy as early as 1896. Arnd Krüger, "'The Olympic Spirit of the Modern World Has Given Us a Symbol of World War': Sport and National Representation at the Eve of World War I," in Arnaud and Wahl, *Sports et relations internationales*, 48.

76. Avery Brundage, "The Greatest Sport Nation in the World," 1942 speech, ABC, Box 244. On nationalism in U.S. press reports of 1912, see Dyreson, *Making the American Team*, 162–164.

77. *NYT*, July 4, 1914, 8.

78. Daily Express, January 1, 1929, quoted in Beck, *Scoring for Britain*, 119–120. See also Richard Holt, "The Foreign Office and the Football Association: British Sport and Appeasement, 1935–1938," in Arnaud and Riordan, *Sport and International Politics*, 51–66; and Arnd Krüger, "'Buying Victories Is Positively Degrading': European Origins of Government Pursuit of National Prestige through Sport," *IJHS* 12, no. 2 (August 1995): 183–200.

79. See Chapter 3.

80. Notes for NBC radio broadcast, April 22, 1936, ABC, Box 250.

81. Per Olof Holmäng, "International Sports Organizations 1919–25: Sweden and the German Question," *IJHS* 9, no. 3 (December 1992): 455–466; Beck, *Scoring for Britain*, 80–84; Coubertin, *Olympic Memoirs*, 93–94, 100.

82. Tensions between El Salvador and Honduras, already high, flared up during preliminary World Cup matches in 1969, where disturbances provided one of the proximate causes of what became known as the "Soccer War." John MacAloon has also suggested that by fomenting nationalist sentiment in Greece, the 1896 Athens Olympics may have helped precipitate war between Greece and Turkey. MacAloon, *This Great Symbol*, 259.

83. See also MacAloon's assessment of Coubertin's and Maurras's views in *This Great Symbol*, 268–269.

2. The Rise of International Sports Organizations

1. Boli and Thomas, *Constructing World Culture*, 34. On the role and significance of international NGOs in world affairs, see also Iriye, *Global Community*, and Clive Archer, *International Organizations*, 2nd ed. (London: Routledge, 1992). Boli and Thomas argue that "the world-polity context that envelops the competitive state system has led to a mutual strengthening of states and transnational structures" (p. 1). They identify five global cultural principles, embodied by international NGOS, that characterize the world polity: universalism, individualism, rational voluntaristic authority, rationalizing progress, and world citizenship (p. 17). As Boli

and Thomas note, the IOC has suffered from legitimacy problems because of its undemocratic structure (p. 40).

2. Norbert Elias, "Introduction," in Elias and Dunning, *Quest for Excitement,* 40.

3. The first book-length overview of international sport organizations, focusing on the contemporary scene, is provided in James E. Thomas and Laurence Chalip, *Sport Governance in the Global Community* (Morgantown, W.Va.: Fitness Information Technology, 1996). The legal aspects are surveyed in James A. R. Nafziger, *International Sports Law* (Dobbs Ferry, N.Y.: Transitional, 1988). A number of studies provide brief historical overviews of the development of international sports organizations, including Barrie Houlihan, *The Government and Politics of Sport* (London: Routledge, 1991), 136–150. The IOC's official history provides much useful information: *1894–1994.* Gordon Harold MacDonald has written a dissertation on IOC-federation relations: "Regime Creation, Maintenance, and Change: A History of Relations between the International Olympic Committee and International Sports Federations, 1894–1968" (Ph.D. diss., University of Western Ontario, 1998). Important theoretical perspectives are provided in Hoberman, "Toward a Theory of Olympic Internationalism," and Eichberg, "Olympic Sport."

4. F. S. L. Lyons, *Internationalism in Europe, 1815–1914* (Leyden: Sythoff, 1963), 381–386. Of the 377 international NGOs formed in these years, only 141, or 37 percent, survived to the middle of the twentieth century. Lyons, *Internationalism in Europe,* 14. As far as I can determine, all the international sports federations formed before 1914 still exist, though several underwent reorganizations after World War I. (The International Boxing Union [Fédération internationale de boxe, amateurs], formed after World War I, was one that did not survive World War II.)

5. Of the more than two hundred sports currently organized at the international level (Boli and Thomas, *Constructing World Culture,* 41), none is more important in terms of numbers of fans and financial power than soccer.

6. Christiane Eisenberg, "Massensport in der Weimarer Republik," *Archiv für Sozialgeschichte* 33 (1993): 142.

7. Bill Murray, *Football: A History of the World's Game* (Aldershot: Scolar, 1994), 14–17, 39. The championships that began in 1871 were restricted to amateurs. In 1888 a professional league was formed, with regularly scheduled meetings, a ranking system, and a separate national championship. On developments in France that led to the establishment of regional and then national championships in the 1890s, see Alfred Wahl, *Les Archives du football: Sport et société en France, 1880–1980* (Paris: Gallimard/Julliard, 1989), 91–96.

8. Eisenberg suggests that the early development of an international network explains why sport is institutionalized in a way that other cultural forms are not. Christiane Eisenberg, "The Rise of Internationalism in Sport," in *The Mechanics of Internationalism: Culture, Society, and Politics from the 1840s to the First World War,* ed. Martin H. Geyer and Johannes Paulmann (New York: Oxford University Press, 2001), 376.

9. Compiled from the Union of International Associations, ed., *Yearbook of International Organizations 1997/98,* vol. 1, 34th ed. (Munich: Saur, 1997). Additional information on international sports federations can be found in the earlier editions of this yearbook, for example *Annuaire de la vie internationale 1908–9* (Brussels, 1909), which reprinted the statutes and regulations of early sports federations, and in the appended lists in *1894–1994,* 2:232–240. Lyons counts twenty-six international sport organizations, without enumerating them individually. It is likely that he included such organizations as the Fédération internationale aéronautique and the Association internationale des automobile-clubs reconnus, which could loosely be considered sports organizations. Lyons, *Internationalism in Europe,* 381. For the purposes of this study, I include only those organizations regulating sports that generally appeared on the program of the Olympic Games.

10. Coubertin, *Olympic Memoirs,* 61.

11. Arnaud, "Sport and International Relations," 20–21.

12. *1894–1994,* 1:55; Müller, *One Hundred Years,* 36.

13. See the list of IOC members, as well as the chart of members from each continent, in Lyberg, *Fabulous 100 Years,* 36–45.

14. *1894–1994,* 1:57–58; Christiane Eisenberg, "The Middle Class and Competition: Some Considerations of the Beginnings of Modern Sport in England and Germany," *IJHS* 7, no. 2 (September 1990): 271–272; Coubertin, *Olympic Memoirs,* 14. MacAloon notes also the influence of French models, notably the Unions de la paix: *This Great Symbol,* 89, 180–181. See also Coubertin's justification for the self-recruiting principle in Coubertin, *Olympic Idea,* 18–19.

15. *1894–1994,* 1:80–87. Coubertin named Demetrios Bikelas, a Greek delegate from the Panhellenic Gymnastic Society, the first president of the IOC; Coubertin initially took the position of secretary-general. As Coubertin later explained, "everything that might help to strengthen the international character of the cycle that was about to start seemed to me of paramount importance." Bikelas helped prepare the Athens Games, but Coubertin kept the reigns of power over the direction of the Olympic movement in his own hands. Coubertin, *Olympic Memoirs,* 13; MacAloon, *This Great Symbol,* 179–180. Coubertin's original intention was to rotate

the presidency every four years in connection with the Games, such that the president would be an IOC member from the country hosting the Games. Thus, Coubertin was president for the 1900 Games held in Paris, and Sloane was offered the presidency preceding the 1904 Games in St. Louis. Sloane turned it down and Coubertin accepted a ten-year term. He would remain as president until resigning in 1925; he died in 1937. *1894–1994,* 1:90.

16. Guttmann, *Games and Empires,* 134–136; Lyberg, *Fabulous 100 Years,* 31–32, 359–372. From early on governments and national Olympic committees sought the prerogative of naming representatives to the IOC, but Coubertin insisted that the IOC had to choose its members to maintain its "total independence." See, for example, Coubertin, *Olympic Memoirs,* 55–56.

17. Quoted in Eugene A. Glader, *Amateurism and Athletics* (West Point, N.Y.: Leisure Press, 1978), 85–86.

18. Müller, *One Hundred Years,* 57–58; Coubertin, *Olympic Memoirs,* 62.

19. Müller, *One Hundred Years,* 63.

20. MacDonald, "Regime Creation," chap. 2. On the vociferous Anglo-American disputes at the 1908 Games, see Dyreson, *Making the American Team,* 136–145, and Coubertin, *Olympic Memoirs,* 54, 57. The 1908 London Games were nonetheless the first for which a rulebook was printed and distributed in advance. MacDonald, "Regime Creation," 23–24, 41.

21. MacAloon, *This Great Symbol,* 198–203, 244–247.

22. John Kieran and Arthur Daley, *The Story of the Olympic Games, 776 B.C.–1960 A.D.* (Philadelphia: Lippincott, 1961), 29. See also Coubertin's description of the position of the Olympics in Paris in 1900 as "humiliated vassal" to the world's fair. The Games were not originally advertised as "Olympic Games" but as "the Competitions of the Exhibition." Coubertin did not even attend the 1904 Games in St. Louis, which he described as "completely lacking in attraction" and overshadowed by the embarrassment of the "Anthropological Days." The 1908 London Games, though also held in conjunction with a world's fair, were not upstaged by it. Coubertin, *Olympic Memoirs,* 35–37, 43, 53.

23. Coubertin, *Olympic Memoirs,* 37.

24. Each member of the committee paid twenty-five francs a year, of which twenty went toward publication of the *Olympic Review* (written by Coubertin) and five went to the IOC. Jean Marion Leiper suggests that the IOC also collected a fee from the organizing committee hosting each Olympiad. Such a fee was instituted in 1949, and Leiper suggests that it existed as early as 1929. "The International Olympic Committee: The Pursuit of Olympism, 1894–1970" (Ph.D. diss., University of Alberta, Canada, 1976), 122–124.

25. Coubertin, *Olympic Memoirs,* 70, 90–91, 128; *1894–1994,* 1:108, 115.
26. Coubertin, *Olympic Idea,* 41–43.
27. In 1915 Coubertin made Lausanne, Switzerland, the "world administrative center and the repository of the archives of modern Olympism." Before then, the IOC had had no permanent headquarters; instead, the registered office was in theory transferred every four years to the country where the next Olympiad was to be held. Coubertin, *Olympic Memoirs,* 94. The IOC's finances remained precarious. In 1938 the devaluation of the Swiss franc left IOC finances "stretched" and caused the discontinuation of the *Olympic Bulletin.* Wolf Lyberg, "The IOC Sessions" (unpublished typescript, 1989, held at IOC), 1:207.
28. Monique Berlioux, "History of the IOC," in *The Olympic Games,* ed. Lord Killanin and John Rodda (New York: Macmillan, 1976), 31.
29. For an overview of IOC-federations conflicts in the 1920s, see MacDonald, "Regime Creation," 45–103.
30. As Coubertin wrote, national Olympic committees "were free to form themselves more or less as they wished . . . [The IOC] interfered neither in their formation nor in their running." For the most part such committees existed on a temporary basis during the immediate run-up to the Games; few countries before World War I had well-established organizations. In the event that more than one committee claimed jurisdiction in a particular country (as happened in several South American countries), the IOC member or members from that country were given the power to decide which one to recognize. Coubertin, *Olympic Memoirs,* 60–62.
31. Florence Carpentier, *Le Comité international Olympique en crises: La Présidence de Henri de Baillet-Latour, 1925–1940* (Paris: L'Harmattan, 2004), 33.
32. *1894–1994,* 1:211–212.
33. Soccer was originally known as Association football. Hence, FIFA is the "international federation for Association football."
34. Unfortunately FIFA's prewar archival holdings are incomplete. Most of FIFA's records dating from before its 1932 move to Zurich do not seem to have been kept, and many of the correspondence files with national associations begin only in 1938 or later. For surveys of FIFA's development, see Pierre Lanfranchi et al., *100 Years of Football: The FIFA Centennial Book* (London: Weidenfeld & Nicolson, 2004); Alfred Wahl, "La Fédération Internationale de Football-Association, 1903–1930," in Arnaud and Wahl, *Sports et relations internationales,* 31–45; and Murray, *Football.*
35. Annual Report of the Secretary-Treasurer, June 7, 1908, and Minutes of the Congress, Vienna, June 7–8, 1908, FIFA, Congress Minutes.
36. *Bulletin officiel de la Fédération internationale de football association,* September 1, 1905.

37. *Fédération internationale de football association, 1904–1929* (n.p., 1929), 31–34; Annual Report of the Secretary-Treasurer, June 7, 1908, FIFA, Congress Minutes.

38. *Bulletin officiel de la Fédération internationale de football association,* September 1, 1905.

39. Annual Report of the Secretary-Treasurer, June 7, 1908, and Minutes of the Congress, Vienna, June 7–8, 1908, FIFA, Congress Minutes.

40. Minutes of the 10th Annual Congress, Copenhagen, May 31–June 1, 1913; and Annual Report of the Secretary-Treasurer for 1912–1913, FIFA, Congress Minutes.

41. Minutes of the 14th Annual Congress, Prague, May 24–26, 1925, FIFA, Congress Minutes.

42. Procès-verbal, Congress, Bern, June 3–4, 1906, FIFA, Congress Minutes. On the history of the World Cup, see Jules Rimet, *L'Histoire merveilleuse de la Coupe du monde* (Monaco: Union Européene d'éditions, 1954). Rimet had a long history of involvement in French football, dating back to his founding of the Parisian football club Red Star in 1897. After World War I he was named head of FIFA and of the French Football Association (the Fédération française de football association).

43. Murray, *Football,* 90; Alfred Wahl and Pierre Lanfranchi, *Les Footballeurs professionels des années trente à nos jours* (Paris, 1995), 41; Tony Mason, *Passion of the People? Football in South America* (London: Verso, 1995), ix, 45–51.

44. Louis Oestrup, 1928, quoted in Mason, *Passion,* 45.

45. Minutes of the 17th Annual Congress, Amsterdam, May 25–26, 1928, FIFA, Congress Minutes. On the Dutch threat, see Minutes of the 21st Annual Congress, Stockholm, May 13–14, 1932, p. 8, FIFA, Congress Minutes.

46. Dietrich Shulze-Marmeling and Hubert Dahlkamp, *Die Geschichte der Fussball-Weltmeisterschaft, 1930–2006* (Göttingen: Werkstatt, 2002), 26.

47. Minutes of the General Committee meeting, Helsinki, June 2, 1927, FIFA, Executive Committee Agendas and Minutes.

48. Minutes of the 19th Annual Congress, Budapest, June 6–7, 1930, FIFA, Congress Minutes.

49. Appendices à l'ordre du jour de la réunion du Comité exécutif, Paris, March 14, 1931, FIFA, Executive Committee Agendas and Minutes.

50. Fédération international de football association, *Anuario 1935* (Zurich: J. Rüegg Söhne, 1935), 13.

51. Minutes of the 21st Annual Congress, Stockholm, May 13–14, 1932, FIFA, Congress Minutes. C. A. W. Hirschman, one of FIFA's founding members, had handled FIFA's day-to-day affairs throughout the 1920s, working part-time out of the Dutch football federation's offices in Amsterdam as hon-

orary secretary-treasurer. Report from the Secretary, 1928–1929, FIFA, Congress Minutes; Procès-verbal de la réunion du Comité exécutif, Paris, December 12, 1931, FIFA, Executive Committee Agendas and Minutes; Report of the Secretary, 1931–1932, FIFA, Congress Minutes; Procès-verbal de la réunion du Comité exécutif, Paris, December 12, 1931, FIFA, Executive Committee Agenda and Minutes. For a more detailed account see Barbara Keys, "The Dictatorship of Sport: Nationalism, Internationalism, and Mass Culture in the 1930s" Ph.D. diss., Harvard University, 2001), 67–68.

52. Indeed, a staff and an office, along with a constitution and a symbol or emblem, are among the attributes necessary to be recognized as an international organization. Archer, *International Organizations,* 2, 33.

53. Procès-verbal de la réunion du Comité exécutif, Stockholm, May 15, 1932, FIFA, Executive Committee Agendas and Minutes.

54. Peter J. Beck, "Going to War, Peaceful Coexistence or Virtual Membership? British Football and FIFA, 1928–46," *IJHS* 17, no. 1 (March 2000): 113–134.

55. On international levies see the Congress minutes and the regulations published in the annual FIFA *Handbook.* In 1934 Schricker noted that levies from international matches "are the principal part of the regular revenues of the Federation," bringing in 20,426 Swiss francs that year. Net receipts from the 1934 World Cup came to 53,225 Swiss francs. Financial Report, 1934, FIFA, Congress Minutes. Federations overseeing sports with less spectator appeal did not collect such fees. As of 1932, for example, the IAAF (the track federation) derived income only from membership fees and from the sale of handbooks. Minutes of the 11th Congress of the IAAF, 1932, IOC, Jeux Olympiques d'été 1932.

56. See the regulations in FIFA's annual *Handbook.* Originally an international match was defined as one played between "a team representing a country versus that of another country." Minutes of the 3rd Congress, Bern, June 3–4, 1906, FIFA, Congress Minutes.

57. Ibid.

58. Minutes of the 13th Congress, Paris, May 24–28, 1924, FIFA, Congress Minutes.

59. Hirschman's remarks at the 1907 Congress, FIFA Archives, Congress Minutes. See also many of the entries in FIFA's *Fédération Internationale de Football Association, 1904–1929.*

60. Minutes of the Meetings of the Executive Committee for Paris, July 5, 1931; Geneva, September 26, 1931; Paris, December 12, 1931, FIFA, Executive Committee Agenda and Minutes.

61. "Question de la personnification civile en Suisse de la F.I.F.A.," Procès-

verbal de la réunion du Comité exécutif, San Remo, February 27–28, 1932, FIFA, Executive Committee Agendas and Minutes. The issue of juridical personality for international organizations was considered seriously only after the founding of the League of Nations and was the subject of considerable legal debate before World War II. Legal personality is not necessary for an organization to function but does confer certain advantages, including allowing an organization to appear in its own rights in legal proceedings, either at the national or international level. More generally it means that rights, obligations, and powers are considered to be vested in the organization itself, rather than collectively in its members. C. F. Amerasinghe, *Principles of the Institutional Law of International Organizations* (Cambridge: Cambridge University Press, 1996), 67–78.

62. MacAloon, *This Great Symbol,* 222.
63. Elisabeth Crawford, *Nationalism and Internationalism in Science, 1880–1939: Four Studies of the Nobel Population* (Cambridge: Cambridge University Press, 1992); André Durand, *From Sarajevo to Hiroshima: History of the International Committee of the Red Cross* (Geneva: Henry Dunant Institute, 1984).
64. "Organization of the NOCs," at www.olympic.org/uk/organisation/noc/index_uk.asp?id_assoc=7 (accessed in July 2005).
65. "Sydney 2000: Did You Know?" at www.olympic.org/uk/games/past/innovations_uk.asp?OLGT=1&OLGY=2000 (accessed in July 2005).
66. Coubertin, *Olympic Memoirs,* 55.
67. Quoted in Leiper, "The International Olympic Committee," 80.
68. Organizing Committee of the Xth Olympiad, "General Regulations and Program of the Olympic Games, 1932," 9, HAA-WB, Box 26.
69. Minutes of 4th Congress, Amsterdam, May 19–20, 1907, FIFA, Congress Minutes.
70. Minutes of 5th Congress, Vienna, June 7–8, 1908, FIFA, Congress Minutes. Note the exception for Britain discussed above.
71. Coubertin, *Olympic Memoirs,* 55.
72. *1894–1994,* 1:82–86.
73. Article 1 of FIFA statutes, in FIFA, *Anuario 1935,* 11.
74. F. J. Wall to Schricker, November 28, 1933, FIFA, Correspondence with English National Association.
75. Coubertin, *Olympic Memoirs,* 55. See also *1894–1904,* 1:104.
76. In 1907, for example, the IOC agreed to offer an award to the nation with the highest medal count. *Revue Olympique* no. 18 (June 1907): 278.
77. MacAloon, *This Great Symbol,* 189.
78. Lyberg, *Fabulous 100 Years,* 237.
79. Jules Rimet/Encyclopédie des Sports Modernes, eds., *Le Football* (Mon-

aco: Union Européenne d'éditions, 1954), 2:177. These numbers did not include colonial associations indirectly affiliated with FIFA through colonial powers (the Belgian Congo association, for example, was affiliated via Belgium). For a list of such indirect affiliates, see, for example Fédération internationale de football association, *Handbook 1937*, 8th ed. (Zurich, 1937), iv–v.

80. François Oppenheim, *Histoire de la natation mondiale et française* (Paris: Chiron, 1977), 56.

81. Coubertin, *Olympic Memoirs*, 136.

82. Ibid. 133, 138–139; *Revue Olympique*, no. 100 (April 1914): 63.

83. Coubertin, *Olympic Memoirs*, 117.

84. Comité international Olympique, *Biographies Olympiques* (Lausanne: Comité international Olympique, n.d. [1986?]), 265–267. On the difficulties of organizing sport in India, see Tata to Baillet-Latour, May 21, 1929, IOC, Correspondance de Baillet-Latour.

85. Unidentified newspaper clipping, IOC, Correspondance de Baillet-Latour.

86. "History of the Far Eastern Athletic Association," *Official Bulletin of the IOC*, 1926, reprinted in *World's Football: Official Bulletin of the Fédération Internationale de Football Association*, no. 16 (July 24,1930). The "Olympic kindergarten" quotation is in Coubertin, *Olympic Memoirs*, 97. For a program and descriptions of ceremonies and events staged in the 1920s, see Far Eastern Athletic Association, *Official Report of the China Contest Committee of the Eighth Far Eastern Championship Games, 1925–1927*, ed. Wm. Z. L. Sung (Shanghai: Oriental Press, 1928).

87. Coubertin, *Olympic Memoirs*, 118–119.

88. Such ambitions had been expressed as early as 1910, when South Africa became the first non-European member. In his annual report for 1909–1910, Secretary-Treasurer C. A. W. Hirschman noted that the federation should aim "to make Association football a universal game and to control it as such." Annual report, May 2, 1910, FIFA, Congress Minutes.

89. Lanfranchi et al., *100 Years of Football*, 68; Jean-Yves Guillain, *La Coupe du monde de football: L'Oeuvre de Jules Rimet* (Paris: Amphora, 1998), 72.

90. Minutes of the Meeting of the General Committee, Berlin, May 21, 1931, FIFA, Executive Committee Agenda and Minutes. The policy of reduced subscription fees was first adopted at the 13th Congress, Paris, May 24–28, 1924.

91. Report of the Secretary, 1938 and 1939, FIFA, Congress Minutes.

92. Coubertin, *Olympic Memoirs*, 135–136. On Germany and the Soviet Union, see Chapters 6 and 7.

93. Kankovszky to Baillet-Latour, September 17, 1937, ABC, Box 42.

94. Jules Rimet, "Introduction et esquisse historique," in *Le Football,* ed. Rimet/Encyclopédie des Sports Modernes, 1:15.

95. Lanfranchi et al., *100 Years of Football,* 126–127, 137, 141.

96. Thierry Terret, *L'Institution et le nageur: Histoire de la Fédération française de natation (1919–1939)* (Lyon: Presses universitaires de Lyon, 1998), 111–112.

3. Democracy and International Sport

1. Baseball, of course, is widely played in parts of Asia and Latin America, and in recent years basketball has developed widespread appeal abroad. On the relationship between sport and Americanization, see Barrie Houlihan, "Homogenization, Americanization, and Creolization of Sport: Varieties of Globalization," *Sociology of Sport Journal* 11 (December 1994): 356–375.

2. This attitude was similar to the business-based internationalism of the 1920s, according to which Americans would transform the world by spreading prosperity, not by meddling in politics. Barry Dean Karl, *The Uneasy State: The United States from 1915 to 1945* (Chicago: University of Chicago Press, 1983).

3. David Riesman and Reuel Denney, "Football in America: A Study in Cultural Diffusion," *American Quarterly* 3 (1951): 309–319; Warren Goldstein, *Playing for Keeps: A History of Early Baseball* (Ithaca, N.Y.: Cornell University Press, 1989); and Elliot Gorn and Warren Goldstein, *A Brief History of American Sports* (New York: Hill and Wang, 1993).

4. Andrei S. Markovits, "The Other 'American Exceptionalism': Why Is There No Soccer in the United States?" *IJHS* 7, no. 2 (September 1990): 230–264, esp. 235. For a similar explanation of the divergence in team sports, see John Sugden, "USA and the World Cup: American Nativism and the Rejection of the People's Game," in *Hosts and Champions: Soccer Cultures, National Identities and the USA World Cup,* ed. John Sugden and Alan Tomlinson (Aldershot, Hants: Arena, 1994), 222–240.

5. Markovits, "The Other 'American Exceptionalism.'"

6. For an extended and intelligent argument about the uniqueness of the U.S. sport experience, see Andrei Markovits and Steven L. Hellerman, *Offside: Soccer and American Exceptionalism* (Princeton, N.J.: Princeton University Press, 2001). For an argument that emphasizes the failures of the globalized soccer world to erode tribal hatreds, see Franklin Foer, *How Soccer Explains the World: An Unlikely Theory of Globalization* (New York: Harper/Perennial, 2004).

7. William Stead, *The Americanization of the World or the Trend of the Twentieth Century* (1902; repr., New York: Garland, 1972). On the early influence of U.S. sport and physical education in Europe, see Arnd Krüger, "'We Are Sure to Have Found the True Reasons for the American Superiority in Sports': The Reciprocal Relationship between the United States and Germany in Physical Culture and Sport," in *Turnen and Sport: The Cross-Cultural Exchange,* ed. Roland Naul (Münster: Waxmann, 1991), 51–80; Dietrich R. Quanz, "The Impact of North American Sport on the Olympic Movement in Germany and Austria-Hungary," in *Turnen and Sport,* 147–163; and Dietrich R. Quanz, "Studien zu Bild und Funktion des amerikanischen Sports in der deutschen Sportentwicklung," in Giselher Spitzer and Dieter Schmidt, eds., *Sport zwischen Eigenständigkeit und Fremdbestimmung: Pädagogische und historische Beiträge aus der Sportwissenschaft. Festschrift für Hajo Bernett* (Bonn: Wegener, 1986), 129–144.

8. On the use of sport as a paradigm for U.S.-style modernity in Weimar Germany, see Frank Becker, *Amerikanismus in Weimar: Sportsymbole und politische Kultur, 1918–1933* (Wiesbaden: Deutscher Universitäts-Verlag, 1993), 30–31. The United States usurped the role of "sport nation" par excellence, but soccer, in which Britain continued to be the dominant power and the global role model in the interwar years, was a major exception.

9. Bertolt Brecht, *Poems, 1913–1956,* ed. John Willett and Ralph Manheim (New York: Methuen, 1976), 170.

10. Frank Costigliola, *Awkward Dominion: American Political, Economic, and Cultural Relations with Europe, 1919–1933* (Ithaca, N.Y.: Cornell University Press, 1984), 167. On U.S. cultural influence in Europe, see also Victoria de Grazia, "Mass Culture and Sovereignty: The American Challenge to European Cinemas, 1920–1960," *Journal of Modern History* 61 (March 1989): 53–87; Akira Iriye, *The Globalizing of America, 1913–1945,* vol. 3 of *The Cambridge History of American Foreign Relations,* ed. William I. Cohen (New York: Cambridge University Press, 1993); Mary Nolan, *Visions of Modernity: American Business and the Modernization of Germany* (New York: Oxford University Press, 1994); and Rob Kroes, *If You've Seen One, You've Seen the Mall: Europeans and American Mass Culture* (Urbana: University of Illinois Press, 1996). On connections between trade and film and on the role of Hollywood films in stimulating the boxing fad in Europe, see Costigliola, *Awkward Dominion,* 168, 176. For one Bolshevik official's strong reaction to the depiction of a football game in a U.S. film, see A. Lunacharskii, *Mysli o sporte* (Moscow: Ogonek, 1930), 16–19. ·

11. Guy Lewis, "Physical Education and Sport in the United States," in *Geschichte der Leibesübungen,* ed. Horst Ueberhorst (Berlin: Bartels & Wernitz, 1972), 4:8, 17–20; Guy Lewis, "World War I," *Geschichte der*

Leibesübungen, 109–122; Eugene T. Lies, *The New Leisure Challenges the Schools: Shall Recreation Enrich or Impoverish Life?* (Washington, D.C.: National Education Association, 1933), 60–64.

12. Benjamin Rader, *American Sports: From the Age of Folk Games to the Age of Televised Sports,* 3rd ed. (Englewood Cliffs, N.J.: Prentice Hall, 1996), 115–116; Gorn and Goldstein, *Brief History of American Sports,* 188–195.

13. William J. Baker, *Sports in the Western World* (Totowa, N.J.: Rowman & Littlefield, 1982), 229–231; Douglas Noverr and Lawrence E. Ziewacz, *The Games They Played: Sports in American History, 1865–1980* (Chicago: Nelson-Hall, 1983), chap. 4.

14. John Wong, "FDR and the New Deal on Sport," *Sport History Review* 29 (1998): 173–174; Donald S. Howard, *The WPA and Federal Relief Policy* (New York: Russell Sage Foundation, 1943), 130, 127.

15. Congress showed little interest in foreign sport ties before the Cold War, though in 1935 Congress did pass one of the first exemptions from taxes or duties granted to a sports organization: PL528 allowed excess money from the Los Angeles Olympic Games to be free of federal taxes. Other sport-related bills, like one to build a national stadium in Washington, D.C., were rare and usually died in committee. Roy Clumpner, "American Government Involvement in Sport," in *The 1984 Olympic Scientific Congress Proceedings,* ed. Gerald Redmond, vol. 7: *Sport and Politics* (Champaign, Ill.: Human Kinetics, 1984), 8, 10; Roy Clumpner, "American Federal Government Involvement in Sport, 1888–1973" (Ph.D. diss., University of Alberta, 1976), 95.

16. In 1930, for example, the U.S. Department of Commerce asked its foreign services to compile information on sports in foreign countries, in response to inquiries from U.S. manufacturers of athletic and sporting goods. Memorandum, April 12, 1930, SDDF 811.4063 Olympic Games/ 44. On the development of official U.S. cultural diplomacy beginning in 1938, see Frank A. Ninkovich, *The Diplomacy of Ideas: U.S. Foreign Policy and Cultural Relations, 1938–1950* (Cambridge: Cambridge University Press, 1981).

17. Address by Asa Bushnell, director of the office's sport section, to the National Collegiate Athletic Association (NCAA), in *Proceedings of the National Convention of the National Collegiate Athletic Association,* 1941, 86–90; Bushnell to Kirby, August 4, 1941, ABC, Box 30.

18. On foreign subsidies see Krüger, "Buying Victories." The U.S. government subsidized the U.S. team competing in the 1920 Antwerp Olympics by commandeering a leaky naval vessel to transport the athletes across the Atlantic. The provision of the ship (offered by the secretary of war and approved by Congress) came about because chaotic conditions in shipping following

wartime disruptions made it difficult for the team to secure transportation. The "subsidy" proved little appreciated, however, as poor conditions on board occasioned many complaints from athletes. American Olympic Committee, *Report: Seventh Olympic Games, Antwerp, Belgium, 1920* (Greenwich, Conn.: Condé Nast, 1921), 18–31. The federal government does provide indirect subsidies to U.S. Olympic teams in the form of tax policies.

19. On monitoring see, for example, Thomson to Brundage, November 4, 1940, ABC, Box 202; letter from Cordell Hull, October 2, 1939, quoted in "Supplemental Report of Avery Brundage on the First Pan American Sport Congress, 18 November 1940," ABC, Box 244. On the State Department and the 1932 Olympics, see Chapter 4.

20. For one notable example of a polo meet, see the description of a visit to Argentina by a U.S. Army polo team, whose members were received by the minister of war and the president. Report of Robert Woods Bliss, Buenos Aires, November 27, 1930, SDDF 835.40634/4. On a similar polo meet between a U.S. Army team and a Mexican Army team, see Patrick Hurley, Secretary of War, to Stimson, March 22, 1930, SDDF 811.40634/1. At one such event Eleanor Roosevelt acted as patroness. Secretary to Mrs. Roosevelt to Sumner Welles, September 5, 1934, SDFF, 811.40634/44. On informal matches during U.S. naval visits to foreign ports see Laurence Duggan to General Strong, June 12, 1939, SDDF 810.40634/11. On MacArthur's role, see American Olympic Committee, *Report: Ninth Olympic Games, Amsterdam, 1928; Second Olympic Winter Sports, St. Moritz, 1928* (New York: American Olympic Committee, 1929).

21. American Olympic Committee, *Report: Seventh Olympic Games,* 17, 84–99; Robert E. Lehr, "The American Olympic Committee, 1896–1940: From Chaos to Order" (Ph.D. diss., Pennsylvania State University, 1985), 58; Robert Korsgaard, "A History of the Amateur Athletic Union of the United States: Of a Type C Project" (typescript, Paul Ziffren Sports Library, Los Angeles, 1952), 313.

22. *NYT,* April 12, 1932, 15, and April 27, 1932, 21.

23. *NYT,* September 3, 1936, 10; September 10, 1936, 2; and September 27, 1936, 5. Owens threw his support to Landon.

24. The U.S. Department of Commerce regretfully squelched the false story, which appeared in the Paris edition of a U.S. newspaper. Mowatt Mitchell, Rome, to Specialties Division, February 17, 1931, Sporting Goods—Italy, File 209/Sporting Goods, Box 850, Record Group 51, General Records of the Bureau of Foreign and Domestic Commerce, National Archives II, College Park, Md.

25. Quoted in Ludwell Denny, *America Conquers Britain* (New York: Knopf, 1930), 405–406.

26. On the Pan-American Games, see Memorandum of Meeting, June 27, 1939, SDDF 812.4063/3. For additional material see also ABC, Box 30.

27. On the AOC, see Lehr, "The American Olympic Committee." (The American Olympic Association and the AOC were distinct but related organizations. For the sake of simplicity, "American Olympic Committee" is used here to refer to both organizations.) On the AAU see Korsgaard, "History of the Amateur Athletic Union," and Arnold William Flath, *A History of Relations between the National Collegiate Athletic Association and the Amateur Athletic Union of the United States (1905–1963)* (Champaign, Ill.: Stites Publishing, 1964). In 1938, the AAU was the U.S. member of the international federations for swimming, track and field, boxing, wrestling, gymnastics, weight lifting, bobsleigh, field handball, ice hockey, and basketball. AAU track rules, 1938, ABC, Box 9.

28. Korsgaard, "History of the Amateur Athletic Union." In cases when all-star teams were assembled, the AAU played a large role in selecting athletes. At other times getting AAU sanction was pro forma. For example, when a Harvard College team competed in England the request was rubber-stamped; see the correspondence in HAA-WB, Box 41.

29. In 1937 the AAU levied a "foreign relations" tax on international competitions, amounting to 5 percent of gross receipts. Under this new policy, the AAU collected thousands of dollars from Swedish, German, and British track associations for tours by U.S. teams in 1938. Amateur Athletic Union of the United States, *Minutes of the Fiftieth Annual Meeting, 1938* (n.p., n.d.), 18, 22. In the case of amateur boxing, the AAU had been taking 10 percent of the "gate" until 1936, when it voted to resolve a promotional dispute by reducing its fee to 5 percent. *NYT*, December 8, 1936, 35.

30. On Brundage (1887–1975) see Allen Guttmann, *The Games Must Go On: Avery Brundage and the Olympic Movement* (New York: Columbia University Press, 1984). Brundage's papers are held at the University of Illinois at Urbana and in microfilm copies at several libraries in Europe, the United States, and Canada; the extensive collection is described in *Avery Brundage Collection, 1908–1975*, comp. Maynard Brichford (Schorndorf: Hofmann, 1977).

31. *NYT*, February 26, 1956. On the false claim, see the draft of a radio address by Kirby, July 15, 1938, USOC, Kirby papers, Box 2, and Lehr, "American Olympic Committee," 39.

32. Some of Kirby's papers are held at USOC. Kirby's autobiography is of little interest: *I Wonder Why?* (New York: Coward-McCann, 1954). On Kirby's character flaws, see John A. Lucas, "Gustavus Town Kirby: Doyen of American Amateur Athletics and His Inadmissability into the International

Olympic Committee," *Stadion* 21/22 (1995–1996): 171–191; USOC, Kirby papers, Box 2; Mahoney to Kirby, January 4, 1940, ABC, Box 30.

33. Brundage was rabidly anti-Roosevelt and felt the New Deal had "half wrecked" the country. Brundage to Edström, December 18, 1940, ABC, Box 42. He was sympathetic to the Nazi regime and maintained close contacts with Nazi sport officials. He revived his friendship with German sport official Carl Diem immediately after the war and tried to intercede to secure the release of Karl Ritter von Halt, a former Nazi sport official who was arrested as a war criminal. Brundage to Diem, August 10, 1946, ABC, Box 22. Kirby was sympathetic to some aspects of the Nazi regime. In February 1939, Kirby called Germany "the fittest, best organized, best equipped nation," which has "reached out into other countries . . . by peaceful but powerful and persuasive methods" to bring "their resources to the support of Germany." He suggested that Germany will "go . . . into the Ukraine, and probably peacefully and by mutual agreement." Meeting of the International Advisory Committee of the World Congresses for Leisure Time and Recreational Activities, London, ABC, Box 30. See also Kirby to Brundage, November 4, 1935, ABC, Box 29. After returning from Germany in 1936, Kirby publicly declared that "everyone in Germany from six to sixty is fit, and fine, well-fed, well-clothed, well-housed, smiling and happy"; he went on to praise Hitler's willingness to listen to criticism. Address to Varsity C Club, Columbia University Club, December 3, 1936, USOC, Kirby papers, Box 7.

34. NBC radio address, April 22, 1936, ABC, Box 40; undated notes (c. 1936), ABC, Box 250; "Talk for German Day," October 4, 1936, USOC, Kirby papers, Box 7.

35. Brundage said, "If more money were spent on sport and recreation which cultivate initiative, mental discipline, self reliance, independence and character building, it would be unnecessary to spend so much on relief, reform, charity, health, etc. . . . Sport does not countenance the 'Owe me a living philosophy' so prevalent today." NBC radio address, April 22, 1936, ABC, Box 40.

36. See, for example, Harald Lechenperg, *Mann gegen Mann: Sport in U.S.A. mit europäischen Augen gesehen* (Berlin: Ullstein, 1936), dustjacket, 8; "Why We Haven't More Olympic Champions," *World Sports* (London) (September 1936): 248.

37. See, for example, "Why America Wins at the Olympics," *Literary Digest,* August 27, 1932, 8.

38. *Amateur Athlete* (January 1938). See also *Amateur Athlete* (March 1940): 3.

39. Brundage, "The Greatest Sport Nation in the World," 1942 speech, ABC,

Box 244. On foreign coaches training in the United States, see, for example, the notice about basketball in *Amateur Athlete* (October 1939): 11.

40. *Amateur Athlete* (March 1941): 26.

41. Nicholas Dawidoff, *The Catcher Was a Spy: The Mysterious Life of Moe Berg* (New York: Pantheon Books, 1994), 92; Robert Obojski, *The Rise of Japanese Baseball Power* (Radnor, Pa.: Chilton Book, 1975), 23–24. Other baseball exchanges in the 1930s include a visit of major-leaguers in 1931, visits by U.S. college teams in 1934 and 1935, and the visit of a Japanese team to the United States in 1935. A dearth of accessible sources on the U.S. side has left this fascinating subject understudied. Baseball's geographic reach was far too limited and its organizers' concerns too overwhelmingly parochial to justify Richard C. Crepeau's claim that baseball was "as active as the business community in expanding American influence around the world in the decades between the wars." Richard C. Crepeau, *Baseball: America's Diamond Mind, 1919–1941* (Orlando: University of Central Florida Press, 1980), 196. On the early appeal of baseball in Japan, see Roden, "Baseball and the Quest for National Dignity."

42. Dawidoff, *Catcher,* 90–91.

43. *NYT,* November 3, 1934, 9.

44. Dawidoff, *Catcher,* 90–92; Obojski, *Rise of Japanese Baseball,* 15; *NYT,* February 24, 1935, 25. One member of the tour, catcher Moe Berg, worked for the U.S. government during World War II, first at the Office of Inter-American Affairs and then the Office of Strategic Services. His first spy mission seems to have been on the 1934 tour of Japan, when he surreptitiously filmed the Tokyo skyline. Dawidoff, *Catcher,* 92–96, 129–137.

45. This summary is compiled primarily from articles in *Amateur Athlete* during the 1930s. See also Brundage, "Greatest Sport Nation." Under the rules of most international federations, every international match required the formal permission of the national body governing that sport in each participating country. As the governing body for most sports, the AAU's permission was therefore required even for tours organized by other groups.

46. *Amateur Athlete* (August 1934): 8.

47. *Amateur Athlete* (September 1938): 10; Amateur Athletic Union of the United States, *Minutes of the Fiftieth Annual Meeting, 1938* (n.p., n.d.), 54, 101–103.

48. For one example, see *Amateur Athlete* (September 1934): 3. On other kinds of cultural emissaries see Victoria de Grazia, "Americanism for Export," *Wedge* 7/8 (1985): 76.

49. See, for example, 1934 Norway report, 857.4064/3, ABC Box 1, which at-

tributed the tour's success to "the careful selection of the team members" and "preparatory care" in ensuring that the athletes and managers behaved with tact and courtesy.

50. In arranging for a U.S. track and field team to tour Sweden in 1931, for example, Sweden's national athletic organization requested the inclusion of Eddie Tolan, an African American track star then at the University of Michigan. The U.S. organizer demurred, advising that including a black athlete would cause "difficulties." Kjellstrom to Bingham, June 17, 1931, HAA-WB, Box 40.

51. Participants typically had their travel costs paid and were given a small stipend for daily expenses, but were forbidden from receiving any compensation for "broken time," or salary lost during competition. Financing for the meets was usually derived from ticket sales. A host organization would offer a "guarantee" to a visiting team, whereby the host agreed to pay a certain amount of money for traveling expenses and daily stipends. When expenses and stipends came to less than the guarantee, the visiting team received the difference. See, for example, the correspondence relating to a Harvard track team's tour of Sweden in 1931 in HAA-WB, Box 40.

52. "American Track and Field Team in Oslo," Report of U.S. Legation, September 10, 1934, 857.4064/3, ABC, Box 1.

53. *Amateur Athlete* (October 1938): 2; *Amateur Athlete* (September–October 1933): 9; *Amateur Athlete* (October 1935): 7.

54. *NYT,* July 30, 1932, 8.

55. *Amateur Athlete* (November 1937): 10.

56. Report of the AOC, 1940, in ABC, Box 20.

57. Complaints about semiprofessionalism in college sport were frequently aired in such European newspapers as the major French sports paper, *L'Auto.* Criticisms of commercialization and the quest for "sensations" were common even in mostly favorable works, such as Lechenperg, *Mann gegen Mann.* See also Jack Lovelock, "Should Britain Imitate American Athletic Methods?" *Amateur Athlete* (June 1938): 4, originally published in *World Sports* (London).

58. Georges Duhamel, *America the Menace: Scenes from the Life of the Future,* trans. Charles Miner Thompson (Boston: Houghton Mifflin, 1931), 152–162. Duhamel acknowledged, however, that the brand of modern sport practiced in the United States was probably the wave of the future. On Duhamel's influence, see Richard Kuisel, *Seducing the French: The Dilemma of Americanization* (Berkeley: University of California Press, 1993), 11.

59. *Amateur Athlete* (December 1938): 61.

60. *New York Herald Tribune,* August 13, 1940, 22; A. C. Gilbert, "The A.A.U.

Convention and the International Metric Distances," in *Bulletin of the Intercollegiate Association of Amateur Athletes of America,* no. 21 (December 21, 1933), 2–4. The sports public seems to have been broadly supportive of the change (*NYT,* March 2, 1933, 16), but the switch was unpopular among the vast majority of AAU constituents whose athletes did not compete at world-record levels and who therefore felt the metric system was irrelevant. Many affiliated organizations chose not to implement the metric system, the NCAA refused to adopt it, and the Intercollegiate Association of Amateur Athletes of America, after initially following the AAU's lead, dropped metrics in 1936. In 1940, with the onset of war in Europe, the AAU quietly reintroduced yards and miles in its indoor championships. *NYT,* March 5, 1934, 22; *New York Herald Tribune,* August 13, 1940, 22. The switch to meters was much more problematic in swimming, where the standard sizes of pools in the United States did not break down into meter increments. As the U.S. representative pointed out at the 1938 meeting of the international swimming federation (FINA), FINA's rules made it impossible to establish one hundred-meter records in pools of twenty-five yards; he therefore successfully pressed the organization to recognize one hundred-yard records. Amateur Athletic Union, *Minutes of the Fiftieth Annual Meeting,* 151.

61. Kirby to Richard Floyd, February 21, 1933, ABC, Box 28.

62. Meeting of the International Advisory Committee of the World Congresses for Leisure Time and Recreational Activities, London, February 1939, ABC, Box 30.

63. Ronald Bergan, *Sports in the Movies* (London: Proteus, 1982), 53.

64. Warren I. Susman, *Culture as History: The Transformation of American Society in the Twentieth Century* (New York: Pantheon, 1984), 153–154, 157, 161–163, 172.

65. John R. Tunis, *Democracy and Sport* (New York: Barnes & Co., 1941).

66. Welcoming remarks, ABC, Box 244. Brundage also claimed that "sport is a typically American enterprise[,] for the same qualities of alertness, decisive action, ability to think quickly that have caused American business and industry to lead [the] world are responsible for our victories and records in the field of sport." Notes (c. 1936), ABC, Box 250.

67. MacArthur's remarks are in AOC, *Report: Ninth Olympic Games,* 6; Johnson is quoted in AAU, *Minutes of the Fiftieth Annual Meeting, 1938,* 201–203.

68. See William J. Baker, *Jesse Owens: An American Life* (New York: Free Press, 1986), 122–156.

69. David Margolick, *Beyond Glory: Joe Louis versus Max Schmeling and a World on the Brink* (New York: Knopf, 2005), 12, 99, 265.

70. AAU, *Minutes of the Fiftieth Annual Meeting,* 147. In 1938 the rule requir-

ing chaperones for married women was repealed, but the proposal to allow women over age twenty-one to travel without a chaperone was rejected. Ibid., 182. The literature on sport and gender issues is substantial. On U.S. women in the 1930s, useful starting points are Susan K. Cahn, *Coming on Strong: Gender and Sexuality in Twentieth Century Sport* (New York: Free Press, 1994), and Allen Guttmann, *Women's Sports: A History* (New York: Columbia University Press, 1991), 135–171.

71. David B. Welky, "Viking Girls, Mermaids and Little Brown Men: U.S. Journalism and the 1932 Olympics," *Journal of Sport History* 24, no. 1 (1997): 28–31.

72. "A suggested general code for amateur competition" (draft), (1934–1935), and questionnaires and the booklet of AOA leaders' statements on amateurism, USOC, Kirby papers, Box 4. For Brundage's views of amateurism, see Guttmann, *The Games Must Go On,* 116–118, 128–131.

73. I base this observation for the most part on extensive reading in the private correspondence of Brundage (in ABC) and Kirby (in USOC).

74. "At the Observation Post," *Literary Digest,* October 6, 1934, 11.

75. *Washington, D.C. Times-Herald,* June 23, 1940, B1.

76. A. E. Hamilton, *Sportsmanship: A Bridge of Understanding between the Nations of the World* (New York: Sportsmanship Brotherhood, 1926), frontispiece, 8–9, 12–13, 23–24, 33, 41; *NYT,* January 12, 1934, 32.

77. *Amateur Athlete* (May 1935): 3.

78. Tunis, *Democracy and Sport,* 15–22. A rare voice worried that if sports champions continue to be produced by the dictatorships, "democracy would look more precarious than it does now." Editorial, *Boston Sunday Globe,* November 14, 1937, reprinted in *Amateur Athlete* (December 1937): 8.

79. *NYT,* July 3, 1937, 1; August 5, 1938, 13; August 14, 1938, V:1; and August 22, 1938, 19.

80. Ibid., October 17, 1937, 38; AAU, *Minutes of the Fiftieth Annual Meeting,* 103.

81. The boycott controversy has generated a vast amount of scholarly ink—far more than other aspects of American participation in international sport in the 1930s. An overview is provided in Allen Guttmann, "The 'Nazi Olympics' and the American Boycott Controversy," in Arnaud and Riordan, *Sport and International Politics,* 31–50. See also Stephen R. Wenn, "A Suitable Policy of Neutrality? FDR and the Question of American Participation in the 1936 Olympics," *IJHS* 8, no. 3 (December 1991): 319–335; Stephen R. Wenn "A Tale of Two Diplomats: George B. Messersmith and Charles H. Sherrill on Proposed American Participation in the 1936 Olympics," *Journal of Sport History* 16, no. 1 (Spring 1989): 27–42; and

George Eisen, "The Voices of Sanity: American Diplomatic Reports from the 1936 Berlin Olympiad," *Journal of Social History* 11 (1984): 56–78.

82. "Move the Olympics!" *Christian Century* (August 7, 1935): 1007.

83. Brundage to Kirby, May 31, 1933, ABC, Box 28, quoted in Guttmann, "The 'Nazi Olympics,'" 34.

84. "Germany Has Violated the Olympic Code! An Open Letter to Dr. Theodor Lewald by Jeremiah T. Mahoney," October 21, 1935, pamphlet issued by the Committee on Fair Play in Sports, USOC, Kirby papers, Box 7. The letter was published in various newspapers.

85. Guttmann, "The 'Nazi Olympics,'" 38–39; American Olympic Committee, *Fair Play for American Athletes* (New York: American Olympic Committee, 1936). One historian has suggested that, in addition to ideological inclination, Brundage's commercial interests may have played a role in his support of Berlin; *NYT*, February 21, 1999, Sports, 1.

86. Remarks to AAU, December 7, 1935, USOC, Kirby papers, Box 7. Kirby also wrote: "I believed that more good would come to the same people of Germany by the example of the American team and of other teams with Jews, Roman Catholics, etc., there on, playing the game in the best sportsmanlike manner and bringing home to the German spectators and the German participants that there were other methods, other points of view toward race and religion than that which their government was endeavoring to force upon them or which they had honestly taken unto themselves." Kirby to Brundage, November 4, 1935, ABC, Box 29.

87. Arnd Krüger, "United States of America: The Crucial Battle," in *The Nazi Olympics: Sport, Politics, and Appeasement in the 1930s*, ed. Arnd Krüger and William Murray (Urbana: University of Illinois Press, 2003), 52; *NYT*, March 23, 1938, 28.

88. *NYT*, July 14, 1936, 23.

89. See the list in Wenn, "Suitable Policy," 333n32.

90. *NYT*, August 16, 1925, 4. The resolution was sent to the Committee on Foreign Relations, where it died. *Congressional Record: Proceedings and Debates of the First Session of the Seventy-fourth Congress of the United States of America* (Washington, D.C.: U.S. Government Printing Office, 1935), vol. 79, pt. 12, 13332; ibid., pt. 13, 14397–14398; ibid., pt. 14, 903. See also ibid., pt. 13, 13747–13749; ibid., pt. 12, 12913.

91. *NYT*, August 14, 1935, 4.

92. Report of George S. Messersmith, "With Reference to American Participation in the Olympic Games to Be Held in Berlin in 1936," November 15, 1935, SDDF 862.4063 Olympic Games/57, 11–12, 10, 11; Wenn, "Tale of Two Diplomats."

93. See, for example Messersmith's report of November 28, 1933, SDDF 862.4063 Olympic Games/1.
94. In a note to Senator Lonergan, for example, Hull used typical language to describe the boycott issue as a private matter, about which any government statement would be inappropriate. Hull to Lonergan, December 12, 1935, SDDF 862.4063 Olympic Games/59. See also Wenn, "Suitable Policy," 320, 327; Krüger, "United States."
95. According to long-standing tradition, the president of the United States held the honorary presidency of the AOC, and the secretaries of state, war, and the navy were honorary vice presidents. Such patronage was common, Hull explained, for organizations promoting religion, peace, or international sports. Press release, April 23, 1936, SDDF 811.43 American Olympic Association/4. See also Wenn, "Suitable Policy," 325–326.
96. Krüger, "United States," 57.
97. See Chapter 6.
98. Morrell Heald and Lawrence S. Kaplan, *Culture and Diplomacy: The American Experience* (Westport, Conn.: Greenwood Press, 1977), 4. U.S. policymakers viewed cultural diplomacy as an effort to impose American values and ideas abroad, with U.S. culture as the universal standard that would foster well-being in all areas of the globe. See Ninkovich, *Diplomacy of Ideas.*
99. Clarence Bush, "Americanism in the Olympic Games" (c. 1935), ABC, Box 232.

4. "Americanizing" the Olympic Games

1. Quoted in Allen Guttmann, *The Olympics: A History of the Modern Games* (Urbana: University of Illinois Press, 1992), 52.
2. *NYT,* July 29, 1932, 1.
3. This description is based on Arthur E. Grix, *Unter Olympiakämpfern und Indianerläufern* (Berlin: Wilhem Limpert, [1935]), 5–6; *NYT,* July 24, 1932, III, 1; *LAT,* July 28, 1932, 1; and photographs of the city in Reemstsma cigarettenfabriken g.m.b.h./Willy Meisl et al., eds., *Die Olympischen Spiele in Los Angeles 1932* (Altona-Bahrenfeld, Reemtsma cigarettenfabriken, 1932), 9–10. On the Biltmore see *LAT,* July 26, 1932, 1. On decorations at the 1928 Amsterdam Olympic Games see *Algemeen Handelsblad* (Amsterdam), Olympisches Beiblatt, July 29, 1928, 1, in Articles de presse, IOC, Jeux Olympiques d'été 1928.
4. Unidentified foreign journalist quoted in "Facts and Figures from the Greatest of All Olympics," *Literary Digest,* August 27, 1932, 34.
5. *1894–1994,* 1:249; Lyberg, *Fabulous 100 Years,* 237, 247.

6. The Dutch parliament, for example, refused to authorize funds for the 1928 Games, on the basis that the Games were pagan, violated the Sabbath, and contradicted the ideals of the ancient Greek Olympics. Legislators also objected to the "indecent" clothing worn by sportswomen. Peter-Jan Mol, "Sport in Amsterdam, Olympism and Other Influences: The Inter-war Years," *IJHS* 17, no. 4 (December 2000): 146.

7. See, for example, the list in Budget 1922, IOC, Jeux Olympiques d'été 1924.

8. "Awarding of 1932 Games Described," *Olympic: Official Publication of the Organizing Committee, Games of the Xth Olympiad, Los Angeles, U.S.A., 1932*, no. 1, p. 1, reproduced in *1894–1994*, 1:289; *1932 OR*, 35–38; William May Garland, "Story of the Origin of the Xth Olympiad Held in Los Angeles, California, in 1932, as Written by William May Garland" (undated typescript), Paul Ziffren Sports Resource Library, Los Angeles.

9. Coubertin, *Olympic Memoirs*, 117.

10. Garland, "Story of the Origin," 25.

11. Coubertin, *Olympism*, 517.

12. David Gebhard and Harriette von Breton, *Los Angeles in the Thirties, 1931–1941*, 2nd ed. (Los Angeles: Hennessey & Ingalls, 1989), 17.

13. *Le Journal* (Paris), August 27, 1936, 1.

14. Jeremy White, "'The Los Angeles Way of Doing Things': The Olympic Village and the Practice of Boosterism in 1932," *Olympika: The International Journal of Olympic Studies* 11 (2002): 80–85.

15. John Lucas, "Prelude to the Games of the Tenth Olympiad in Los Angeles, 1932," *Southern California Quarterly* 64, no. 4 (Winter 1982): 313–314; John E. Findling and Kimberly D. Pelle, eds., *Historical Dictionary of the Modern Olympic Movement* (Westport, Conn.: Greenwood Press, 1996), 75–78.

16. Findling and Pelle, *Historical Dictionary*, 75–78.

17. *NYT*, July 23, 1932, 8.

18. *OR 1932*, 47, 374–375.

19. Ibid., 59, 61–94. In accordance with Olympic procedures, the organizing committee operated independently of the AOC, which was responsible for selecting and funding the U.S. team. The AOC, a predominantly East Coast organization, was often suspicious and resentful of Garland and his West Coast associates.

20. Netherlands Olympic Committee, *The Ninth Olympiad: Official Report of the Olympic Games of 1928 Celebrated at Amsterdam*, ed. G. Van Rossem, trans. Sydney W. Fleming (Amsterdam: J. H. de Bussy, 1929), 940–941; *OR 1932*, 89–166. According to Wolf Lyberg, at the 1928 Games "nothing seemed to have worked as it should, and schedules were not adhered to particularly, to the great annoyance of the press which had deadlines to meet." Lyberg, *Fabulous 100 Years*, 199.

21. *OR 1932*, 90–100, 110; Guttmann, *The Olympics*, 52; *NYT*, July 17, 1932, III, 8; *LAT*, July 17, 1932, II, 4.

22. *LAT*, July 17, 1932, II, 4; Netherlands Olympic Committee, *Ninth Olympiad*, App. IV; *1894–1994*, 1:257.

23. Hartley D'Oyley Price, "The Tenth Olympic Games," *Journal of Health and Physical Education* 3 (November 1932): 3.

24. *OR 1932*, 335–362; *LAT*, July 30, 1932, 1; and July 31, 1932, 24.

25. *OR 1932*, 45, 209–210. In fact, the Amsterdam organizers had also published similar news releases.

26. Findling and Pelle, *Historical Dictionary*, 76; *OR 1932*, 211.

27. The 840-page official report of the 1932 Games has considerable detail on these technical arrangements. *OR 1932*, 89–166. The *LAT* reported 850 accredited newspaper correspondents. *LAT*, August 14, 1932, II, 4. Roughly five hundred of the journalists were American, according to a clipping from *L'Auto*, August 6, 1932, in Articles de presse 1931–1932, IOC, Jeux Olympiques d'été 1932. For the quotation see *OR 1932*, 166.

28. *LAT*, August 14, 1932, II, 4.

29. See especially *La Gazzetta dello sport*.

30. A typical list of advance complaints included the tiring voyage, the strange food (especially the lack of wine due to Prohibition), mediocre lodging, and high temperatures. *L'Echo de Paris*, July 11, 1932, 4.

31. Grix, *Unter Olympiakämpfern*; Arthur E. Grix, *Olympische Tage in Los Angeles* (Berlin: Emil Wernitz, 1932); Emil Andersen ("Mr. Smile"), *Med Danske Idraetsmaend til Olympiske lege* (Copenhagen: Gyldendalske, 1932), see esp. 55, 106.

32. Findling and Pelle, *Historical Dictionary*, 75–83; *LAT*, August 4, 1932, 9.

33. John McCoy, "Radio Sport Broadcasting in the United States, Britain and Australia, 1920–1956, and Its Influence on the Olympic Games," *Journal of Olympic History* 5, no. 1 (Spring 1997): 22.

34. *LAT*, August 5, 1932, 12, and August 7, 1932, VIa, 5.

35. Findling and Pelle, *Historical Dictionary*, 75–83; *OR 1932*, 329–330; *LAT*, July 24, 1932, II, 3; III, 1; July 31, 1932, 5; and August 3, 1932, 10.

36. *LAT*, August 2, 1932, 13; Guttmann, *Olympics*, 51.

37. *LAT*, July 16, 1932, 7. See also *LAT*, July 30, 1932, 11, and the report that the foreign athletes knew "as much about Garbo, Dietrich, Gary Cooper, Norma Shearer and the rest of them as any gaga American." *LAT*, July 24, 1932, III, 13.

38. *Athens to Atlanta: 100 Years of Glory* (Colorado Springs: U.S. Olympic Committee, 1993), 106–107; David Fury, *Johnny Weissmuller: "Twice the Hero"* (Minneapolis, Minn.: Artist's Press, 2000), 146–149.

39. *Mermaids on Parade*, 130, 114. Holm made a lot of money swimming in

the Billy Rose Aquacades with Johnny Weissmuller and Buster Crabbe. Ibid., 132–134.

40. *LAT,* July 26, 1932, 1; *LAT,* August 4, 1932, 2.

41. *LAT,* August 15, 1932, II, 1; July 17, 1932, II, 5; July 24, 1932, II, 3; and July 24, 1932, VIa, 3.

42. *LAT,* July 17, 1932, II, 5, and July 26, 1932, 6.

43. See, for example *LAT,* July 19, 1932, II, 7; July 31, 1932, II, 5; and August 7, 1932, VIa, 5.

44. *LAT,* August 3, 1932, 10; quotation in *Congressional Report* no. 2443, January 30, 1931, in SDDF 811.4063 Olympic Games/143.

45. *LAT,* August 5, 1932, 12.

46. Ibid., July 26, 1932, 1, and August 3, 1932, 1.

47. May Co. advertisement, *LAT,* July 24, 1932, III, 20; *LAT,* July 22, 1932, II, 8.

48. *OR 1932,* 30, 175, 220 (quotation on p. 175); Jonathan Robert Paul, "Melting Resources: A Historical Analysis of the 1932 Olympic Winter and Summer Games" (Master's thesis, University of Windsor, Canada, 2004), 100–102.

49. Robert K. Barney, Stephen R. Wenn, and Scott G. Martyn, *Selling the Five Rings: The International Olympic Committee and the Rise of Olympic Commercialism* (Salt Lake City: University of Utah Press, 2002), 27–28.

50. List of TOP Sponsors, provided by the Department of Communications, IOC, March 2001.

51. Items no. 0024233 and 0031417 in the IOC's Département Collections/ Expositions, Lausanne, Switzerland.

52. This generalization is based on a comparison of the publications of the 1928 and 1932 Games held at the IOC Archives: Jeux Olympiques 1928, Programmes officiels, *De Olympiade,* and Jeux Olympiques 1932, Rapports, règlement et programme officiel.

53. Items no. 0084029, 0060826, 0060964, 0061498, 0061501, 0061532, 0069485 in the IOC's Département Collections/Expositions, Lausanne, Switzerland; *OR 1932,* 173–175, 216–220; *Postal History and Vignettes of the Xth Olympiad, Los Angeles, 1932, and the III. Winter Olympic Games* (Cleveland, Ohio: Sports Philatelists International, 1976,) 164–173; Dyreson, "Marketing National Identity," 26–27; Gebhard and von Breton, *Los Angeles in the Thirties,* 16.

54. Grix, *Unter Olympiakämpfern,* 6; *LAT,* July 31, 1932, 5.

55. Barney et al., *Selling the Five Rings,* 34–36.

56. *Postal History.* For a list of some of the private advertisers who put out Olympic vignettes, see pp. 164–173.

57. *Mermaids on Parade,* 151, 160.

58. F. S. Palazzini, *Coca-Cola Superstar: The Drink That Became a Business Em-*

pire (London: Columbus Books, 1989), 32; Paul Arnoldussen, *Amsterdam 1928: Het verhaal van de IXe Olympiade* (Amsterdam: Thomas Rap, 1994), 196–197. Thanks to Jeff Vanke for a translation of the latter. See also International Olympic Committee, Department of Communications, Public Information Factsheet, "Long-Time Worldwide Olympic Partners (TOP)," March 12, 2002.

59. "Coca-Cola and the Olympic Movement: A Long-Standing Partnership," undated brochure provided to the author by the Coca-Cola™ Company. Johnny Weissmuller became the first Olympic athlete to endorse Coke in 1934. He and Maureen O'Sullivan appeared on Coke serving trays and posters. Palazzini, *Coca-Cola Superstar,* 116.

60. *NYT,* July 13, 1932, 21.

61. *LAT,* July 24, 1932, VIa 3.

62. *NYT,* July 20, 1932, 3; *LAT,* July 20, 1932, II, 9; Hoover to Stimson, December 13, 1929, SDDF 811.4063 Olympic Games/2. According to an unsourced report, Hoover told friends, "It's a crazy thing. And it takes some gall to expect me to be part of it." Al J. Stump, "The Olympics That Almost Wasn't," *American Heritage* 33, no. 5 (1932): 67.

63. *LAT,* July 30, 1932, 1, and July 30, 1932, 1. The press also reported that Hoover "broke bread" with the athletes, partaking of a special loaf of bread from the Olympic Village that was flown in from Los Angeles and presented to the White House by Representative Harry Englebright of California; *NYT,* July 30, 1932, 10.

64. *NYT,* July 10, 1932, 2, and July 20, 1932, 3; *LAT,* July 20, 1932, II, 9.

65. *LAT,* July 24, 1932, II, 3; July 31, 1932, 5; and August 3, 1932, 10.

66. Garland to Stimson, January 20, 1930, SDDF 811.4063 Olympic Games/10; Memorandum, September 8, 1931, SDDF 811.4063 Olympic Games/Lake Placid/44; Memorandum, August 27, 1931, SDDF 811.4063 Olympic Games/ 171. The invitations, like those to similar international cultural events, were transmitted by the State Department on behalf of the organizers.

67. *OR 1932,* 767–768; *1894–1994,* 1:254.

68. *OR 1932,* 233; *1894–1994,* 1:253–254. Similar facilities, on a much smaller scale, had existed in 1906 and 1924, though most teams had preferred to stay in hotels. The organizing committee had also proposed such facilities for the 1928 Games but the visiting teams declined.

69. British Olympic Association, *Official Report of the Xth Olympiad, 1932* (London: British Olympic Assocation, 1932), 23–24; *LAT,* July 16, 1932, 7.

70. *OR 1932,* 235.

71. *NYT,* June 19, 1932, VI, 6f; April 13, 1932, 15; and March 22, 1932, 25.

72. See Susan E. Cayleff, *Babe: The Life and Legend of Babe Didrikson Zaharias* (Urbana: University of Illinois Press, 1995); Welky, "Viking Girls."

73. Fr.-M. Messerli, *Impressions et images mouvantes recueillies en faisant le tour du monde* (Lausanne: Éditions Haeschel-Dufey, 1936), 57.

74. Guttmann, *The Olympics*, 52; *Le Matin*, August 9, 1932, 1. For the story behind China's one-man team in 1932, see Morris, *Marrow of the Nation*, 167–171.

75. This figure is based on my tally of the roster of official registrants in *OR 1932*, 793–814.

76. *LAT*, July 19, 1932, II, 7.

77. *NYT*, June 12, 1932, III, 3, and July 19, 1932, 23.

78. Ibid., October 9, 1932, 7; Eriko Yamamoto, "Cheers for Japanese Athletes: The 1932 Los Angeles Olympics and the Japanese American Community," *Pacific Historical Review* 69, no. 3 (August 2000): 417–418.

79. Editorial, *LAT*, August 14, 1932, II, 4.

80. *NYT*, October 9, 1932, 7.

81. Dick Schapp, quoted in Guttmann, *Olympics*, 52.

82. *Amateur Athlete* (December 1937): 8; "Swimming Japan: What Can It Do in the Coming Olympiad?" *Journal of Health and Physical Education* 3, no. 6 (June 1932): 20–22; Ben Grady, "Americans, Japanese, and Swimming," *Journal of Health and Physical Education* 5, no. 4 (April 1934): 57–58. On press treatment of women and nonwhites, see Welky, "Viking Girls," 40.

83. *NYT*, August 21, 1982, E6, and September 11, 1932, E5.

84. Allen Guttmann and Lee Thompson, *Japanese Sports: A History* (Honolulu: University of Hawaii Press, 2001), 123.

85. *NYT*, September 3, 1932, 10.

86. *OR 1932*, 749–764.

87. *LAT*, August 2, 1932, 1, and August 4, 1932, 8.

88. *OR 1932*, 324.

89. *Proceedings of the First International Recreation Congress, July 23–29, 1932, Los Angeles, California* (n.p., National Recreation Association, 1933); *NYT*, July 25, 1932, 14; Memorandum, February 4, 1931, Division of International Conferences and Protocol, SDDF 540.6 B1/7.

90. *International Olympics Conference on Physical Education, 1932: Supplement to the Proceedings of the Institute of International Relations, 9th Session* (n.p., 1932). The organizers had intended to hold an International Congress of Physical Education and Sports but had to scale back their plans due to the Depression.

91. *LAT*, July 29, 1932, 13.

92. The only exception was a melee at a water polo competition, at which the Brazilian team mobbed the Hungarian referee. *LAT*, August 14, 1932, VIa, 3.

93. *LAT*, August 4, 1932, VIa, 7. For a summary of the Games' successes, see the editorial in the *LAT*, August 14, 1932, II, 4. Other home papers were

ostentatious in praise. Arthur Daley of the *NYT* called the Games "the mightiest of all," with better facilities, larger stadia, and "close to perfect" organization. *NYT,* July 24, 1932, III, 1.

94. Report of IOC Session, Vienna, 1933, in *Bulletin officiel du Comité international Olympique* no. 24 (September 1933): 6; "Facts and Figures," 34; *London Times,* August 15, 1932, 12b; Japanese journalist quoted in *LAT,* July 30, 1932, 14; Grix, *Unter Olympiakämpfern,* 11; German NOC quoted in *1894–1994,* 1:257; German official quoted in "Facts and Figures," 34; *L'Echo de Paris,* August 15, 1932, 4.

95. *London Times,* August 8, 1932, 11c, and August 9, 1932, 4g.

96. "Facts and Figures," 34.

97. At the 1912 Stockholm Games, receipts had exceeded expenses (not including the costs of the new stadium) by a small margin. Coubertin, *Olympic Memoirs,* 80. After the 1932 Games the roughly $1.5 million in "profit" (it was a profit only if state and local government funds to build facilities were excluded from costs) led to an unseemly squabble. Both the state of California, hoping to recoup part of the $1 million it had provided for facilities construction, and the American Olympic Association, arguing that the surplus should be remitted to the IOC, filed suit against the organizing committee, which retained the funds. In a ruling finally sustained by the California Supreme Court in 1935, the organizing committee prevailed, and distributed the surplus among the state, city, and county. Correspondence from Combs to Kirby and Brundage, 1933–1935, USOC, Kirby Papers, Box 1; Garland to Baillet-Latour, March 30, 1933, IOC, Jeux Olympiques d'été 1932.

98. *OR 1932,* 41–42.

99. See Chapter 6.

5. Dictatorship and International Sport

1. Victoria de Grazia sees the German cultural industry as the most powerful competitor of the U.S. model in the 1930s. In the case of film, U.S. imports to Germany dropped rapidly from sixty-four in 1933 to twenty in 1939, when Goebbels tried to ban U.S. films altogether. Nazi cinema, though largely apolitical and influenced by American styles, did, in de Grazia's view, represent a successful nationalist alternative to the internationally dominant Hollywood system. De Grazia, "Mass Culture and Sovereignty," 53–87.

2. Michael H. Kater, "Forbidden Fruit? Jazz in the Third Reich," *American Historical Review* 94, no. 1 (February 1989): 13; Detlev Peukert, *Inside Nazi Germany: Conformity, Opposition, and Racism in Everyday Life,* trans. Richard Deveson (New Haven, Conn.: Yale University Press, 1987, 77.

3. Hans Dieter Schäfer, "Amerikanismus im Dritten Reich," in *National-sozialismus und Modernisierung,* ed. Michael Prinz and Rainer Zitelman (Darmstadt: Wissenschaftliche Buchgesellschaft, 1991), 204–205.

4. Margolick, *Beyond Glory,* 68.

5. Volker Kluge, *Max Schmeling: Eine Biographie in 15 Runden* (Berlin: Aufbau, 2004), 286; *NYT,* June 23, 1938, 14; Margolick, *Beyond Glory,* 289–291. Schmeling's nickname refers to his dark hair, the *Uhlanen* (nineteenth-century Prussian cavalry lancers), and the Rhineland, where Schmeling, originally from Hamburg, began his boxing career. Max Schmeling, *Max Schmeling: An Autobiography,* trans. George B. von der Lippe (Chicago: Bonus Books, 1988), 7–9. The 1938 bout was for the world championship; the 1936 bout was not. Schmeling should have fought the current titleholder, James Braddock, after beating Louis in 1936, but Schmeling and his manager were outmaneuvered in negotiations that dragged on for more than a year. (Then, as now, boxing promoters chose contenders more on the basis of commercial considerations than on athletic merit.) Ultimately, it was Louis who fought (and beat) Braddock for the title in 1937, and Louis was defending his title in the 1938 rematch with Schmeling. For details see Jeffrey T. Sammons, *Beyond the Ring: The Role of Boxing in American Society* (Urbana: University of Illinois Press, 1988), 79–117.

6. The list of attendees is culled from *NYT,* June 23, 1938, 1, 14–15, and Schmeling, *Max Schmeling.* For final attendance and gate figures, see Sammons, *Beyond the Ring,* 117, and Margolick, *Beyond Glory,* 7, 291.

7. *NYT,* June 23, 1938, 1, 14; Margolick, *Beyond Glory,* 296–302.

8. Quoted in Sammons, *Beyond the Ring,* 115.

9. *NYT,* June 23, 1938, 20.

10. Margolick, *Beyond Glory,* 203–208.

11. Schmeling, *Max Schmeling,* 152; Sammons, *Beyond the Ring,* 114; Anthony Edmonds, "Second Louis-Schmeling Fight: Sport, Symbol, and Culture," *Journal of Popular Culture* (Summer 1973): 44; compare Margolick, *Beyond Glory,* 258.

12. *Charlotte Observer,* June 24, 1938, sec. 2, 11, quoted in Sammons, *Beyond the Ring,* 116.

13. June 24, 1938, entry, Joseph Goebbels, *Die Tagebücher von Joseph Goebbels: Sämtliche Fragmente. Teil I: Aufzeichnungen 1924–1941,* ed. Elke Fröhlich (Munich: K. G. Saur, 1987), 3:465.

14. Ivone Kirkpatrick, British Embassy, Berlin, to W. Strang, June 27, 1938, minute, Vansittart, July 6, 1938, Public Records Office, London, FO 371/21781/C6586, quoted in Beck, *Scoring for Britain,* 239.

15. June 20, 1936, and June 21, 1936, entries, Goebbels, *Tagebücher,* 2:630.

16. June 28, 1936, entry, in Goebbels, *Tagebücher,* 2:635; Schmeling, *Max Schmeling,* 130–131.

17. Stanley McClatchie, *Sieh: das Herz Europas* (Berlin: H. Hoffman, 1936), 96, in Reinhard Rürup, *1936: Die Olympischen Spiele und der National-sozialismus: Eine Dokumentation* (Berlin: Argon, 1996), 159.

18. Siegfried Gerhmann, "Symbol of National Resurrection: Max Schmeling, German Sports Idol," in *European Heroes: Myth, Identity, Sport,* ed. Richard Holt, J. A. Mangan, and Pierre Lanfranchi (London: Frank Cass, 1996), 110.

19. Schmeling, *Max Schmeling,* 1–2, and throughout (see especially the photographs); David Bathrick, "Max Schmeling on the Canvas: Boxing as an Icon of Weimar Culture," *New German Critique* 51 (Fall 1990): 113.

20. After the 1936 victory Goebbels was so overcome by enthusiasm that he waived the taxes on Schmeling's earnings. June 26, 1936, entry, Goebbels, *Tagebücher,* 2:633. See also Birk Meinhardt, *Boxen in Deutschland* (Hamburg: Rotbuch, 1996), 93–94. The regime treated professional boxing as a business and did not subject professional boxers to the stringent oversight of the Nazi sport apparatus. Schmeling's choice of fights was not subject to approval by the Nazi hierarchy, but the government did play a role in negotiations regarding the financing of certain international fights, in part because of their implications for foreign currency earnings. (The regime's economic policies included strict controls on foreign trade and foreign exchange, in an effort to get foreign currency to purchase vital raw materials.)

21. Schmeling, *Max Schmeling,* 86–87, 93–94, 109–110. It is worth noting that the letter Schmeling delivered did not change Brundage's views; he was already determined to resist the boycott. Unlike Weimar politicians, Hitler courted athletes, as well as actors and artists, with flowers and invitations. Schmeling writes that he had long wanted to meet Reich President Hindenburg but that Hindenburg received only athletes with aristocratic credentials, like the equestrian Carl-Friedrich von Langen and the tennis star Gottfried von Cramm. In his autobiography, Schmeling claims that he resisted Nazi pressure to abandon his American Jewish manager, Joe Jacobs. Schmeling, *Max Schmeling,* 102–105.

22. Margolick, *Beyond Glory,* 209–210; "Financing of a Proposed Braddock-Schmeling Bout for the World's Championship in Berlin This Summer," report by Donald Jenkins, American Consul General, Berlin, to State Department, February 1, 1937, SDDF 862.4066/1.

23. Quotations in Kluge, *Max Schmeling,* 291–292.

24. Quoted in *NYT,* June 24, 1938, 22.

25. In 1933 Schmeling also fought Max Baer, an American who passed himself off as Jewish, though he was not. Margolick, *Beyond Glory,* 30.

26. In the United States before the 1880s, black and white heavyweights had competed freely, but when John L. Sullivan won the title he refused to fight black challengers. Jim Jeffries, another white champion, likewise refused to fight blacks until 1910, when Jack Johnson defeated him in a contest framed as a battle of the races. See Gail Bederman, *Manliness and Civilization: A Cultural History of Gender and Race in the United States, 1880–1917* (Chicago: University of Chicago Press, 1995), 1–2, and Al-Tony Gilmore, *Bad Nigger! The National Impact of Jack Johnson* (Port Washington, N.Y.: Kennikat Press, 1975). On Johnson's career and racism in American boxing, see Sammons, *Beyond the Ring*, ch. 2.

27. On the British ban see Patrick F. McDevitt, *May the Best Man Win: Sport, Masculinity and Nationalism in Great Britain and the Empire, 1880–1935* (New York: Palgrave Macmillan, 2004), 58–80.

28. Quotations in Margolick, *Beyond Glory*, 92, 137.

29. Quotations from *Nationalsozialistische Monatshefte* (1933) and *Völkische Beobachter* (1932) in Hans Joachim Teichler, "Coubertin und das Dritte Reich," *Sportwissenschaft* 12 (1982): 19.

30. Christiane Eisenberg, "German Workers and 'English Sport': Some Notes on the Limits of Cultural Transfer in the Nineteenth and Early-Twentieth Centuries," in *Labor and Leisure in Historical Perspective, Thirteenth to Twentieth Centuries (Vierteljahrschrift für Sozial- und Wirtschaftsgeschichte, Beihefte No. 116)*, ed. Ian Blanchard (Stuttgart: Franz Steiner, 1994), 156.

31. Speech of February 10, 1933, in Adolf Hitler, *Reden und Proklamationen, 1932–1945*, ed. Max Domarus (Wurzburg: Schmidt, Neustadt a.d. Aisch, 1962), 1:206.

32. Christiane Eisenberg, "Charismatic Nationalist Leader: *Turnvater* Jahr," in Holt, Mangan, and Lanfranchi, *European Heroes*, 14–27; John M. Hoberman, *Sport and Political Ideology* (Austin: University of Texas Press, 1984), 100–101; George L. Mosse, *The Nationalization of the Masses: Political Symbolism and Mass Movements in Germany from the Napoleonic Wars through the Third Reich* (Ithaca, N.Y.: Cornell University Press, 1975), 75. On the militaristic connotations that inspired Jahn's neologism, see Christiane Eisenberg, *"English Sports" und deutsche Bürger: eine Gesellschaftsgeschichte 1800–1939* (Paderborn: Schoningh, 1999), 112.

33. Mosse, *Nationalization of the Masses*, 128, 75, 82–83.

34. Ibid., 127.

35. On the political transformation of *Turnen*, see Michael Krüger, *Körperkultur und Nationsbildung: Die Geschichte des Turnens in der Reichgründung-sära* (Schorndorf: Hofmann, 1996), or the highly condensed summary presented in Michael Krüger, "Body Culture and Nation Building: The History of Gymnastics in Germany in the Period of Its Foundation as a

Nation-State," *IJHS* 13, no. 3 (December 1996): 409–417. See also Daniel McMillan, "Germany Incarnate: Politics, Gender and Sociability in the Gymnastics Movement, 1811–1871" (Ph.D. diss., Columbia University, 1996); and Rudy Koshar, *Social Life, Local Politics, and Nazism: Marburg, 1880–1935* (Chapel Hill: University of North Carolina Press, 1986), 109–114, 255.

36. Mosse, *Nationalization of the Masses,* 134; Arnd Krüger, "*Sieg Heil* to the Most Glorious Era of German Sport: Continuity and Change in the Modern German Sports Movement," *IJHS* 4, no. 1 (May 1987): 7. Note that the Germanness of *Turnen* did not prevent the system from being used as a model for similar nation-building enterprises, as in the Sokol in Czechoslovakia.

37. On English sports in Germany, see Eisenberg, *"English Sports"*; Eisenberg, "German Workers and 'English Sport,'" 149–159; and Eisenberg, "Middle Class and Competition," 265–282.

38. Edmund Neuendorff, *Geschichte der neueren deutschen Leibesübungen vom Beginn des 18. Jahrhunderts bis zur Gegenwart* (Dresden: Limpert, 1934), 4:486, quoted in Guttmann, *Games and Empires,* 144.

39. Quoted in Guttmann, *Games and Empires,* 144–145. Christiane Eisenberg sees this *Kulturkampf* as a conflict between adherents of tradition and modernity within the middle class; *"English Sports,"* 250–253.

40. Schmeling, *Max Schmeling,* 7–9; see Eisenberg, "Massensport," 139, 165.

41. Eisenberg, "Massensport," 171–172. The extensive use of sport and physical education for paramilitary aims in the 1920s is detailed in Hermann Bach, "Volks- und Wehrsport in der Weimarer Republik," *Sportwissenschaft* 11 (1981): 273–294.

42. Carl Diem, "Der Austritt der Deutschen Turnerschaft aus dem Deutschen Reichausschuß für Leibesübungen" (1925), in PAdAA, Gesandtschaft Bern, 2321, Aktenzeichen XII 20a Pkt 664, Sport, Verschiedenes, 1925–1938. The Turnerschaft stayed out from 1924 until 1926.

43. Hans Joachim Teichler, *Internationale Sportpolitik im Dritten Reich* (Schorndorf: Karl Hofmann, 1991), 38–44.

44. Diem, "Der Austritt"; Carl Diem, *Weltgeschichte des Sports und der Leibeserziehung* (Stuttgart: Cotta, 1960), 996.

45. Hans Joachim Teichler, "Sport unter der Herrschaft der Ideologie—Sport im Nationalsozialismus," in *Körper, Kultur und Ideologie: Sport und Zeitgeist im 19. und 20. Jahrhundert,* ed. Irene Diekmann and H. Joachim Teichler (Bodenheim bei Mainz: Philo, 1997), 100.

46. Adolf Hitler, *Mein Kampf,* trans. Ralph Manheim (Boston: Houghton Mifflin, 1971), 408–409.

47. Teichler, "Sport unter der Herrschaft," 101. According to Arnd Krüger, the

Völkischer Beobachter used the news service of the anti-Semitic Deutscher Turnerbund (an offshoot of the Turnerschaft) for ideological statements relating to sport. Krüger, "Sieg Heil," 12; Hajo Bernett, ed., *Der Sport im Kreuzfeuer der Kritik: Kritische Texte aus 100 Jahren deutscher Sportgeschichte* (Schorndorf: Karl Hofmann, 1982), 211.

48. *Der völkische Beobachter,* no. 88, April 17, 1929, quoted in Teichler, *Internationale Sportpolitik,* 45.

49. Bernett, *Sport im Kreuzfeuer der Kritik,* 212–213.

50. *Der völkische Beobachter,* no. 214, September 14, 1928, quoted in Teichler, *Internationale Sportpolitik,* 45.

51. *Der völkische Beobachter,* September 22–23, 1928 (Bayern-Ausgabe), quoted in Alkemeyer, *Körper, Kult, und Politik,* 234. On the Nazis' sharp reversal of the Weimar Republic's energetic cultivation of cultural internationalism, see also Iriye, *Cultural Internationalism,* 94–95.

52. Teichler, "Sport unter der Herrschaft," 104–105; Alkemeyer, *Körper, Kult und Politik,* 237.

53. Hajo Bernett, *Sportpolitik im Dritten Reich* (Schorndorf: Karl Hofmann, 1971), 44n80; Arnd Krüger, "The Role of Sport in German International Politics, 1918–1945," in Arnaud and Riordan, *Sport and International Politics,* 85; Diem, *Weltgeschichte des Sports,* 996.

54. Eisenberg, *"English Sports,"* 393.

55. Arnd Krüger, "Der Einfluß des faschistischen Sportmodells Italiens auf den nationalistischen Sport," in *Sport und Politik 1918–1939/40: Proceedings, ICOSH Seminar,* ed. A. Morgan Olsen (Otta, Norway: Engers Boktrykkeri A/S, 1986), 226–232.

56. G. A. Carr, "The Synchronization of Sport and Physical Education under National Socialism," *Canadian Journal of History of Sport and Physical Education* 10, no. 2 (December 1979): 15–35; Bernett, *Sportpolitik im Dritten Reich,* 19–37.

57. Bernett, *Sportpolitik im Dritten Reich,* 120. On the organizational structure of Nazi sport and physical education, see Hajo Bernett, *Der Weg des Sports in die nationalsozialistische Diktatur: Die Entstehung des Deutschen (Nationalsozialistischen) Reichsbundes für Leibesübungen* (Schorndorf: Karl Hofmann, 1983).

58. Carr, "Synchronization of Sport," 30.

59. Hajo Bernett, *Sportunterricht an der nationalsozialistischen Schule: Der Schulsport an den höheren Schulen Preußens 1933–1940* (Sankt Augustin: Richarz, 1985).

60. Hans von Tschammer und Osten, "Leibeserziehung bedeutet Erziehung des gesamtem Menschen von Leibe aus," *Leibesübungen und körperliche Erziehung* 10/11 (1933): 218.

61. *Der völkische Beobachter,* no. 87, March 22, 1937, 135. On women and sport under the Nazis, see Michaela Czech, *Frauen und Sport im national-sozialistischen Deutschland. Eine Untersuchung zur weiblichen Sportrealität in einem patriarchalen Herrschaftssystem* (Berlin: Tischler, 1994), and Gertrud Pfister, "Conflicting Femininities: The Discourse on the Female Body and the Physical Education of Girls in National Socialism," *Sport History Review* 28 (1997): 89–107.

62. Bruno Malitz, *Die Leibesübungen in der nationalsozialistischen Idee,* 2nd ed. (Munich: Frz. Eher Nachf., 1934), 23. This seventy-page booklet was published as volume 46 of the "Nationalsozialistische Bibliothek." Malitz, a former sprinter, was the sport editor of *Start und Ziel* and the sport expert of an SA brigade in Berlin. He was executed as a war criminal in 1948. Bernett, *Sport im Kreuzfeuer,* 214.

63. Malitz, *Leibesübungen,* 29–31, 47, 64.

64. *Das Archiv* (1935), 1934, quoted in Teichler, "Sport unter der Herrschaft," 104.

65. See the table in Teichler, *Internationale Sportpolitik,* 117. Unfortunately Teichler lumps the 1920s together, though it seems probable that international contacts would have dramatically increased as the decade progressed. Even so, the numbers under the Nazis after 1934 represent a substantial increase from the thirty or so meets that occurred annually in the early 1930s.

66. Teichler, "Sport unter der Herrschaft," 103, 107; Teichler, *Internationale Sportpolitik,* 105–117.

67. Unfortunately a full picture of the reasons for the regime's embrace of international sport and its aims in promoting it is difficult to reconstruct because many of the key sources are not available. Hans Joachim Teichler, whose dissertation is a thorough and impressively researched examination of the Nazis' international sport policy, concludes that many collections have been lost without a trace, including the records of the Deutscher Reichsbund für Leibesübungen (the central sport body) and its foreign department, as well as of the individual sport associations, the Reich Sport Office established in 1936, and the Propaganda Ministry's Foreign Sports section. Teichler, *Internationale Sportpolitik,* 16–17.

68. American Consul, Raymond H. Geist, Berlin, to Secretary of State, December 5, 1933, "The reorganization of German sport and its part in the political scheme of the Hitler Government" (twenty-one-page report marked "strictly confidential"), SDDF 862.4063/5, p. 15.

69. Foreign Ministry Nr. VI C 4328/33, July 31, 1933, PAdAA, Botschaft Rom.

70. Foreign Ministry to all missions, February 19, 1935, 2321 Aktenzeichen (Az) XII 20a Pkt 664, PAdAA, Gesandschaft Bern, Sport, Verschiedenes.

71. See Bern to Foreign Ministry, June 9, 1941, 3373 808 no. 2, PAdAA, Gesandschaft Bern.

72. Foreign Ministry to all missions, March 21, 1935, PAdAA, Gesandschaft Bern.

73. Teichler, "Sport unter der Herrschaft," 103–104.

74. "Grüner Tisch—Grüner Rasen," *Frankfurter Zeitung,* nr. 658, December 21, 1936.

75. International Großdeutschlandfahrt des Deutschen Radfahrer-Verbandes to Dörnberg, February 9, 1939, PAdAA, Sportwesen 2, Italien.

76. Brian Stoddart, "Sport, Cultural Politics and International Relations: England versus Germany, 1935," in *Olympic Scientific Congress, 1984, Official Report: Sport History,* ed. Norbert Müller and Joachim K. Rühl (Niedernhausen: Schors, 1985), 393; Richard Holt, "The Foreign Office and the Football Association, 1935–1938," in Arnaud and Riordan, *Sport and International Politics,* 53–57.

77. Friedrich Hartmannsgruber, ed., *Die Regierung Hitler: Akten der Reichskanzlei* (Munich: R. Oldenbourg, 1999), 2:1153.

78. Stoddart, "Sport, Cultural Politics, and International Relations," 401–404.

79. Krüger, "Role of Sport," 91.

80. Tschammer had hoped to be appointed to the IOC himself, but according to Arnd Krüger, Diem and Lewald successfully pushed for Reichenau instead. Krüger, "Role of Sport," 89. Diem had tried to convince the IOC to make Lewald a vice president, to make it more difficult for the Nazis to remove him from the organizing committee, but the IOC refused. Edström to Baillet-Latour, April 1, 1937, ABC, Box 42.

81. Karl Lennartz, "Difficult Times: Baillet-Latour and Germany, 1931–1942," *Olympika: The International Journal of Olympic Studies* 3 (1994): 102–103. The IOC took no position on the Olympic Institute. Lyberg, "IOC Sessions," 1:207.

82. The last issue of the *Olympic Bulletin* appeared in January 1938. The transfer of the IOC's official Olympic news to *Olympische Rundschau* was, according to IOC minutes, motivated by financial difficulties. Diem agreed to distribute the *Olympische Rundschau* free of charge to all Olympic members. Lyberg, "IOC Sessions," 1:207.

83. Lennartz, "Difficult Times," 102–103. The Olympic Diploma was awarded to Riefenstahl at the 1939 session in London; Lyberg, "IOC Sessions," 217.

84. Teichler, *Internationale Sportpolitik,* 291.

85. Quoted in Lennartz, "Difficult Times," 103. See also Teichler, *Internationale Sportpolitik,* 291–295.

86. Lennartz, "Difficult Times," 104. Baillet-Latour died in January 1942, and Sigfrid Edström, a Swede, assumed de jure leadership of the IOC for the

duration of the war. Karl Ritter von Halt attended Baillet-Latour's funeral as a representative of the German government, and both Hitler and Goebbels sent wreaths. Lyberg, "IOC Sessions," 222.

87. Newspaper clipping, unlabeled, November 1940, in IOC, Correspondance de Baillet-Latour.

88. Guttmann, "Nazi Olympics," 40.

89. See the correspondence of secretary Ivo Schricker with Nazi sport authorities in FIFA, correspondence with German National Association. Schricker, for example, broke federation rules in admitting to membership newly created Nazi-controlled national associations in occupied countries (for example Slovakia and Norway).

90. Edström to Brundage, August 19, 1942, January 19, 1942, and November 25, 1941, ABC, Box 42.

91. See de Grazia, "Mass Culture and Sovereignty."

92. Protocol of Amt Körperliche Ertüchtigung (Hamburg) conference, December 3–4, 1938, in Hajo Bernett, *Untersuchungen zur Zeitgeschichte des Sports* (Stuttgart: Karl Hofmann, 1973), 107.

6. Between Nazism and Olympism

1. Germany had been excluded from the Olympics until 1928, not by any official mandate of the IOC but by the host cities (Antwerp in 1920, Paris in 1924), which simply did not invite the defeated rival.

2. *Preussische Zeitung,* July 31, 1932, quoted in *LAT,* August 1, 1932, 14.

3. Baillet-Latour (to Coubertin, perhaps), August 11, 1932, IOC, Correspondance de Baillet-Latour.

4. Arnd Krüger, *Die Olympischen Spiele 1936 und die Weltmeinung: Ihre außenpolitische Bedeutung unter besonderer Berücksichtigung der USA* (Berlin: Bartels & Wernitz, 1972), 31, 50–52.

5. Guttmann, "Nazi Olympics," 32.

6. Karl-Heinz Minuth, ed., *Die Regierung Hitler, Teil 1: 1933/34* (Boppard am Rhein: Boldt, 1983), 234n3. The meeting took place on March 16, 1933.

7. Conversation with Goebbels, October 10, 1936, recorded by Lewald, quoted in Arnd Krüger, "The 1936 Olympics–Berlin," in *The Modern Olympics,* ed. Peter J. Graham and Horst Ueberhorst (West Point, N.Y.: Leisure Press, 1976), 178.

8. Richard Mandell, *The Nazi Olympics* (New York: Macmillan, 1971), 70; Arnd Krüger, "Germany: The Propaganda Machine," in Krüger and Murray, *Nazi Olympics,* 29. Diem was the single most important sports administrator in German history, from the Kaisserreich, when he was in charge of preparations for the 1916 Olympic Games in Berlin, and during the

Weimar period, when he headed the Deutsche Hochschule für Leibesübungen, through the postwar period, when he played a key role in re-
building German sport. On his controversial role under the Nazis, see
Hans Joachim Teichler, "Die Rolle Carl Diems in der Zeit und im
zeitlichen Umfeld des NS-Regimes," *Sozial- und Zeitgeschichte des Sports*
10 (1996): 56–74.

9. Arnd Krüger, "'Once the Olympics Are Through, We'll Beat Up the Jew':
German Jewish Sport 1898–1938 and the Anti-Semitic Discourse," *Journal of Sport History* 26, no. 2 (Summer 1999): 355–357.

10. Baillet-Latour to Lewald, Mecklenburg, and Ritter von Halt, May 3, 1933,
in Minuth, *Die Regierung Hitler,* 1:434–435. Lewald called Baillet-Latour's
tone "impertinent" in a letter to Staatssekretär Lammers, May 15, 1933
(ibid., 1:454).

11. Mandell, *Nazi Olympics,* 70.

12. Teichler, *Internationale Sportpolitik,* 83. See also Minuth, *Die Regierung
Hitler,* 1:454n4.

13. *NYT,* June 8, 1933, 1; Baillet-Latour quoted in Krüger, "United States," 50.

14. Baillet-Latour to Brundage, May 26, 1934, reproduced in Rürup, *1936,* 56.

15. Baillet-Latour to Berdez, December 8, 1933, IOC, Correspondance de
Baillet-Latour/Berdez.

16. Edström to Kirby, May 17, 1934, letter countersigned by Baillet-Latour,
USOC, Kirby papers, box 6.

17. *NYT,* October 22, 1935, 1; Baillet-Latour (to Coubertin, perhaps), March
27, 1935, IOC, Correspondance de Baillet-Latour.

18. Pfundtner to Lammers, September 3, 1935, Re: Participation of Jews in
the Olympic Games, in Hartmannsgruber, *Die Regierung Hitler,* 2:769;
Krüger, "'Once the Olympics Are Through,'" 359; Guttmann, "Nazi
Olympics," 41.

19. *NYT,* October 22, 1935, 1.

20. Ibid., July 30, 1936, 1, and November 11, 1936, 34; John Lucas, "Ernest
Less Jahncke: The Expelling of an IOC Member," *Stadion* 17, no. 1
(1991): 53–78; Carpentier, *Comité international Olympique,* 106.

21. Messersmith to State Department, November 15, 1935, "With reference to
American participation in the Olympic Games to be held in Berlin in
1936," SDDF 862.4063 Olympic Games/57.

22. On the boycott debate in the United States, see Chapter 3. On other countries, see Krüger and Murray, *Nazi Olympics,* 91–97, 169, 217–220.

23. David K. Wiggins, *Glory Bound: Black Athletes in a White America* (Syracuse, N.Y.: Syracuse University Press, 1997), 72–73.

24. Rürup, *1936,* 53, 57, 74–76, 98. Neither Ball nor Mayer were Jewish according to the Jewish definition, which recognizes as Jews only those born

to Jewish mothers. When Mayer arrived in Germany in February 1936, the press was ordered not to mention her "non-Aryan" descent. Krüger, "Germany," 26, 30.

25. Krüger, "Germany," 24, 33–34. See also Lewald's warning in May 1935 that anti-Semitic propaganda in Garmisch-Partenkirchen was a threat to the Games, in Hartmannsgruber, *Die Regierung Hitler,* 2:1091, and Krüger, "United States," 59. On the Winter Games, which were in many ways a dress rehearsal for Berlin, see Mandell, *Nazi Olympics,* 95–106.

26. Teichler, *Internationale Sportpolitik,* 164-166; Rürup, *1936,* 132, 140 (race researcher quotation on p. 201); Victor Klemperer, *I Will Bear Witness: A Diary of the Nazi Years,* trans. Martin Chalmers (New York: Random House, 1998), 182. According to the *New York Times, Der Stürmer* appeared despite the ban. *NYT,* August 21, 1936, 4.

27. *NYT,* July 26, 1936, VII, 10.

28. Ibid., August 16, 1936, IV, 1.

29. *OR 1936,* 44.

30. *Olympic Games 1936: Official Publication of the Publicity Commission for the XI. Olympic Games, Berlin 1936,* no. 2 (July 1935): 14; Mandell, *Nazi Olympics,* 44; *NYT,* August 4, 1936, 23.

31. *NYT,* August 4, 1936, 23, and August 16,1936, IV, 5.

32. *OR 1936,* 376–378.

33. Board of Education, *Physical Education in Germany,* Board of Education Educational Pamphlets, no. 109 (London: His Majesty's Stationery Office, 1938), 40. This is the report of the "British Physical Training Delegation" that toured Germany in November 1936, under the auspices of the German Academic Exchange Service and the Reich Ministry of Education. The delegation's conclusions were extremely favorable.

34. *OR 1936,* 135–137.

35. Albert Speer, *Inside the Third Reich,* trans. Richard and Clara Winston (New York: Macmillan, 1970), 80.

36. Board of Education, *Physical Education in Germany,* 40.

37. *OR 1936,* 166–182, 373; *NYT,* December 22, 1936, 12.

38. Rürup, *1936,* 109.

39. *NYT,* August 30, 1936, V, 1; *OR 1936,* 225–226.

40. *OR 1936,* 86–94, 122–139; Krüger, "Germany," 32. In another connection to Krupp, on August 1 an Olympic torch was used to light a new "Olympic Blast Furnace 4" at the Krupp factories in Essen. Rürup, *1936,* 114.

41. *OR 1936,* 276–281.

42. Krüger, "Germany," 21; *OR 1936,* 373.

43. *OR 1936,* 301–306.

44. "Address of the Reich Sports Leader," July 29, 1936, IOC, Correspondance de Baillet-Latour.

45. *OR 1936*, 355–363; *NYT*, July 26, 1936, V, 1.

46. *OR 1936*, 42.

47. Ibid., 362.

48. *NYT*, July 31, 1936, 13.

49. *OR 1936*, 309–311.

50. *NYT*, July 31, 1936, 13.

51. Krüger, "Germany," 34. The estimate was made by Victor Boin, the Belgian president of the international sportswriters union.

52. *NYT*, July 19, 1936, 17.

53. Ibid.; *OR 1936*, 335–341.

54. *NYT*, July 26, 1936, IX, 7, and August 2, 1936, V, 3.

55. *OR 1936*, 342–343; Mandell, *Nazi Olympics*, 138–139; Stephen R. Wenn, "A History of the International Olympic Committee and Television, 1936–1980" (Ph.D. diss., Pennsylvania State University, 1993).

56. *OR 1936*, 498–500.

57. Ibid., 424, 417–419; Krüger, *Olympischen Spiele*, 228. Countries sending the most visitors were Czechoslovakia, the United States, Sweden, and Great Britain (p. 419). The official report's estimate of the total number of visitors is based on records of hotels and pensions; uncounted others stayed with friends and relatives (p. 417).

58. *NYT*, August 8, 1936, 6. Mussolini did not attend the Games but his sons Bruno and Vittorio did. *NYT*, August 7, 1936, 12.

59. *NYT*, July 27, 1936, 11, and July 28, 1936, 12.

60. Pendergrast, *For God, Country, and Coca-Cola*, 220–226; Helmut Fritz, *Das Evangelium der Erfrischung: Coca-Colas Weltmission* (Reinbek bei Hamburg: Rowohlt, 1985), 74; Jeff R. Schutts, "'Die erfrischende Pause': Marketing Coca-Cola in Hitler's Germany," in *Selling Modernity: Cultures of Advertising in Twentieth Century Germany*, ed. Jonathan Wiesen, Jonathan Zatlin, and Pamela Swett (Durham, N.C.: Duke University Press, forthcoming); Rürup, *1936*, 82; and David Clay Large, *Nazi Games: The 1936 German Olympics* (New York: W. W. Norton, forthcoming).

61. July 29, 1936 and August 1, 1936 entries, Goebbels, *Tagebücher*, 2: 649–651.

62. Headline in *Le Jour*, July 29, 1936, quoted in William Murray, "France: Liberty, Equality, and the Pursuit of Fraternity," in Krüger and Murray, *Nazi Olympics*, 99.

63. By central decree, Jews in the city were permitted to hang the Olympic flag and the flags of participating nations, but not the swastika. Rürup, *1936*, 83.

64. Mandell, *Nazi Olympics*, 138–143; *OR 1936*, 374–375, 458–459; *NYT* December 19, 1936, 4; Krüger "Germany," 25–27; Alkemeyer, *Körper, Kult und Politik*, 309; Teichler, *Internationale Sportpolitik*, 164–166; Schmeling, *Max Schmeling*, 135; David Clay Large, *Berlin* (New York: Basic Books, 2000), 295; Klemperer, *I Will Bear Witness*, 182; Rürup, *1936*, 132–135, 140.

65. *NYT*, July 18, 1932, 13. The Associated Press report remarked that "there was no immediate reaction except on the faces of the visitors who read the proclamation."

66. *NYT*, July 6, 1936, 6.

67. Ibid., July 13, 1936, 10, and August 16, 1936, V, 2.

68. *OR 1936*, 544–546, 575; quotation on 544.

69. The official tally showed 4,793 competitors representing 50 nations entered for the competitions, of which 3,949 competitors from 49 countries competed (Jamaica's entry was added to that of Great Britain). *OR 1936*, 596–598.

70. *NYT*, August 4, 1936, 23. In the Olympic salute the right arm is raised level with the shoulder and held sidewise, rather than forward as in the Nazi salute. Not surprisingly, the Olympic salute was not used again after World War II.

71. Mandell, *Nazi Olympics*, 146–154.

72. John Weitz, *Hitler's Diplomat: The Life and Times of Joachim von Ribbentrop* (New York: Ticknor & Fields, 1992), 109–112; André François-Poncet, *The Fateful Years* (New York: Harcourt, Brace, 1949), 206; William E. Dodd Jr., *Ambassador Dodd's Diary, 1933–1938*, ed. William E. Dodd Jr. and Martha Dodd (New York: Harcourt, Brace & Co., 1941), 340; Mandell, *Nazi Olympics*, 155–158; Goebbels, *Tagebücher*, 2:651, 662; Rob Burns, ed., *German Cultural Studies: An Introduction* (New York: Oxford University Press, 1995), 117; Rürup, *1936*, 118.

73. William Manchester, *The Arms of Krupp, 1587–1968* (Boston: Little, Brown, 1968), 376; Krüger, *Olympischen Spiele*, 228; Krüger, "Germany," 28.

74. Quoted in *NYT*, August 17, 1936, 12.

75. *NYT*, August 7, 1936, 12; Krüger, "The Role of Sport in German International Politics, 1918–1945," in Arnaud and Riordan, *Sport and International Politics*, 88.

76. Rürup, *1936*, 162.

77. Wiggins, *Glory Bound*, 73.

78. Martha Dodd, *Through Embassy Eyes* (New York: Harcourt, Brace, 1939), 211. Owens was greeted on his return as a national hero (*NYT*, August 26, 1926, 27), but racism limited his subsequent opportunities.

79. On Riefenstahl, see Cooper C. Graham, *Leni Riefenstahl and Olympia* (Metuchen, N.J.: Scarecrow Press, 1986).

80. William J. Baker, *Jesse Owens: An American Life* (New York: Free Press, 1986), 90–91. The myth was created by U.S. journalists covering the Games, and although Owens at first disputed it, he eventually found it easier to pretend it was true.

81. Speer, *Inside the Third Reich,* 73. See also Dodd, *Through Embassy Eyes,* 212.

82. August 5, 1936 entry, Goebbels, *Tagebücher,* 2:655.

83. Press instructions cited in Krüger, "Germany," 25; Rürup, *1936,* 161.

84. Speer, *Inside the Third Reich,* 73.

85. August 3, 1936, entry, Goebbels, *Tagebücher,* 2:654.

86. August 15, 1936, entry in Goebbels, *Tagebücher,* 2:662; see also August 12, 1936 entry in ibid., 2:660.

87. *NYT,* August 18, 1936, 18.

88. William E. Dodd, Berlin, to State Department, "The Olympic Games," September 2, 1936, 2, 5, 7–8, SDDF 862.4063 Olympic Games.

89. Rürup, *1936,* 106.

90. Krüger, "Germany," 35; Krüger, *Die Olympischen Spiele.*

91. *OR 1936,* 541.

92. See, for example, Alkemeyer, *Körper, Kult und Politik,* Peter Reichel, *Der schöne Schein des Dritten Reiches: Faszination und Gewalt des Faschismus* (Munich: Carl Hanser, 1991), 263–270.

93. Eisenberg, *"English Sports,"* 411–419; Rürup, *1936,* 113; United Press report quoted in Lipstadt, *Beyond Belief,* 81.

94. For an opposing view, see Large, *Nazi Games.*

95. *NYT,* August 16, 1936, IV, 5.

96. Marty Glickman with Stan Isaacs, *Fastest Kid on the Block: The Marty Glickman Story* (Syracuse, N.Y.: Syracuse University Press, 1996), 170. Glickman claimed that Brundage and the track coach kept him and Sam Stoller, both Jews, off the final four hundred-meter relay team in order not to "embarrass their Nazi friends by having two Jewish athletes stand on the winner's podium to be cheered" (p. 29). There is no direct evidence to back this claim; the two spots were filled by Jesse Owens and Ralph Metcalfe, both black and both better sprinters. On the controversy see Krüger, "United States," 62.

7. The Soviet Union and the Triumph of Soccer

1. Katerina Clark, *Petersburg: Crucible of Cultural Revolution* (Cambridge, Mass.: Harvard University Press, 1995), 165–180; Jeffrey Brooks, "Official Xenophobia and Popular Cosmopolitanism in Early Soviet Russia," *American Historical Review* 97, no. 5 (December 1992): 1431–1448.

2. S. Frederick Starr, *Red and Hot: The Fate of Jazz in the Soviet Union, 1917–1980* (New York: Oxford University Press 1983), 107–180; Sheila Fitzpatrick, ed., *Stalinism: New Directions* (New York: Routledge, 2000), 190–193, 217; David L. Hoffmann, *Stalinist Values: The Cultural Norms of Soviet Modernity, 1917–1941* (Ithaca, N.Y.: Cornell University Press, 2003), 37; Denise J. Youngblood, *Movies for the Masses: Popular Cinema and Soviet Society in the 1920s* (Cambridge: Cambridge University Press, 1992), 174, 213. More broadly, as Stephen Kotkin has argued, despite its pursuit of a distinctively illiberal version of modernity, the Soviet Union was enmeshed in the international modernizing trends that propelled the spread of mass politics, mass production, mass culture, and mass consumption throughout Europe and the United States. Stephen Kotkin, "'Modern Times': The Soviet Union and the Interwar Conjuncture," *Kritika* 2, no. 1 (Winter 2001): 111–164.

3. De Grazia, "Mass Culture and Sovereignty," 53–87.

4. In fascist Italy, for example, the government promoted noncompetitive, mass-participation sport designed to discourage aggressive individuality and to prepare participants for work and war, a system with many elements in common with early Soviet physical culture. To avoid "contamination," a separate organ supervised high-level competitive sport, including preparation for the Olympics and professional competitions. In the 1930s, however, elite sport triumphed over mass sport. Victoria de Grazia, *The Culture of Consent: Mass Organization of Leisure in Fascist Italy* (Cambridge: Cambridge University Press, 1981), 172–177.

5. The Soviet shift from mass to elite sport in the 1930s has long been recognized by historians of Soviet sport (see the earliest account in Henry Morton, *Soviet Sport: Mirror of Soviet Society* [New York: Collier, 1963], 35). This chapter addresses the causes and consequences of this shift, and its international dimension, based on the recently opened records of the main government organ for sport (the All-Union Committee on Physical Culture and Sport and its predecessors). Despite the opening of the Russian archives, however, it remains difficult to elucidate sport-related decision making at the highest levels of party and state because key collections were destroyed. In particular the prewar secret documents of the Committee on Physical Culture—including most of its correspondence with the highest levels of party and state—were burned in the months following the German invasion in 1941. See the lists of burned documents in GARF, f. 7576, op. 29, d. 2.

6. The classic statement on the Great Retreat is Nicholas Timasheff, *The Great Retreat: The Growth and Decline of Communism in Russia* (New York: Dutton, 1946).

7. David Hoffmann similarly situates Stalinist population politics in a European context, arguing that Stalinist pronatalism reflected a new type of population politics practiced in the modern era and that Stalinist policies, though shaped by culture and ideology, should be seen as part of a broader trend toward state management of population. David Hoffman, "Mothers in the Motherland: Stalinist Pronatalism in Its Pan-European Context," *Journal of Social History* 34, no. 1 (Fall 2000): 35–54.

8. Catriona Kelly and David Shepherd, eds., *Constructing Russian Culture in the Age of Revolution, 1881–1940* (Oxford, England: Oxford University Press, 1998), 75–77; James Riordan, *Sport in Soviet Society: Development of Sport and Physical Education in Russia and the USSR* (Cambridge: Cambridge University Press, 1977), 31–37; V. I. Koloskov, ed., *Sto let rossiiskomu futbolu* (Moscow: Rossiiskii fultbol'nyi soiuz, 1997), 32–35.

9. A. V. Lunacharskii, *Mysli o sporte* (Moscow: Ogonek, 1930), 24–26, 40–42; Riordan, *Sport in Soviet Society,* 94–105.

10. A. A. Zikmund, *Osnovy sovetskoi sistemy fizkul'tury* (Moscow, 1926), 21, quoted in N. F. Kulinko, *Istoriia fizicheskoi kul'tury i sporta* (Orenburg: Orenburgskoe knizhnoe izd-vo), 193.

11. Koloskov, *Sto let,* 56–57; Kulinko, *Istoriia fizicheskoi kul'tury,* 192.

12. Lunacharskii, *Mysli o sporte,* 24–26, 40–42.

13. For an overview of the relationship between the Sportintern and the socialist sport international, see David Steinberg, "The Workers' Sport Internationals, 1920–1928," *Journal of Contemporary History* 13, no. 2 (April 1978): 233–251.

14. For a brief overview of Sportintern policy, see André Gounot, "Between Revolutionary Demands and Diplomatic Necessity: The Uneasy Relationship between Soviet Sport and Worker and Bourgeois Sport in Europe from 1920 to 1937," in Arnaud and Riordan, *Sport and International Politics,* 184–209.

15. The Supreme Council for Physical Culture, established in 1923, was replaced in 1930 by the All-Union Council of Physical Culture attached to the Central Executive Committee. In 1936 the Council was reconstituted as the All-Union Committee on Physical Culture and Sport, its enhanced standing reflected in its direct subordination to the Council of People's Commissars (or Sovnarkom, the highest executive organ of the government). (For ease of reference, both the council and the committee are referred to here as the "Physical Culture Council.") Similar but not equivalent to the ministries for sport established in many European countries in this period, the council's powers were limited and its authority was contested by the Komsomol, the Central Trade Union Council, and the Commissariats of Health, Education, and Defense, which also had important independent roles in sport policy.

16. RGASPI, f. 537, op. 1, d. 105, l. 79; RGASPI, f. 537, op. 1, d. 126, ll. 64–65; RGASPI, f. 537, op. 1, d. 75, l. 70; RGASPI, f. 537, op. 1, d. 125, l. 93. For one Sportintern official's criticisms of bourgeois deviations within the Sportintern, see Bruno Lieske to the Sportintern Presidium, August 1925, RGASPI, f. 537, op. 1, d. 104, ll. 26–57.

17. Boris Bazhanov, *Vospominaniia byvshego sekretaria Stalina* (Paris: Tret'ia volna, 1980), 235. Bazhanov was a member of the Physical Culture Council and a secretary to Stalin who fled the USSR in the late 1920s. He claimed (many years later) to have interceded with Stalin, who cared little about sport, when this dispute arose in 1925–1926.

18. See, for example, Gounot, "Between Revolutionary Demands," 191–192.

19. See, for example, a 1921 Sportintern report calling for international matches to showcase "achieved successes"; RGASPI, f. 537, op. 1, d. 71, ll. 39–40.

20. Koloskov, *Sto let,* 56–58; Robert Edelman, *Serious Fun: A History of Spectator Sports in the USSR* (New York: Oxford University Press, 1993), 30, 48–53; Andrei Starostin, *Bol'shoi futbol* (Moscow: Molodaia gvardiia, 1959), 24. As Edelman notes, the largest arena in Moscow before 1928 was built in 1926 by the food workers' union, with 15,000 seats. Before 1926, the largest arena had five thousand seats "on rickety wooden bleachers"; these venues had few or no amenities like scoreboards, restrooms, and changing rooms.

21. See, for example, M. Kedrov, *Boevye zadachi Krasnogo Sportinterna* (Moscow: Fizkul'tura i sport, 1930), 38, 41.

22. Quoted in Koloskov, *Sto let,* 73.

23. *Krasnyi sport,* October 16, 1927, quoted in Edelman, *Serious Fun,* 49.

24. Quoted in Koloskov, *Sto let,* 74.

25. Some physical culture activists felt betrayed by the reversal in policy and criticized the new line as a *smena vekh,* or a retreat from revolutionary principles in the name of nationalism. Stenogram of meeting of representatives of physical culture soviets, April 12, 1934, GARF, f. 7576, op. 1, d. 186, ll. 32–33.

26. Kedrov, *Boevye zadachi,* 21. In advocating meets with members of bourgeois clubs, Kedrov noted that "even raising the issue of joint competitions with workers from bourgeois groups undoubtedly will provoke heated debate within our ranks."

27. Physical Culture Council to Commissariat of Foreign Affairs, August 13, 1933, GARF, f. 7576, op. 2, d. 137.

28. *Krasnyi sport,* December 31, 1933, 1; July 24, 1934, 3; and June 21, 1934, 1.

29. Ibid., July 31, 1934, 1; October 22, 1934, 3–4; and January 1, 1937, 1.

[Emphasis added.] See also *Pravda,* April 13, 1935: "In the near future we must make the USSR the country of all world records."

30. GARF, f. 7576, op. 2, d. 108.

31. VOKS even created a sport section; GARF, f. 7576, op. 2, d. 248, l. 225. The Commissariat of Foreign Affairs seems to have been less enthusiastic about sport. One request to the Commissariat for assistance in getting literature on foreign sport was met with a curt refusal. Snegov to Potemkin/NKID, May 23, 1939, GARF, f. 7576, op. 1, d. 403, l. 42. One former Physical Culture Council official who later emigrated recalled that Foreign Department employees were carefully screened because they worked with foreign materials. Even so, foreign newspapers and journals arrived at the department with articles and photos already cut out by censors, who feared that such publications revealed too much about life abroad. F. Legostaev, *Fizicheskoe vospitanie i sport v SSSR* (Munich: Institut po izucheniiu istorii i kul'tury, 1952), 28.

32. *Sport in the Soviet Union* (Moscow: Intourist, [1937]); Intourist to Snegov, June 23, 1939, GARF, f. 7576, op. 1, d. 403, l. 11. In the latter memo, Intourist complained that foreign tourists show a great interest in Soviet sport but that it is very difficult for them to get tickets to games, lamenting both the loss of hard currency and the opportunity to showcase Soviet achievements.

33. Snegov to Central Committee, July 3, 1940, GARF, f. 7576, op. 29, d. 1, ll. 15–16, 39. Complaints were voiced throughout the 1930s about *Krasnyi sports* low circulation and deficiencies in its presentation of sport events. GARF, f. 7576, op. 1, d. 295, ll. 35, 37.

34. Stenogram of VKFK meeting on organizing the physical culture exhibit for the Paris Exhibition, December 13, 1936, GARF, f. 7576, op. 1, d. 268, l. 23.

35. Karpov and Polliak to Zelikov, [1938], GARF, f. 7576, op. 2, d. 176, ll. 32–33.

36. Stenogram of meeting of Council Presidium, November 28, 1934, GARF, f. 7576, op. 1, d. 182, l. 5.

37. *Krasnyi sport,* October 22, 1934, 3.

38. As a condition of the trip, Czech authorities insisted that Soviet athletes refrain from participating in political demonstrations of any kind. When some track and field athletes who were also part of the delegation did participate in a protest, they were arrested and deported. Aleksandr Starostin, *Rasskaz kapitana* (Moscow: Molodaia gvardiia, 1935), 9, 67–69.

39. Ibid., 3.

40. Stenogram of meeting of players who went to Czechoslovakia, November 22, 1934, GARF, f. 7576, op. 2, d. 160, ll. 2, 8, 16–18.

41. Procès-verbal de la réunion du Comité exécutif, Paris, November 17, 1934, FIFA, Executive Committee Agendas and Minutes, 1927–1943.
42. Stenogram of meeting of players, l. 53.
43. Kharchenko and Demin to Antipov, Kosarev, Shvernik, and Iagoda, RGASPI, f. 1-m, op. 21, d. 250, l. 3.
44. List of international sport contacts, GARF, f. 7576, op. 2, d. 197, ll. 20–35; *Krasnyi sport*, August 9, 1935, 1, and August 31, 1935, 1. For a detailed description of the 1935 meets, including tables comparing Soviet and world records in various sports, see Ivan Kharchenko, *Sovetskii sport na pod"eme* (Moscow: Fizkul'tura i turizm, 1936).
45. On May 23, 1937, calling the continued existence of the Sportintern "inexpedient," the Presidium of the Executive Committee of the Comintern transferred responsibility for sport work directly to national communist parties and established a special sport commission under the Secretariat of the Executive Committee. The Secretariat of the Sportintern was relegated to "an auxiliary organ of the Comintern for sport activity," whose main duty was to collect information and issue a sport journal. Resolution on the transformation of the Sportintern Secretariat into an auxiliary organ of the Comintern for sport, May 23, 1937, RGASPI, f. 495, op. 2, d. 255, ll. 4, 15–16. At Dimitrov's order, the disbanding of the Sportintern was kept secret. That the Sportintern had ceased to function was therefore not publicly known at the time, and scholars have sometimes erroneously suggested that the organization lasted into the war years. (The Popular Front policy of conciliation with the "bourgeoisie" also rendered superfluous the Red International of Labor Unions, or Profintern, another Comintern auxiliary. It began the process of dissolution in 1936.)
46. Stenogram of meeting of Presidium of Comintern Executive Committee, March 22, 1937, RGASPI, f. 495, op. 2, d. 251, ll. 10–20, 77.
47. Appeal, July 8, 1936, RGASPI, f. 495, op. 20, d. 868, l. 210.
48. Draft resolution of the Secretariat of Comintern Executive Committee on tasks of the Sportintern, c. April 1937, RGASPI, f. 495, op. 2, d. 252, l. 51.
49. The French organizers of the 1924 Paris Games were "likely" to invite the USSR, but the French Council of Ministers judged the invitation inappropriate. Pierre Arnaud, "French Sport and the Emergence of Authoritarian Regimes, 1919–1939," in Arnaud and Riordan, *Sport and International Politics,* 131. The assertion in one source (Koloskov, *Sto let,* 62) that the IOC invited the Soviets to participate in 1924 seems unlikely; more probable is that some preliminary feelers or rumors of a possible invitation reached the Soviets. According to one source, the Los Angeles Organizing Committee, eager to ensure maximum participation in the Games after the onset of the Depression, initiated discussions with Ivan Zholdak, general secretary of

the Sportintern, about the possibility of Soviet participation. Nikolai Niko-
laevich Bugrov, "Mezhdunarodnye sviazi sovestskikh sportivnykh organi-
zatsii na sluzhbe sotsial'nogo progressa i uprocheniia vseobshchego mira
(1917–1967)" (Ph.D. diss., GTsOLIFK, Moscow, 1971), 87, citing notes of
a discussion with Zholdak. A 1931 letter from the Los Angeles Organizing
Committee secretary lends some support to the idea that the committee
was interested in Soviet participation but was instructed by the IOC that
the USSR was "not to be considered" for participation. Farmer to Baillet-
Latour, November 19, 1931, IOC, Jeux olympiques 1932.

50. Berdez to Baillet-Latour, January 7, 1934, and Baillet-Latour to Berdez,
January 17, 1934, IOC, Correspondance de Baillet-Latour. For a highly
critical assessment of the IOC's flirtation with fascism in the 1930s, see
John Hoberman, "Toward a Theory of Olympic Internationalism," *Journal
of Sport History* 22, no. 1 (Spring 1995): 1–37.

51. Procès-verbal de la réunion du Comité d'urgence, Paris, October 7, 1934,
FIFA, Comité d'urgence, Correspondence, 1932–1950; Circular from
Schricker to Executive Committee members, October 19, 1934, FIFA, Ex-
ecutive Committee Agendas and Minutes, 1927–1943. See also Beck,
Scoring for Britain, 231.

52. Procès-verbal de la réunion du Comité exécutif, November 28, 1936,
Frankfurt, Annexe No. II.1, FIFA, Executive Committee Agendas and
Minutes, 1927–1943. The Basque professionals who visited the USSR in
1937 played without FIFA sanction.

53. Translated excerpts from Vienna's *Sport-Tageblatt* and *Prager Tageblatt,*
July 17, 1937, in GARF, f. 7576, op. 1, d. 328, ll. 4–5. In 1944 Sigfrid Es-
tröm, the head of the IAAF, wrote that "the Russians have been invited
several times in earlier years to become members of IAAF but have refused." Edström to Brundage, May 19, 1944, ABC, Box 42.

54. Karpov and Polliak to Zelikov, [1938], GARF, f. 7576, op. 2, d. 176, ll. 32–33.

55. Translation of article from *L'Auto,* January 24, 1936, in RGASPI, f. 1-m, op.
21, d. 283, ll. 36–37.

56. Stenogram of meeting of Presidium of Comintern Executive Committee,
March 22, 1937, RGASPI, f. 495, op. 2, d. 251, l. 110.

57. Karpov and Polliak to Zelikov, [1938], GARF, f. 7576, op. 2, d. 176, ll.
32–33. On Soviet views of Schricker see RGASPI, f. 495, op. 2, d. 251, l.
33, and RGASPI, f. 495, op. 20, d. 871, ll. 156–157.

58. According to Swedish press reports, Pelikan visited Moscow and proposed
that the Soviet Union join FIFA and compete in the 1940 Helsinki
Olympic Games, on condition that the regime agree to join the IOC, to respect amateur rules, to uphold the regulations of international federations
in refraining from the use of sport as political propaganda, and to main-

tain ties with workers' sports associations only as permitted on a case-by-case basis by international federations. Kristina Exner-Carl, *Sport und Politik in den Beziehungen Finnlands zur Sowjetunion, 1940–1952* (Wiesbaden: Harrassowitz, 1997), 55–58, summarizing a report in the Stockholm sports paper *Idrottsbladet* from October 12, 1938, with the headline "The Soviet Union breaks its isolation! It will be allowed to start in Helsinki and become a member of FIFA when it meets four conditions." The newspaper article also claimed that Soviet authorities had discussed the participation of a Soviet soccer team at the Olympics with the Finnish Olympic Committee, but Exner-Carl found no reports of any such discussions in the committee's protocols.

59. Zelikov to Kosior, September 10, 1938, GARF, f. 7576, op. 1, d. 377, ll. 77–78. The text of the technical agreement is not in the council's files, but according to the assessment offered by the council's foreign department, it offered the Soviet Union "the opportunity to meet with the strongest representatives of international soccer (the most popular sport in the USSR), without depending politically or practically on the leadership of FIFA." The department also recommended joining the international federations for track and field and for skating, because "Soviet sportsmen occupy a respected place in these sports and the Scandinavian leadership of these associations is friendly toward the USSR." Karpov and Polliak to Zelikov, [1938], GARF, f. 7576, op. 2, d. 176, ll. 32–33. The Politburo had discussed joining the International Shooting Union as early as 1935 (the result is unknown). Protocol no. 31, July 28, 1935, and no. 32, August 31, 1935, RGASPI, f. 17, op. 3, d. 969.

60. Proposals for international sport matches had to be approved by the Politburo; see, for example, the resolution approving the match against Racing Club: RGASPI, f. 17, op. 3, d. 974, l. 11.

61. John McCannon, *Red Arctic: Polar Exploration and the Myth of the North in the Soviet Union, 1932–1939* (New York: Oxford University Press, 1998), 70, 96–98; protocol of April 20, 1936 Politburo meeting, RGASPI, f. 17, op. 3, d. 976, l. 49.

62. Christiane Eisenberg, "Football in Germany: Beginnings, 1890–1914," *IJHS* 8, no. 2 (1991): 206.

63. Murray, *Football*, 90; Wahl and Lanfranchi, *Les Footballeurs professionnels*, 41.

64. Koloskov, *Sto let*, 60–61; Edelman, *Serious Fun*, 44–47.

65. Starostin to Kosarev and Mantsev, [February 15, 1936], GARF, f. 7576, op. 1, d. 275, ll. 33–34. See also the description of press accounts of a Komsomol's Central Committee meeting at which Nikolai Starostin presented his proposal, in Edelman, *Serious Fun*, 60.

66. Koloskov, *Sto let*, 77–78. On the formation of the league, see also Edel-

man, *Serious Fun*, 51, 57–62. Sport societies were established in 1935 and organized sport along production (rather than territorial or sport) principles: thus, individual trade unions organized multisport societies. Societies were also run by the secret police (Dinamo), the Red Army (Central House), and the producers' cooperatives (Spartak).

67. Edelman, *Serious Fun*, 66.
68. *Krasnyi sport*, March 25, 1940, 3.
69. Riordan, *Sport in Soviet Society*, 127, 133.
70. See Edelman, *Serious Fun*, 61.
71. Ibid., 64–65. According to Nikolai Starostin, Beria attended almost every Dinamo match after he was appointed head of the secret police (Dinamo's sponsor). On Beria's interest in soccer and his postwar vendetta against Starostin, see Nikolai Starostin, *Futbol skvoz' gody* (Moscow: Sovetskaia Rossiia, 1989), 49ff.; for a summary in English of Starostin's account, see James Riordan, "The Strange Story of Nikolai Starostin, Football and Lavrentii Beria," *Europe-Asia Studies* 46, no. 4 (1994): 681–690. In 1939 Beria forced Spartak to replay a semifinal match against his favorite team, Dinamo Tblisi, after Spartak had already gone on to win the final, because of a disputed goal. See Edelman, *Serious Fun*, 65; Starostin, *Futbol skvoz' gody*, 51ff.
72. M. D. Romm, "Sistema 'Dubl'-ve' v futbole, ee vozniknovenie i vliianie na taktiku igry," *Teoriia i praktika fizicheskoi kul'tury* (May 1938): 40; Aleksandr Starostin, *Rasskaz kapitana* (Moscow: Molodaia gvardia, 1935), 59–60.
73. Beria to Stalin, August 16, 1938, GARF, f. 7576, op. 1, d. 375, ll. 13–14; Zelikov to Molotov, October 7, 1938, GARF, f. 7576, op. 1, d. 375, ll. 3–3ob, 6–7; Zelikov to Sovnarkom, [1938], GARF, f. 7576, op. 1, d. 375, ll. 8–11.
74. These problems were widely discussed in the press and were the subject of many Komsomol discussions in 1939; see the reports in RGASPI, f. 1-m, op. 23, d. 1365.
75. *Pravda*, August 5, 1937, 4.
76. Nikolai, Aleksandr, Andrei, and Petr Starostin to Molotov, September 3, 1937, RGASPI, f. 1-m, op. 23, d. 1268, ll. 11–13.
77. G. I. Znamenskii to Knopova, September 18, 1937, RGASPI, f. 1-m, op. 23, d. 1268, ll. 22–23.
78. S. Znamenskii to Knopova, [September 1937], RGASPI, f. 1-m, op. 23, d. 1268, ll. 29–31. Nikolai Starostin was finally arrested during the war. He claimed that Beria, an avid fan of Spartak's major rival, the Dinamo society of the secret police, was irked by Spartak's success in the late 1930s but could not take revenge until the war. See Starostin, *Futbol skvoz' gody*, 49ff; Edelman, *Serious Fun*, 77; and Riordan, "Strange Story," 681–690.
79. *Krasnyi sport*, February 1, 1938, 1.
80. Ibid., January 3, 1939, 1, 3.

81. Ibid., September 15, 1940, 3, noted the lack of serious international matches in 1938 and 1939.
82. *Pravda,* July 6, 1938, 6; list of sport contacts, GARF, f. 7576, op. 2, d. 197, ll. 20–35. French, Czech, and Norwegian athletes in various sports visited the USSR in 1938.
83. Memo to Vyshinskii, [June 1939], GARF, f. 7576, op. 2, d. 192, l. 5.
84. Plan of international sport meetings for 1940, [1939], GARF, f. 7576, op. 2, d. 205, ll. 3–4; Legostaev, *Fizicheskoe vospitanie,* 27. The large number of meets described for the years 1938–1940 in F. I. Samoukov, V. V. Stolbov, and N. I. Toropov, eds., *Fizicheskaia kul'tura i sport v SSSR* (Moscow: Fizkul'tura i sport, 1967), 158, most likely refers to matches proposed, not held. The claim that in 1939–1940 "some 250 German athletes competed in the USSR and 175 Soviet athletes competed in Germany" and that "more sports contests took place between Soviet and German athletes during 1940 than between the athletes of the USSR and all 'bourgeois' states in all the preceding years since 1917" is incorrect; James Riordan, "The Sports Policy of the Soviet Union, 1917–1941," in Arnaud and Riordan, *Sport and International Politics,* 77. The thrust of Nazi foreign sport policy in these years was directed toward other countries; see Teichler, *Internationale Sportpolitik,* pt. 3.
85. N. N. Romanov, *Trudnye dorogi k olimpu* (Moscow: Fizkul'tura i sport, 1987), 16. For unknown reasons, an attempt to hold a similar soccer match in November 1939 had fallen through. Schricker to Andrejevìc, November 7, 1939, FIFA, Andrejevìc dossier.
86. Starostin, *Futbol skvoz' gody,* 60; Starostin, *Bol'shoi futbol,* 212.
87. GARF, f. 7576, op. 2, d. 233, ll. 4–5, 19, 11; Romanov, *Trudnye dorogi,* 16.
88. Andrejevìc to Schricker, August 17, 1940, FIFA, Andrejevìc dossier. As Gabriel Gorodetsky notes, "In the absence of any tangible leverage on Bulgaria, Stalin continued to rally the reliable popular support there. King Boris was unable to restrain the tumultuous reception given to the Soviet national soccer team." He cites the record of a August 15, 1940, meeting between the Soviet ambassador in Bulgaria (Lavrishchev) and the Bulgarian foreign minister (Ivan Popov). Gabriel Gorodetsky, *Grand Delusion: Stalin and the German Invasion of Russia* (New Haven, Conn.: Yale University Press, 1999), 43.
89. Andrejevìc to Schricker, August 17, 1940, FIFA, Andrejevìc dossier; Romanov, *Trudnye dorogi,* 16. The matches were followed with considerable interest by FIFA's leaders, who still hoped the Soviets would join the organization. Indeed it seems they had hoped to reinitiate contact with the Soviets in Sofia only to find that their intermediary was prevented from getting there in time. M. Andrejevìc, the Yugloslav member of FIFA's Ex-

ecutive Committee, reported that the Soviets played extremely well and with great technical sophistication, though probably not at the level of the best Central European professionals. Andrejevìc to Schricker, July 3, 1940; Schricker to Andrejevìc, July 8, 1940, FIFA Archives, Andrejevìc dossier. Both Andrejevìc and Schricker expressed the desire to see the Soviets join. Andrejevìc hoped to convince FIFA to extend a general, open-ended permission for meets against Soviet teams, in view of the likelihood that for political reasons Yugoslavia would also wish to engage in sport relations with the Soviets. See, for example, Schricker to Seeldrayers, June 18, 1940, FIFA, Seeldrayers dossier.

90. RGASPI, f. 1-m, op. 23, d. 1434, ll. 102–123. Note that the security plan for 1930 matches against Austrian and Swiss workers' teams, at which up to 80,000 spectators were expected, called for only forty-two policemen. VSFK to the militsiia (AOMS), June 12, 1930, GARF, f. 7576, op. 1, d. 53, l. 20.

91. See the list of dates of Politburo resolutions permitting entry into various federations, RGASPI, f. 17, op. 132, d. 99, l. 97.

92. Apollonov to Suslov, July 7, 1948, RGASPI, f. 17, op. 132, d. 99, ll. 1–2; report of Soviet sport delegation to London, August 25, 1948, RGASPI, f. 17, op. 132, d. 99, ll. 44-59; Sobolev to Klochko, October 4, 1948, RGASPI, f. 17, op. 132, d. 99, ll. 87–90.

93. Report of Soviet sport delegation to London, August 25, 1948, RGASPI, f. 17, op. 132, d. 99, ll. 44–59; Mikhailov to Malenkov, June 4, 1949, RGASPI, f. 17, op. 132, d. 267, ll. 40–41. On Soviet entry into the Olympics see also Romanov, *Trudnye dorogi*.

94. Snegov to Vyshinskii, June 1939, GARF, f. 7576, op. 2., d. 192, l. 8; A. P. Pustovalov, *Za mirovye sportivnye rekordy* (Moscow 1941), 6; Legostaev, *Fizicheskoe vospitanie,* 26.

95. Many reports and meetings on such issues were sponsored by the Komsomol in 1939; see the report to the Party Central Committee, October 19, 1939, RGASPI, f. 1-m, op. 23, d. 1365, ll. 36–42; and the report of November 19, 1939, RGASPI, f. 1-m, op. 23, d. 1365, ll. 58–62.

96. *Krasnyi sport,* March 25, 1940, 3.

Conclusion

1. Brundage, "Greatest Sport Nation in the World," 1942, ABC, Box 244.

2. John MacAloon has likened sport to "a world language with many dialects," like music or capitalism. John J. MacAloon, "Double Visions: Olympic Games and American Culture," in *The Olympic Games, Ancient and Modern,* ed. W. Lindsay Adams and Larry R. Gerlach (Boston: Pearson Custom Publishing, 2002), 182–183.

3. As John Bale and Chris Philo have noted, "the prevailing notion of sport is only one way in which the moving, physical body can be configured in modernity." Nonsport forms of physical activity include experiential forms of body culture like "fun running" and the New Games movement of the 1970s. See the introduction to Eichberg, *Body Cultures,* 16; and, on New Games, Karl-Heinrich Bette, *Körperspuren: Zur Semantik und Paradoxie moderner Körperlichkeit* (Berlin: Walter de Gruyter, 1989), 239–244.

4. Arnd Krüger and James Riordan, eds., *The Story of Worker Sport* (Champaign, Ill.: Human Kinetics, 1996); Stephen G. Jones, "The European Workers' Sport Movement and Organized Labour in Britain between the Wars," *European History Quarterly* 18, no. 1 (January 1988): 3–32; David A. Steinberg, "The Workers' Sport Internationals," *Journal of Contemporary History* 13 (1978): 233–251. See also William J. Morgan, *Leftist Theories of Sport: A Critique and Reconstruction* (Urbana: University of Illinois Press, 1994), and Bero Rigauer, *Sport and Work,* trans. Allen Guttmann (New York: Columbia University Press, 1981).

5. See, for example, Margaret P. Karns and Karen A. Mingst, *International Organizations: The Politics and Processes of Global Governance* (Boulder, Colo.: Lynne Rienner, 2004), 12–13.

6. See Arnd Krüger, "Germany," 22. It is worth noting, however, that neither Helen Mayer nor Rudi Ball were considered Jewish under Jewish law. Large, *Nazi Games.*

7. *NYT,* October 9, 1932, 7; Doris Pieroth, *Their Day in the Sun: Women of the 1932 Olympic Games* (Seattle: University of Washington Press, 1996), 47; Large, *Berlin,* 295; Rürup, *1936,* 134.

8. See Speer, *Inside the Third Reich,* 69–70.

9. I thank Frank Ninkovich for making this point to me.

10. Walter Schiffer, *The Legal Community of Mankind: A Critical Analysis of the Modern Concept of World Organization* (New York: Columbia University Press, 1954), 196.

11. Militarized views of sport were most overt in the dictatorships, like Nazi Germany and the Soviet Union, but were also prevalent in the United States.

12. On the debate over sport and the prevention of conflict, see, for example, Peter Beck, "Confronting George Orwell: Philip Noel-Baker on International Sport as Peacemaker," *European Sports History Review* 5 (2003): 187–207.

13. In addition to undeniably transnational sports—track, swimming, tennis, soccer, and the like—there are, of course, still sports that are unique to individual countries, such as Australian rules football. Such sports, however, adhere to a common vernacular of modern sport. The rules are

different, but the underpinning is the same. The use of the clock, the arrangement of the field, the architecture of the stadia, and the way points are scored are similar enough to other sports that an outsider can appreciate the game; whereas an outsider looking at some other form of physical culture would be mystified as to how to appreciate it. (I would note that cricket—though clearly an international sport—marks an exception: temporally and spatially it harkens back to a preindustrial era, which makes it, as a sport, unusually inaccessible to outsiders.) However much individual countries may (justifiably) celebrate national styles of play, a Martian visiting Earth would likely be struck above all by the commonalities in sports as compared to other forms of physical culture.

14. On this point see also MacAloon, *This Great Symbol,* 267, and Geyer and Paulmann, *Mechanics of Internationalism,* 6–7.

15. See, for example, Benedict Anderson, *Imagined Communities: Reflections on the Origin and Spread of Nationalism,* rev. ed. (London: Verso, 1991), 97; Anthony D. Smith, *Nationalism: Theory, Ideology, History* (New York: Polity Press), 139.

16. Anderson, *Imagined Communities,* 97.

17. John W. Meyer, John Boli, George M. Thomas, and Francisco O. Ramirez, "World Society and the Nation-State," *American Journal of Sociology* 103, no. 1 (July 1997): 144–145; and Connie L. McNeely, *Constructing the Nation-State: International Organization and Prescriptive Action* (Westport, Conn.: Greenwood Press, 1995), 17. On international influences on the construction of nationalism, and especially the use of a transnational discourse of national self-determination to legitimize anticolonial movements, see Erez Manela, "The Wilsonian Moment: Self-Determination and the International Origins of Anticolonial Nationalism, 1917-1920" (Ph.D. diss., Yale University, 2003), 25, 29. See also Afshin Marashi, "Performing the Nation: The Shah's Official State Visit to Kemalist Turkey, June to July 1934" in *The Making of Modern Iran: State and Society Under Riza Shah, 1921–1941,* ed. Stephanie Cronin (London: Routledge/Curzon, 2003), 99–119.

18. McNeely, *Constructing the Nation-State,* 24.

Bibliography

Archives

United States

Harvard University Archives, Cambridge, Massachusetts
Harvard Athletic Association
Records of the Harvard Athletic Association, 1868–1977
    Records relating to international track meets, 1923–1939
Records of William J. Bingham, Director of Athletics, 1925–1948
    Boxes 26, 40, 41

U.S. Olympic Committee Archives, Colorado Springs, Colorado
Gustavus Town Kirby Papers
Minutes of the Meetings of the American Olympic Association and Its
    Executive Committee

University of Illinois Archives, Urbana
Avery Brundage Collection
[See: *Avery Brundage Collection, 1908–1975.* Compiled by Maynard
    Brichford. Schorndorf: Hofmann, 1977. Microfilm copies of the collec-
    tion are also held by the Paul Ziffren Sports Resource Library in Los
    Angeles; the International Olympic Committee Archives in Lausanne,
    Switzerland; the Carl-Diem-Institut in Cologne, Germany; and the
    Weldon Library at the University of Western Ontario, Canada.]

National Archives, College Park, Maryland
Record Group 51, General Records of the Bureau of Foreign and Domestic
    Commerce
    Sporting Goods
Record Group 59, State Department Decimal Files
    800.406
    811.406
    811.43 American Olympic Association

861.406 Soviet Union: Internal Affairs
862.406 Germany: Internal Affairs
862.4063 Olympic Games
032 Japanese Baseball Team

Germany

Politisches Archiv des Auswärtiges Amts (PAdAA), Bonn [now Berlin]
Politische Abteilung IV, Rußland: Gesundheitswesen 10 (1923–1934)
Inland I Partei
Gesandtschaft Paris
Gesandschaft Preßburg
Botschaft Rom

Bundesarchiv (BA), Berlin
Rk 43 II Reichskanzlei
Abteilung R, Personalakten: Hans von Tschammer und Osten, Karl Ritter
    von Halt

Russia

*GARF—Gosudarstvennyi arkhiv Rossiisskoi Federatsii (State Archives of the
Russian Federation), Moscow*
f. 5451   Vsesouiznyi tsentral'nyi soiuz profsoiuzov
f. 7576   Vsesoiuznyi komitet po fizicheskoi kul'ture
f. 8009   Narkomzdrav (Commissariat of Health)
f. 9480   Gruppovoi fond tsentral'nykh sportivnykh obshchestv profsoiuzov

*RGASPI—Rossiiskii gosudarstvennyi arkhiv sotsial'no-politicheskoi istorii
(Russian State Archive of Socio-Political History; the former Central Party
Archives, also formerly known as RTsKhIDNI, Rossiiskii tsentr dlia khraneniia
i izucheniia dokumentov noveishei istorii), Moscow*
f. 1-m   Tsentral'nyi komitet VLKSM (formerly held at TsKhDMO)
f. 17   Tsentral'nyi komitet VKP(b)
f. 495   Komintern
f. 533   Kommunisticheskii International Molodezhi
f. 534   Profintern
f. 537   Krasnyi Sportivnyi International

*TsGAMO—Tsentral'nyi gosudarstvennyi arkhiv Moskovskoi oblasti (Central
State Archives for Moscow oblast'), Moscow*
f. 6835   Spartak, 1934–1937, 1939

TsMAM—Tsentral'nyi munitsipal'nyi arkhiv Moskvy (Central Municipal Archives of Moscow)
f. 457   Spartak
f. 1067   Dinamo

Switzerland

Fédération Internationale de Football Association Archives, Zurich
Executive Committee Agendas and Minutes, 1927–1943
Comité d'urgence, Correspondence, 1932–1950
Activities Reports/Ordinary Congress Minutes, 1904–1938
Dossiers individuels, Membres du Comité Exécutif
Correspondence with Afffiliated National Associations

International Olympic Committee Archives, Lausanne
Correspondance, Présidents: Pierre de Coubertin, Henri de Baillet-Latour, Sigfrid Edström
Correspondance, Membres: Clarence Aberdare, Jiri Guth-Jarkovsky, William May Garland, Jigoro Kana, Baron Alphert Schimmelpennick van der Oye, Soyeshima, Tata, Blonay
Correspondance, Comités nationales olympiques: USSR, USA, China, Japan
Correspondance, Fédérations internationales: International Amateur Athletic Federation, Fédération internationale de football association, Federation international de natation amateur, International Skating Union
Jeux Olympiques d'été (1920, 1924, 1928, 1932, 1936, 1940)
Minutes and Procès-verbal of IOC Sessions
Villes candidates (1932, 1936, 1940)

Selected Readings

1894–1994, The International Olympic Committee—One Hundred Years. The Idea—The Presidents—The Achievements. 3 vols. Lausanne: International Olympic Committee, 1994.

Arnaud, Pierre, and James Riordan, eds. *Sport and International Politics: The Impact of Fascism and Communism on Sport.* London: E & FN Spon/Routledge, 1998.

Beck, Peter J. *Scoring for Britain: International Football and International Politics, 1900–1939.* London: Frank Cass, 1999.

Coubertin, Pierre de. *Olympic Memoirs.* Lausanne: International Olympic Committee, 1989.

Dyreson, Mark. "Marketing National Identity: The Olympic Games of 1932 and American Culture." *Olympika: The International Journal of Olympic Studies* 4 (1995): 23–48.

Edelman, Robert. *Serious Fun: A History of Spectator Sports in the USSR.* New York: Oxford University Press, 1993.

Eichberg, Henning. *Body Cultures: Essays on Sport, Space and Identity,* ed. John Bale and Chris Philo. London: Routledge, 1998.

———. "Olympic Sport—Neocolonialism and Alternatives." *International Review for Sociology of Sport* 19, no. 1 (1984): 97–105.

Eisenberg, Christiane. *"English Sports" und deutsche Bürger. Eine Gesellschaftsgeschichte 1800–1939.* Paderborn: Schöningh, 1999.

Elias, Norbert, and Eric Dunning. *Quest for Excitement: Sport and Leisure in the Civilizing Process.* New York: Basil Blackwell, 1986.

Gorn, Elliot J., and Warren Goldstein. *A Brief History of American Sports.* New York: Hill & Wang, 1993.

Guttmann, Allen. *Games and Empires: Modern Sports and Cultural Imperialism.* New York: Columbia University Press, 1994.

———. *From Ritual to Record: The Nature of Modern Sports.* New York: Columbia University Press, 1978.

Hoberman, John M. *Sport and Political Ideology.* London: Heinemann, 1984.

———. "Toward a Theory of Olympic Internationalism." *Journal of Sport History* 22, no. 1 (Spring 1995): 1–37.

Iriye, Akira. *Global Community: The Role of International Organizations in the Making of the Contemporary World.* Berkeley: University of California Press, 2002.

Koloskov, V. I., ed. *Sto let russiiskomu futbolu.* Moscow: Rossiiskii futbol'nyi soiuz, 1997.

Krüger, Arnd. *Die Olympischen Spiele 1936 und die Weltmeinung: Ihre außenpolitische Bedeutung unter besonderer Berücksichtigung der USA.* Berlin: Bartels und Wernitz, 1972.

Krüger, Arnd, and William Murray, eds. *The Nazi Olympics: Sport, Politics, and Appeasement in the 1930s.* Urbana: University of Illinois Press, 2003.

Lanfranchi, Pierre, Christiane Eisenberg, Tony Mason, and Alfred Wahl. *100 Years of Football: The Football Centennial Book.* London: Weidenfeld & Nicolson, 2004.

Legostaev, F. *Fizicheskoe vospitanie i sport v SSSR.* Munich: Institut po izucheniiu istorii i kul'tury SSSR, 1952.

MacAloon, John J. *This Great Symbol: Pierre de Coubertin and the Origins of the Modern Olympic Games.* Chicago: University of Chicago Press, 1981.

————. "The Turn of Two Centuries: Sport and the Politics of Intercultural Relations." In *Sport . . . The Third Millenium: Proceedings of the International Symposium,* ed. Fernand Landry, Marc Landry, and Magdaleine Yerles (Sainte-Foy, Canada: Les Presses de l'Université Laval, 1991), 31–44.

Margolick, David. *Beyond Glory: Joe Louis versus Max Schmeling and a World on the Brink.* New York: Alfred A. Knopf, 2005.

Markovits, Andrei S. "The Other 'American Exceptionalism': Why Is There No Soccer in the United States?" *International Journal of the History of Sport* 7, no. 2 (September 1990): 230–264.

Mandell, Richard. *The Nazi Olympics.* New York: Macmillan, 1971.

Morton, Henry W. *Soviet Sport: Mirror of Soviet Society.* New York: Collier Books, 1963.

Müller, Norbert. *One Hundred Years of Olympic Congresses, 1894–1994: History, Objectives, Achievements,* trans. Ingrid Sonnleitner-Hauber. Lausanne: International Olympic Committee, 1994.

Murray, Bill. *Football: A History of the World Game.* Aldershot: Scolar, 1994.

Ninkovich, Frank A. "Culture, Power, and Civilization: The Place of Culture in the Study of International Relations." In *On Cultural Ground: Essays in International History,* ed. Robert David Johnson (Chicago: Imprint Publications, 1994), 1–22.

Riordan, James. *Sport in Soviet Society: Development of Sport and Physical Education in Russian and the USSR.* New York: Cambridge University Press, 1977.

Riordan, Jim, and Arnd Krüger, eds. *The International Politics of Sport in the 20th Century.* London: E & FN Spon, 1999.

Romanov, A. O. *Mezhdunarodnoe sportivnoe dvizhenie.* Moscow: Fizkul'tura i sport, 1973.

Steinberg, D. A. "The Workers' Sport Internationals, 1920–1928." *Journal of Contemporary History* 13 (1978): 233–251.

Teichler, Hans Joachim. *Internationale Sportpolitik im Dritten Reich.* Schorndorf: Karl Hofmann, 1991.

Tomlinson, John. *Globalization and Culture.* Chicago: University of Chicago Press, 1999.

Tunis, John R. *Democracy and Sport.* New York: A. S. Barnes, 1941.

Index

AAU. *See* Amateur Athletic Union
Afghanistan, 59
Africa, 28, 60–61
African Americans. *See* Blacks
African Games, 61
Albers, Hans, 119
All-Russian Football Union, 160, 161
All-Union Society for Cultural Relations Abroad (VOKS), 165, 177
Amateur Athlete, 77
Amateur Athletic Association, 43
Amateur Athletic Union (AAU): adopts metric system, 79; on Americanism, 88–89; and 1936 Olympics, 87; and female competitors, 82; and Gus Kirby, 74; and international meets, 44, 72–73, 77; military representation in, 71; relations with dictatorships, 84–85; standardization proposal by, 47
Amateurism: and class, 12, 22, 81; and national sport organizations, 43, 82; and Olympics, 31, 32–33, 43; in soccer, 52, 54
Ambassadors, athletes as, 77. *See also* Foreign policy, sport as instrument of
American culture, international influence of, 5, 15, 64–66, 68–69, 115–116, 158–159, 187–188
American Federation of Labor, 83
Americanism: as exemplar of modernity, 68–69, 187; sport as expression of, 77, 80–84, 88–89
Americanization, 68, 89, 91, 184
Americanization of the World, The (Stead), 68

American Olympic Committee (AOC), 71, 72, 73, 82
Amsterdam (1928) Olympic Games, 52–53, 71, 92, 96, 104, 124
Anderson, Benedict, 189
Angriff, Der, 120, 150, 155
Antipov, Nikolai, 166
Anti-Semitism: and Baillet-Latour, 131; in German sport, 123–125, 129, 137; masking of, at 1936 Olympics, 87, 141, 149, 157, 185; Nuremberg Laws, 139; and participation in 1936 Olympics, 85, 125, 136, 138, 141; and United States, 87, 139, 140. *See also* Jews
Antwerp (1920) Olympic Games, 38, 92, 93
AOC (American Olympic Committee), 71, 72, 73, 82
Appadurai, Arjun, 8
Archery, 45
Argentina, 52, 146
Aristocrats, 45–46, 47
Association football. *See* Soccer
Athens (1896) Olympic Games, 32, 35–36, 47, 56, 104, 204n82
Athens (2004) Olympic Games, 7
Australia, 46, 58
Austria, 52
Austro-Hungarian Empire, 58
Aviation, 172

Baillet-Latour, Henri de: and Berlin Olympics, 138, 139, 141, 150; and Hitler, 152, 154, 156; and IOC, 47,